DAILY LIFE OF

WOMEN IN CHAUCER'S ENGLAND

I0641471

Recent Titles in
The Greenwood Press Daily Life Through History Series

DAILY LIFE OF

WOMEN IN CHAUCER'S ENGLAND

JENNIFER C. EDWARDS

The Greenwood Press Daily Life Through History Series

BLOOMSBURY ACADEMIC
NEW YORK • LONDON • OXFORD • NEW DELHI • SYDNEY

BLOOMSBURY ACADEMIC
Bloomsbury Publishing Inc, 1359 Broadway, New York, NY 10018, USA
Bloomsbury Publishing Plc, 50 Bedford Square, London, WC1B 3DP, UK
Bloomsbury Publishing Ireland, 29 Earlsfort Terrace, Dublin 2, D02 AY28, Ireland

BLOOMSBURY, BLOOMSBURY ACADEMIC and the Diana logo are trademarks of
Bloomsbury Publishing Plc

First published in the United States of America by ABC-CLIO 2022
Paperback edition published by Bloomsbury Academic 2026

Copyright © Bloomsbury Publishing Inc, 2025

COVER PHOTO: Three women of 14th-century England, 1386–1399.
(Chronicle/Alamy Stock Photo)

All rights reserved. No part of this publication may be: i) reproduced or transmitted in
any form, electronic or mechanical, including photocopying, recording or by means of
any information storage or retrieval system without prior permission in writing from
the publishers; or ii) used or reproduced in any way for the training, development or
operation of artificial intelligence (AI) technologies, including generative AI technologies.
The rights holders expressly reserve this publication from the text and data mining
exception as per Article 4(3) of the Digital Single Market Directive (EU) 2019/790.

Bloomsbury Publishing Inc does not have any control over, or responsibility for,
any third-party websites referred to or in this book. All internet addresses given
in this book were correct at the time of going to press. The author and publisher
regret any inconvenience caused if addresses have changed or sites have ceased
to exist, but can accept no responsibility for any such changes.

Library of Congress Cataloging-in-Publication Data
Names: Edwards, Jennifer C., author.
Title: Daily life of women in Chaucer's England / Jennifer C. Edwards.
Description: Santa Barbara, California : Greenwood, [2022] |
Series: The Greenwood Press daily life through history series |
Includes bibliographical references.
Identifiers: LCCN 2022000460 (print) | LCCN 2022000461 (ebook) |
ISBN 9781440870545 (hardcover ; alk. paper) | ISBN 9781440870552 (ebook)
Subjects: LCSH: Women—History—Middle Ages, 500–1500. |
Women—England—History—To 1500. | Women—England— Social conditions.
Classification: LCC HQ1147.G7 E39 2022 (print) | LCC HQ1147. G7 (ebook) |
DDC 305.4094209/02—dc23/eng/20220118
LC record available at https://lccn.loc.gov/2022000460
LC ebook record available at https://lccn.loc.gov/2022000461

ISBN: HB: 978-1-4408-7054-5
PB: 979-8-2164-4333-9
ePDF: 978-1-4408-7055-2
eBook: 979-8-2160-7154-9

Series: The Greenwood Press Daily Life Through History Series

For product safety related questions contact productsafety@bloomsbury.com.

To find out more about our authors and books visit www.bloomsbury.com
and sign up for our newsletters.

CONTENTS

PREFACE

This book examines the lives of women in England during the fourteenth and fifteenth centuries, a period known as the late Middle Ages. Late Medieval England was governed by a king and a small aristocracy that controlled most of the land. The majority of Medieval English people lived and worked on rural estates, but there were a number of cities that offered alternate lives for merchants, artisans, and servants. Over six chapters, the book details the experiences of women from different status groups through the female life cycle: from birth to childhood, marriage and/or motherhood, widowhood, and death. While this cycle defined the lives of many women, there were a number who reached for spiritual lives that stood outside of it, with perhaps 10 percent of women living as virgins or chaste women devoted to their Christian faith as either nuns, anchoresses, beguines, or tertiaries. Sources are more plentiful for wealthy or noblewomen, but with creative and sophisticated use of sources, historians have recovered details about women from even the poorest segments of medieval society.

Women's lives in the medieval past were not easy, and this book examines them with a focus on truth, even when that includes tackling difficult subjects. I have attempted to present women's lives with a focus on accuracy, but there will be topics that present challenges for some students. Teachers might wish to prepare students for sections on domestic violence, infanticide, abortion, and sexual assault. They may also have groups who need guidance approaching the material in chapter 5.

CHAPTER SKETCH

Chapter 1

The book begins with a discussion of marriage, an institution that defined the lives of 80–90 percent of medieval women during the late Middle Ages in England. Chapter 1 details norms and expectations, the negotiations for dower and dowry in arranging a marriage, and the shape of the wedding ceremony. It also examines expectations for marital relations, including the hope of love and affection, as well as how medieval people resolved problematic marriages at a time when divorce was not a usual option. This chapter also introduces the contrast between the legal, economic, and cultural positions of married women, femes covert, covered by their husbands versus the freedom of femes sole, singlewomen. Last, the chapter examines life after marriage and the prospect of widowhood.

Chapter 2

Since most married women's lives were tied to their reproductive goals, chapter 2 focuses on motherhood. This begins with a study of women's health centered on gynecology and obstetrics and then moves into pregnancy and childbirth. Since medieval women also understood methods to space out their pregnancies, or avoid them altogether, the chapter also discusses contraception and abortifacients. Two rituals that surrounded pregnancy, baptism and churching, deserve special attention, as do women's roles in raising children. While most medieval mothers were married, there were a significant number of single mothers, who conclude the chapter.

Chapter 3

While the lives of royal and noblewomen included the same life cycle concerns of other medieval women, their elevated status shaped their lives in very different ways, and chapter 3 focuses on these aristocratic women. Extant sources document the lives of these women more thoroughly. The first part of the chapter examines the lives of aristocratic women in general, while the second part focuses on the experiences of specific royal women. The third part examines specific queens of England chronologically. These women are among the most studied in the Middle Ages, on whom a class biographical project might focus.

Chapter 4

England in the later Middle Ages was predominantly rural, although it had some significant cities such as London, York, Norwich, Lincoln, and so on. Chapter 4 examines the contrast between urban and rural life for women. Much of the chapter focuses on work, describing the rhythm of women's labor in villages and on estates and then as part of the urban world of merchant and artisan shops. This chapter also provides an opportunity to look more closely at medieval women's households, clothing, food and drink, and their domestic lives in general. Singlewomen appear also in chapters 1, 2, and 5, but this chapter examines the labor of singlewomen, especially in the urban context. Finally, the chapter discusses medieval women's experience of disease and disability as well as the ceremonies surrounding death and burial.

Chapter 5

Many of the topics in these chapters overlap with one another, and that is especially true for chapter 5, which focuses on sex and sexuality in women's lives. Some of the sections in this chapter discuss topics that are controversial in the present, and teachers may wish to screen this material to ensure that it is appropriate for their students. This chapter introduces the concept of sex, gender, and sexuality as used by historians and examines norms during the Middle Ages. There was some discussion of sex within marriage already in chapter 1, but this chapter examines sex outside of marriage, especially adultery, fornication, and concubinage. It pays special attention to the lives of concubines and the institution of prostitution as well as to sexual assault and domestic violence. The chapter concludes with a consideration of homosexuality, searching for evidence of same-sex desire and relationships in medieval sources, and on cross-dressing, which medieval people tended to see as connected to prostitution.

Chapter 6

Chapter 6 examines medieval women's religious lives. While conversion to Christianity was slow in England, by the late Middle Ages, most of England was Christian. Pagan ideas perhaps lingered in certain shrines and practices, but these had become Christianized sufficiently by this period. The small Jewish population in England had been exiled in 1290 and not permitted to return, so during the fourteenth and fifteenth centuries, on which this book focuses, England was primarily a Christian kingdom. The chapter begins with a focus on lay spirituality and religious practice, especially for churchgoing. Religion shaped the calendar for English women of all status groups. The cult of the saints and the phenomenon of pilgrimage greatly defined this era, especially for women. Then the chapter looks at some more specific groups of women who devoted their lives to religious work: nuns, anchorites, beguines, and tertiaries. Finally, the chapter looks at women's roles in some late medieval heresies and considers the background of Jews before their expulsion from England.

There are several themes that run throughout the book, such as legal history and the laws and customs that defined and governed women's lives. These issues appear in their specific contexts. For example, the laws and expectations governing marriage appear in chapter 1, the laws regarding prostitution in chapter 5, and the laws governing infanticide in chapter 2. Norms and laws may have set the parameters for medieval men and women, but cases appearing before ecclesiastical and secular courts offer richer detail on how well these expectations matched reality. Legal records, thus, are crucial sources throughout these six chapters.

ACKNOWLEDGMENTS

This book has taken shape during the COVID-19 pandemic in a New York City apartment where my children play, learn, eat, and sleep steps away from my desk. Writing about the daily lives of women who lived seven centuries ago, I have been struck by small similarities as my life became increasingly interwoven with familial and domestic tasks. Washing my family's laundry in our bathtub; making bread from scratch; banging pots and pans in ritual celebration with my neighbors; taking primary responsibility for the education of my young children; becoming ever more a nagging, shrewish scold; and trying to concoct entertainment that did not involve screens felt like a very small degree of kinship with the women whose lives I tried to pin to these pages.

Much of the research was thus conducted online, and I am intensely grateful to the Manhattan College interlibrary loan department and to Fordham University's library document delivery service for their assistance. Access to Fordham was possible due to time as a Medieval Fellow with Fordham University's Center for Medieval Studies and the generous help of Nicholas Paul and Christina Bruno. I benefited enormously from the fellowship of Fordham's medievalists, who were unfailingly welcoming and kind, including Maryanne Kowaleski, Wolfgang Mueller, Heather Hill, Sally Gordon, and many others. Much that I have learned about medieval women is due to the inspiring collegiality of the Society for Medieval Feminist Scholarship, with scholars too many to name.

A Manhattan College sabbatical year gave me the space to finish this project, and I am grateful to my Manhattan colleagues, especially Paul Droubie, Adam Arenson, Nefertiti Takla, Lydia Crafts, Deirdre O'Leary, Natalia Imperatori-Lee, Evelyn Scaramella, Kerri Mulqueen, Ashley Cross, and Maeve Adams, for their cheer, support, shared exhaustion, and fear during the terrifying months of the pandemic. While we saw little of each other off-screen, the frequent, or even occasional, small messages provided great comfort. I appreciate also the thoughtful comments, excellent questions, patience, and good cheer of Manhattan College students in my Premodern Women and Gender course during the book's production.

And, finally, I am grateful to my husband, Scott, and sons, Sebastian and Logan, for the time they gave me to write, in a space somewhat adjacent to the chaos. While I could not have a room of my own, it appears that a writing nook sufficed. This book is for them.

INTRODUCTION

CHAUCER

This book examines the daily lives of women in the age of Geoffrey Chaucer, an important English author who lived from the 1340s to 1400 and is buried in Poet's Corner at Westminster Abbey. He was an author who wrote poetry in the English vernacular as well as a public servant who studied law and served at the courts of Edward III and his son John of Gaunt. Chaucer served as comptroller for the port of London; he fought in the Hundred Years War, was captured, and was ransomed. He had notable female patrons, including Alice Perrers, Edward III's mistress, and Elizabeth de Burgh, wife of Edward's son Lionel, Duke of Clarence. Chaucer's family used their connections to the court circle well: Geoffrey's granddaughter Alice Chaucer married William de la Pole, Duke of Suffolk. During his travels in the service of the king and well-connected men, Chaucer met Dante Alighieri, another vernacular poet, and may have learned from his style.

Among this praise, it is important to also note that Chaucer was accused by Cecily Chaumpaigne of *raptus*, which can mean sexual assault or kidnapping or seduction. We do not know much about the incident beyond a document in which Chaumpaigne released him from her charge of *raptus* in 1380. This document suggests that she had previously made a formal allegation but was persuaded to withdraw it, perhaps due to a settlement. This is important context for understanding some of Chaucer's comments about women and sex, but as an allegation, not an admission or conviction, it challenges historians with how to treat Chaucer, a man with influence within his own time and our own.

Chaucer composed many works over the course of his career; the first significant one was *The Book of the Duchess*, but others followed, including *Parliament of Fowls*, *The Legend of Good Women*, and *Troilus of Criseyde*. He also worked as a translator of other poems, such as the French *Romance of the Rose*. These works were significant contributions to English literature and served a broad audience literate but unable to read in Latin. Since women were increasingly becoming literate but not educated in Latin, a great poet writing in English made literature more available to them and encouraged others to write in the vernacular.

Geoffrey Chaucer's most famous work is *The Canterbury Tales*, the story of a group of pilgrims en route to the shrine of Saint Thomas Becket in Canterbury, telling one another stories. The structure introduces details about the narrators who then each tell their stories. Unfortunately, Chaucer died before finishing *The Canterbury Tales*. He encased in his prologue and in the stories commentaries on English society, culture, and politics, lampooning corruption and immorality and hypocrisy. He told many stories about women, in *The Canterbury Tales* and beyond them, that give us insight into fourteenth- and fifteenth-century values, gender roles, misogyny, and ideals.

It made sense for Chaucer to pick a pilgrimage as the activity through which he could examine a broad variety of people in *The Canterbury Tales*, since pilgrimage was an opportunity available to most Christians in medieval England. Those with wealth and time and able bodies might go farther, to Rome or Jerusalem or Compostela, while the poor working person or the disabled or ill person might visit a local shrine. Those who could not travel at all might take a mental pilgrimage, envisioning their steps along the way and saying the prayers they intended the saint to hear at home. Misfortune touches all people, and medieval Christians believed that visits to saints' shrines might bring them the answers to their prayers.

Medieval women sought the assistance of saints when struggling for a pregnancy or when pregnant and hoping for a safe delivery. They gifted their girdles to statues of the Virgin Mary in thanks for a healthy child. People praying for a miraculous cure of an injury or an illness gave their crutches to churches. Penitents of means atoning for sins built churches and chapels to house new shrines.

Craftsmen used their wealth and influence through their guilds to found and decorate chapels in their local churches. Cathedrals housing ancient relics had to create special doors through which to welcome pilgrims because there were so many, and demand for access was so fierce. Medieval towns filled with shrines to new saints and anchor-holds housing hermits who seemed like saints-in-waiting, to whom many flocked for advice or connection. The year filled with days of the saints' feasts for celebration and devotion. Medieval England teemed with saints, and with people moving to see them.

One of the more prolific female pilgrims from this period, Margery Kempe, sometimes reads as a Chaucer character. Larger than life, with her many faults laid out in her autobiography for the world to see, Margery was deeply committed to her faith and to her mission of understanding her usefulness to God. She also exemplifies many of the themes and topics of this book. Margery was a wife, a mother (fourteen times over!), and the daughter of an important urban family who lived in relative comfort as a member of a working family, as well as a visionary, a pilgrim, and a woman who desired chastity to focus on a life of devotion. She begged her husband to free her from the sexual duties of their marriage, which he finally did when she stopped taking meals with him, demonstrating the importance of sharing bed and table within a marriage. And Margery devoted the next portion of her life to her faith—traveling to Canterbury, Rome, and Jerusalem on pilgrimage, receiving visions from God, visiting a famous anchoress to receive her approval, and even debating with priests and bishops and friars about spirituality. Margery and Chaucer's Wife of Bath might have had quite a lark on pilgrimage together. Alison, the Wife of Bath, may have joined Margery's companions in abandoning her, finding Margery's exuberant crying exhausting, and Margery might have found Alison's notions on marriage and partner selection scandalous. But the two women likely would have shared gossip, faith, the experience of being a wife and running a household, and a sense of the world while journeying to a destination they both valued to petition the saints for a better future.

GEOGRAPHY OF ENGLAND

Britain is an island divided from the European continent to the south by the English Channel and east by the North Sea, from Ireland by the Irish Sea to the west, and, at some distance, from Iceland to the north by the North Atlantic Ocean. In the Middle Ages, three kingdoms occupied the island of Britain: Wales to the west, Scotland to the north, and England in the south and east. England fought to control the rest of Britain through campaign, marriage, and diplomacy. England's border with Wales was mostly defined by the River Severn as well as by a series of motte-and-bailey castles, called marches and ruled by marcher lords, the origin of the title marquis. Scotland's border shifted in this period, but was marked by a line of Scottish marches north of Northumberland. Hadrian's Wall in the north of England marks a convenient northern border, but England pushed this past the River Tweed and sometimes up to the Firth of Forth.

WOMEN'S LIVES

Women's lives in late medieval England differed by region, social and economic status, and profession, but they were all shaped by three commonalities: the life cycle, the church, and patriarchy.

Life Cycle

In the female life cycle of the Middle Ages, girls were born and raised in the nuclear family until their teen years, when they might marry, leave home for work in a town or as an apprentice, or embrace a religious vocation. Women who married also sought to have children and, if fertile, might have a dozen or more pregnancies between their teen years and their early thirties. While the maternal death rate was quite high, the age differential between men and women at marriage meant that women often outlived their husbands. Widows, especially young and/or wealthy ones, were encouraged to remarry and spin that loop of the life cycle again. Women who committed themselves to holy lives skipped marriage, motherhood, and widowhood, but all women eventually faced the end of their lives. Wealthy or elite widows or singlewomen might make a will in their own names to dispose of their property, while lower-status women might make their wishes known to their loved ones before their death. Christians practiced burial rather than cremation, expecting to bury themselves in a church cemetery or, if more privileged, inside the church itself.

The household was the basic unit of medieval English society. The household typically meant the nuclear family but might also include further generations. Many households also included servants, even among peasant villagers. Servants could be hired on as day laborers during times of extra work, such as the harvest, or for yearlong contracts that began at Michaelmas, September 29, and included clothing, housing, board, and wages. Older children or young adults often took work as servants to set money aside for marriage or to set up their own businesses, and there were people who devoted themselves to lifelong careers in service. While considered members of the household in which they worked, servants could not expect to inherit family property. They might receive a bequest in a will, however, and these were often specified for female servants as a contribution toward their dowry.

Within this life cycle there were status-based distinctions. Medieval clerics divided their world into three estates or orders based on their function in society and ranked the social order with themselves at the top: those who pray (*oratores*), meaning monastics and priests; those who fight (*bellatores*), the nobles who governed and waged war; and those who work (*laboratores*), peasant farmers. Urban artisans, merchants, and service workers were not included in this vision of medieval society, but if they were, they would join the peasants at the bottom. This system was interdependent, with workers providing food for the nobles who provided military protection and clerics who prayed for the community, but also strictly hierarchical. There was little opportunity for social mobility outside the towns, where it remained difficult to change one's station.

Church

England was a multilingual place in the Middle Ages. The Christian church used Latin, which the common people all encountered as the language of the weekly mass, and most official records were still written in Latin. French was a common language used by the nobility, who often enjoyed songs, poems, and other literature in French. Depending on the part of England, Gaelic could be used near the borders with Scotland or Welsh on the borders with Wales. English was the common vernacular, however, and in the fourteenth and fifteenth centuries, great works of literature, such as those by Geoffrey Chaucer, John Gower, and Thomas Malory, came to be written in English. Not always ranked with "great works of literature," there were also important works by female authors writing in English, such as Margery Kempe, Julian of Norwich, and Katherine of Sutton. There was even a heretical group, the Lollards, that pressed for translation of the Bible into English.

While there was greater racial and ethnic diversity in medieval England than scholars of previous generations have described, the kingdom was overwhelmingly Christian. Muslims rarely visited

England, and Edward I had expelled the Jewish population, about three thousand people, from England in 1290. Jews were not permitted to return to England legally until the seventeenth century, leaving the realm religiously homogenous. Even Christians who followed the Eastern Orthodox interpretation of Christianity were unlikely to visit England beyond London. The Christian church in England looked to Rome and the pope for guidance on practice and theology, with the archbishop of Canterbury and archbishop of York guiding the church more locally. Orthodox practice in England thus followed the Latin rites.

The church was deeply involved in everyday life, as it governed morality through canon law and church courts that were responsible for punishing those who violated Christian laws about sex, marriage, and a wide number of sins. The seven sacraments, with few exceptions, required clerical intervention: baptism, Eucharist, penance, confirmation, marriage, ordination, and extreme unction. Interaction with the church also shaped Christians' lives, from their own baptism to the baptism of their children and neighbors, always a time of celebration. Marriage was a sacrament that ushered women into the next phase of their lives, and a postnatal purification ritual called churching celebrated their recovery after childbirth. Alternatively, formal vows allowed women to put aside traditional expectations of marriage and motherhood to embrace a life of prayer, chastity, and devotion to faith. Christians sought confession and the last rites when sick and dying, to prepare their souls for death.

The church was also a powerful presence in Christians' lives through pilgrimage and the cult of the saints, holy men and women who, while dead, were believed to be intercessors who carried messages sent in prayer and who worked miracles for petitioners. The church calendar was filled with holy days devoted to these saints with celebrations that included prayers but also church ales and feasting. Christians marked time by the liturgical calendar, whether in Advent or Passiontide or another season of the church calendar. They also marked time based on the number of years in the king's reign, but within the year, holy days and church celebrations more clearly fixed events in memories.

Patriarchy

In the "Wife of Bath's" prologue in Chaucer's *The Canterbury Tales*, Alison reveals that her fifth husband had a book with misogynist portrayals of women and that this book enraged her so much that she tore out pages from it, starting a violent fight between them. This misogynist little book is not unusual, as many medieval authors had misogynist ideas, and England was a patriarchy, a system in which men hold power as men and women remain subordinate to them.

Wealthy or noblewomen lived more privileged lives than peasant men, but both noble and peasant women experienced the disadvantages of patriarchy. In medieval England royal women could not rule even when their claims to power were better than those of men, as demonstrated by the rejection of Henry I's heir Matilda in favor of her cousin Stephen, described below, or Isabella's need to govern in the name of her son Edward III when she—with the assistance of a lover—deposed her husband Edward II. Edward III declared himself the king of France through his mother's claim as princess, but was dismissed because women could neither rule in France nor pass on their claims to the throne.

On a less exalted level, married women in England were legally "covered" by their husbands through the legal concept of coverture, meaning that their property, inheritance, and even their debt was under the power of their husband and they could not transact their own business independently without his permission. Female adultery was harshly punished, and rape was perceived as a crime against the female victim's father or husband, or no crime at all if she became pregnant as a result since then she must have "enjoyed" it. Women on manors who had sex outside of marriage were charged a steep fine, while their male partners were not, even when identified. Women's wage for the same work was about 79 percent that of male colleagues. Women were not free to make their own decisions or to govern their own lives, and their competence to hold power was suspicious. Men even speculated what machinations were afoot in the birthing chamber—a rare all-female space—to the point that they sought control over childbirth by the end of this period.

In addition, patriarchy is a system that constrains men as it does women. It is a system that prioritizes, or even only permits, heteronormative, masculine, cisgendered values and so oppresses men who do not fit those expectations. Even those who do "fit in" to patriarchal norms could find certain customs onerous, such as the expectation that men were responsible for controlling their wives and responsible under the law for their crimes and debts. While men occupied the position of power, not all men desired responsibility for others or control over them.

Also important is that some women enforced patriarchy over both men and women. Women participated in the system that oppressed them, scolding men who did not act in masculine ways, and women did not seek to overturn patriarchy in this period. Even Christine de Pisan, a prolific Italian author writing in the French court during the fourteenth and fifteenth centuries, who wrote many pages defending women's competence and pushing back against anti-feminine attacks, did not argue that men and women should be equal or that women should upset a patriarchal system. Much of Christine's advice to the women in her *City of Ladies* was to be ladylike, embracing feminine virtues. Women participated in public shaming rituals meant to keep transgressors in their place and caution against future transgressions.

The medieval English good wife was expected to be obedient, passive, chaste, and quiet. Women who scolded, gossiped, nagged, or fornicated were a threat to proper male control of society. There were formal mechanisms for punishing some of these transgressions, there were more informal public shaming rituals to pressure women and men to enforce norms in their homes, and there were warnings—in parish sermons, in art, in literature—that there were punishments looming in the afterlife for improper women.

That said, this patriarchal model that expected women to be subject to male authority made room for women's agency, even women's power, and offered women respect within patriarchy. While the system created subordinate roles for women, and set up parameters for women's appropriate behavior, it also praised women who fulfilled these roles, emphasized women's admirable qualities, and gave them space to excel within this limited model. There were, without doubt, misogynous trends within medieval society, but there were also thinkers and writers who defended women. Christine de Pisan engaged with a debate about misogyny in a popular poem, the *Romance of the Rose*, and focused several of her books on demonstrating the ways that women were praiseworthy, most notably in *The Book of the City of Ladies* and *The Treasury of the City of Ladies*. Neither of these books argued a feminist position, a modern notion about equality between the sexes, but they did argue a pro-feminine position that pointed out the errors of misogyny. These books, while written in French, were popular in England. Although Chaucer showed Alison burning the misogynist book her husband had read and getting her control back, this is not a positive portrayal, and he did not seem to intend Alison as an exemplar for other women to follow.

Another such example of praise for women is the poem "Women Are Worthy," in which the poet declared that he praises women because his mother was a woman, because the Virgin Mary was a woman, and because women do the work, such as laundry and raising the children. He suggested that women are worthy because they serve men, "And yet she has but care and woe" (Salisbury 2002).[1] Women, according to the poet, were worthy because they cleaned the clothes and sang the children to sleep and served men night and day, for which she received no thanks. The *Ballad of a Tyrannical Husband* put it another way, praying to God to protect all women, "For much they are blamed and sometimes with wrong" (Salisbury 2002).

POLITICAL BACKGROUND

The political story of England in the fourteenth and fifteenth centuries has complicated roots stretching back to the eleventh century, because the kings of England had balanced hopes of conquering Britain against maintaining their territorial interests in France since the eleventh century. When William, Duke of Normandy (c. 1028–1087), conquered England in 1066, known as the Norman conquest, he created a legacy for his heirs that persisted for generations. While William did not leave Normandy and the English throne to a single heir, the English monarchs remained embroiled in contests for French possessions for the rest of the period discussed here. The many generations of intermarriages between the English royal family and French noblewomen further complicated claims to land, title, and the French throne.

The marriage of William's granddaughter, Empress Matilda (c. 1102–1167), to Geoffrey, Count of Anjou, Touraine, and Maine (1113–1151), gave her son Henry claim to enormous territories in France as well as Matilda's powerful claim on the English throne, as discussed in chapter 3. As King Henry I's (1068–1135) only surviving child, Matilda should have inherited the throne herself and become England's first ruling queen since the conquest, but her cousin Stephen seized it, causing decades of strife between the cousins and their supporters. Matilda was not able to secure the throne for herself, but did win her son Henry (1133–1189) the right to inherit it from Stephen, which Henry did in 1154. For his part, Henry had recently snapped up the most eligible woman in Europe,

---

[1] I have modernized the language of any quotation originally in Middle English.

Eleanor (1122–1204), the heiress to the wealthy county of Poitou and duchy of Aquitaine, in 1152, right after her marriage to King of France Louis VII (1120–1180) was annulled. When they became King Henry II and Queen Eleanor in 1154, this couple controlled all of England and most of western France. While their sons, Richard the Lionheart (1157–1199) and John (1166–1216) managed to lose control of many of these massive estates in France to Louis's son Philip II (1165–1223), known as Philip Augustus, the idea of their family, the Plantagenets, regaining past glory remained a dream for generations.

Wars in Britain

The Hundred Years War was waged in France and so affected the English primarily in its expense and its periodic need for soldiers, leaving women alone to maintain the household and businesses, sometimes permanently. England's kings also invested in wars closer to home, in wars of expansion against the Scots to the north and the Welsh to the west. These were also expensive endeavors, and to finance them, kings raised special taxes and drafted young men into their armies. The wars were not popular due to their expense, the loss of men in the countryside, and the food that the king seized to feed his armies under his rights of purveyance. The wars continued through the Great Famine, when there was little food to spare, and helped to destabilize the kingdom.

King Edward I (1239–1307) pushed the development of a national monarchy with the use of Parliament and an extensive engagement in wars of conquest. The great-grandson of Henry II, Edward had Henry's energy and acumen in exploiting institutions to his benefit. Parliament was a representative body Edward called on to raise funds for his wars, engaging the leading powers of the kingdom in the process. Since Plantagenet lands in France were securely controlled by the French at this time, Edward looked to the rest of Britain and to Ireland to expand his rule, another thing he had in common with Henry II.

As with France, the wars England waged with Wales and Scotland had women at their center. In 1258 Llywelyn II governed as the Prince of Wales, who intended to marry Eleanor, the daughter of Simon de Montfort, Earl of Leicester, but Edward seized her en route to Wales in 1275, causing Llywelyn to complain to the pope. Edward invaded Wales and forced Llywelyn to submit to him in 1277 before allowing the marriage to go forward. Eleanor died in childbirth in 1282 leaving a daughter, Gwenllian (1282–1337). Edward and Llywelyn again went to war later that year, and Llywelyn died in battle, Gwenllian was forced into the Gilbertine Priory at Sempringham, and Edward claimed the country under the 1284 Statutes of Wales, attaching the title "Prince of Wales" to the oldest son of a reigning English monarch.

Affairs in Scotland in the thirteenth century were less unified than in Wales, as Scotland was governed by a council of leaders who came together in support of King Alexander III, but were thrown into chaos by his 1286 death. There had been many intermarriages between Scottish and English ruling families, and Alexander had married Margaret, daughter of Henry III and sister of Edward I. Like Llywelyn, Alexander lost his wife in childbirth, and his only living child was a daughter, Margaret, whom he married to the king of Norway. Margaret herself died in childbirth in 1283, leaving only a daughter also named Margaret, sometimes called the Maid of Norway, who inherited the kingdom from Alexander in 1286. This deeply interested Edward, who betrothed his son, the future Edward II, to Margaret. When she died returning to Scotland in 1290, civil war broke out in Scotland, and Edward seized his opportunity to become deeply involved in Scottish politics. His further engagements there are convoluted, but by 1297, Edward had seized control as well as key symbols of Scotland, such as the stone of scone that remained in England until the twentieth century. As part of the conflicts, Edward had the daughters of leading Scots held in cages on the walls of Berwick Castle, a humiliation that long offended their countrymen. Edward died fighting against Scotland, and his son Edward II suffered a major defeat at the Battle of Bannockburn in 1314, leaving Scotland independent for the rest of the Middle Ages.

Hundred Years War

After the death of the Maid of Norway, the English connection with France was renewed when Edward II married Isabella, daughter of King Philip IV (1268–1314) of France, giving her son Edward III (1312–1377) a direct claim to the French throne when Isabella's three brothers became king and died in quick succession without sons, leaving France without a clear heir by 1328. When Edward III pressed that claim, he initiated an intermittent conflict that lasted over a century, known as the Hundred Years War (1337–1453). In order to dismiss the English claim to the throne, French political theorists resurrected and breathed new life into a concept known as the Salic Law, which they claimed barred women from ruling in France and prohibited women from passing down claims to the throne to their children. This theoretically invalidated Edward's claim and the claim of any of his children, but it did little to stop English monarchs from pursuing the French throne militarily.

Edward III and his son Edward (1330–1376), known as the Black Prince of Wales, had successes during their campaigns in France. At the major victory of the Battle of Crécy in 1346, English longbows proved devastatingly effective against the French mounted armored knights and helped to raise the status to a class of yeomen in England. At the Battle of Poitiers (also known as the Battle of Tours) in 1356, several French noblemen including the king of France, John II, were captured. Noblemen defeated in battle provided lucrative opportunities for their captors, and the phrase "a king's ransom," meaning an impressive fortune, accurately reflected the ransom John's captors could claim.

When Edward III died in 1377, England had a dynastic issue the opposite of the one France had following Philip: Edward left too many sons behind. Since his eldest, the Black Prince, had died in 1376, the throne went to the Black Prince's infant son, who became Richard II, but the kingdom was controlled by the new king's uncles, the Dukes of Lancaster and York. Rivalries between them created a number of problems, and Richard had a difficult time imposing his will. Richard also suffered some military defeats, and in 1399 his cousin Henry Bolingbroke, son of Edward III's son John of Gaunt, seized the throne. Henry IV was not interested in war in England, but his son, Henry V was, with glorious victories in France such as the Battle of Agincourt in 1415. The 1420 Treaty of Troyes made Henry V the heir of the French king, Charles VI, and arranged a marriage between Henry and Charles's daughter Catherine. Unfortunately, Henry and Charles both died in 1422, which left another infant king, Henry VI, and both countries in the charge of Henry's uncle, John of Lancaster, Duke of Bedford.

This last phase of the Hundred Years War was primarily the effort of Charles VI's son, the future Charles VII, to reclaim the throne from the English. Joan of Arc was a crucial figure in this struggle. Joan was a nineteen-year-old peasant woman who claimed to hear the voices of saints, which identified the crown prince to her. She won Charles's trust and command of a portion of his army, with which she had several victories. Charles was crowned through her efforts in 1429. Joan was captured and handed over to the English in 1430 and endured a lengthy trial that resulted in her conviction for heresy, and she was burned at the stake. Charles later regretted not intervening to save Joan and reversed this declaration of heresy. He spent much of the rest of his reign fighting to recapture France, and by 1453 the English were left with only Calais. Joan served as one of Christine de Pisan's many examples of a competent, powerful woman.

Cousins' War

The dynastic issues that caused the intermittent struggles of the Hundred Years War continued in England beyond the fighting in France, creating an internal conflict called the Wars of the Roses. This was ultimately a conflict between cousins, all descendants of Edward III, the house of York, represented by the white rose, and the house of Lancaster, represented by the red rose. Again, women were central to the story.

Henry VI became king as an infant and was a weak, uncertain ruler partially due to an unknown mental illness he suffered that made him unable to govern for long periods of time. His wife, Margaret of Anjou, tried to govern during this time but was challenged by Richard, Duke of York, and Richard Neville, Earl of Warwick. The Duke of York's supporters argued that he had a better claim to the throne than Henry did, since Richard's mother was descended from Edward III's third son while Henry was descended from Edward III's fourth son, but English inheritance did not typically recognize a claim through female descent when there was a male option. In any case, the Yorks pressed their claim, and Richard's son became Edward IV at age nineteen. The house of York defeated the house of Lancaster, which sought support in France.

Edward married Elizabeth Woodville, a member of the gentry and a Lancastrian supporter, which upset several of his followers and even his brothers. Elizabeth had a large and ambitious family that caused friction within the Yorkist side; marrying Elizabeth also meant Edward lost the opportunity to use his marriage to make a diplomatic connection with an established royal family, such as the kings of France. When Edward died in 1483, Elizabeth fled into sanctuary while his young sons mysteriously disappeared in the Tower of London, and Edward's brother seized the throne as Richard III. Richard was later challenged by Henry Tudor, a new representative of the house of Lancaster.

When Henry V had died in 1422, his widow Catherine of Valois remained in England, marrying a marcher lord in Wales, Owen Tudor, with whom she had two sons. One of these sons, Edmund Tudor, married Margaret of Beaufort, who was descended from John of Gaunt, Edward III's third son and Henry V's grandfather. Margaret's son Henry was raised by his uncle in Wales and in France, much of the time in hiding or exile due to his excellent claim to the throne that rivaled that of the Yorks and also descended through the female line. Henry returned in 1485 to challenge Richard III at the Battle of Bosworth Field, where Richard died and Henry started a new dynasty as Henry VII: the Tudors. Henry wisely married Edward IV's daughter, Elizabeth of York, uniting the two houses and healing these dynastic conflicts.

CRISES OF THE FOURTEENTH CENTURY

The population of England in 1300 was about six million, its highest point between then and the mid-eighteenth century. The start of this period was a time of socioeconomic crisis, which soon encountered a major health crisis, and these were interwoven with political and religious crises across Western Europe and much of the Mediterranean world. In terms of the economy, England's population stretched it past its breaking point. The arable land did not produce quite enough food, the labor market was so overwhelmed that wages stayed too low to support a family, and rents were too high. England was primed for catastrophe, and the fourteenth century delivered.

In addition to the Hundred Years War and the wars of Britain, the fourteenth century brought three major crises: the Great Famine, the Black Death, and the Avignon Papacy. These crises were crucial background for many of the other issues discussed in this book, not always making their presence known loudly in the day-to-day affairs of medieval English women, but always providing a context for cultural and social patterns in their lives.

Great Famine

Before even the devastation of the Black Death, England suffered a period of starvation known as the Great Famine, starting in 1315. England was already at the edge of what population its arable land could continue to support, since crop yields were quite low and a portion of each crop's yield had to be set aside each year for the next year's seed. Changes in climate at the start of the fourteenth century, combined with years of bad weather, meant persistent crop failures that threw off this balance and left the population starving and malnourished, a perfect canvas for a health disaster that arrived midcentury.

In the early fourteenth century, Europe experienced unusually heavy rain that even left its mark on trees. Dendochronologists, scientists who study tree rings, have found that trees alive in this period experienced substantial growth between 1315 and 1317, showing those to be the years with the heaviest rainfall of the millennium. Those heavy rains meant crop failures for multiple years, a snowballing problem that meant starvation each year and no seeds to plant the next. Climactic change, and perhaps this heavy period of rains, led to the seas rising on the coast of England and the erosion of some coastal farmlands. The rains were followed in England by diseases that affected the animals, causing their numbers to drop significantly as well. Fewer animals meant less meat, but it also meant less power to pull the plow and less fertilizer for the fields. The population declined by somewhere between 10 and 25 percent during this Great Famine. The elderly, the very young, and anyone else in weak health were those most likely to die, and the population that survived had health problems and trauma that persisted. The urban population especially suffered, since they were not involved in producing much of their own food. As with the Black Death, this was not an isolated period of suffering, but there were ripple effects in the following years, with drought in 1325–1326 and further animal diseases during the same years.

The Black Death

The Black Death refers to the initial outbreak of plague, in England lasting from 1348 to 1350. Plague returned periodically throughout the Middle Ages and even through the seventeenth century, but had its most cataclysmic demographic, social, and cultural impact in this first wave. Historians call this fourteenth-century outbreak the Second Pandemic caused by the plague bacillus *Yersenia pestis*, or *Y. pestis*, with the First Pandemic known as the plague of the Byzantine emperor Justinian in the sixth century, and a Third Pandemic that struck in the nineteenth century. The Black Death killed as much as 40–60 percent of the population of Europe, with devastation that continued through subsequent outbreaks. The disease seems to have originated in the Tibetan plateau and then moved into England via trade routes over land and by seaports.

Y. pestis is carried in the stomachs of certain insects, especially the mosquito, and possibly the louse, to a human population by commensal animals, most popularly but not exclusively the black rat. Other animals known to effectively host infected fleas are other rodents, such as marmots; other small animals, such as rabbits; ruminants, such as goats and camels; and these animals' predators, such as mountain lions. Study of the plague is complicated, as it involves research into many variables: the bacillus, the insect vector, the animal that carries the insect, and the human illness.

There are four strains of plague caused by *Y. pestis*: bubonic, septicemic, pneumonic, and gastrointestinal. Bubonic and septicemic plague infections require a bite from an infected flea, while pneumonic is passed from human to human via water droplets, and gastrointestinal through ingestion. Bubonic is the most iconic form of infection and causes the patient's lymph nodes to swell into lumps, called buboes. These might burst or be cut open to release fluid, aiding in recovery. Septicemic is the most frightening, as patients develop no symptoms, and the plague bacillus invades patients' bloodstreams so quickly that they die in their sleep never knowing they were sick.

Because the plague kills so quickly, it does not leave clear markers on skeletons, which made the disease difficult for bioarchaeologists to confirm and study. The innovative study of ancient DNA, or aDNA, however, has made it possible to confirm that plague burial pits, such as the mass cemeteries in West Smithfield outside London, are filled with skeletons that bear evidence of *Y. pestis*. Scientists have been able to find remnants of the bacillus in the dentin of medieval skeletons' teeth, to sequence the *Y. pestis* genome, and to confirm not only that *Y. pestis* infected Europeans in the mid-fourteenth century, but also that it was the same plague that infected people in the sixth-century First Pandemic and nineteenth-century Third Pandemic. The resilience of plague over these millennia is as impressive as the scientific work that has mapped its phylogenetic tree.

Beyond the medicine, plague's impact on late medieval England was significant. It created an economic and social crisis by quickly changing the demographics of the kingdom, raising expectations of the laboring poor of higher wages, greater mobility, and improved conditions, all of which were crushed by aristocratic efforts to control the economy and freeze social mobility. That said, serfdom was seriously weakened by the events of the fourteenth century and had largely disappeared by the middle of the fifteenth century. With such a major and sudden demographic change, the period after 1350 must be understood through the lens of the pandemic catastrophe. The plague had an impact on art, culture, women's work, and even the family. Finally, while this book focuses on England, it is important to see the plague as a global event affecting at least Europe, Asia, and Africa.

Avignon Papacy

There was a significant crisis in the leadership of the Western church starting in the fourteenth century. The bishop of Rome claimed to be the head of the church hierarchy based on the leadership of Peter among the apostles, and this claim was well accepted in the West by the late Middle Ages although contested by the Byzantine emperor and the eastern patriarchs. The bishop of Rome, the pope, was elected by a college of cardinals. In the early fourteenth century, the pope was Boniface VIII who had a number of problems with the king of France, Philip IV, to the point that in 1303, the king's troops assaulted the pope, and he died soon after. Boniface's successor soon died as well, and in 1305 one of Philip's allies, Bertrand de Got, was elected pope, as Clement V. In 1309 Clement moved his curia to a papal palace in Avignon, on land held by the pope but surrounded by the kingdom of France. This began the Avignon Papacy, an eighty-year period in which the popes ruled from Avignon and during which all the popes elected were French and seemed to support French interests. This was so upsetting to many people—including most of the English since it extended over the time of the Hundred Years War when England was at war with France—that it was called the "Babylonian Captivity," referring to the time when the Babylonians captured the leaders of Judea and held them separately from their people.

Pope Gregory XI (r. 1370–1378) returned to Rome in 1377 and died there, which is when matters went from bad to worse. The conclave elected an Italian, Urban VI, but then the French cardinals held a second conclave and elected a Frenchman, Clement VII, leaving the church with *two* popes, each declaring the other an antipope. This Great Schism lasted from 1378 to 1415, when matters were finally resolved by the Council of Constance, which ended both lines of the papacy and elected Pope Martin V in 1417.

The Avignon Papacy and the Great Schism are important for showing the turmoil and failure in leadership that plagued the fourteenth century, a time when social, economic, and health crises required strong, reliable, and consistent direction.

WRITING AND SOURCES

More medieval women in the later Middle Ages were educated and literate than in previous centuries, although not by the standards of their time. Literacy for medieval people usually meant the ability to read Latin, which some women could do, but more commonly, women learned to read in the vernacular. The education of elite women included learning multiple languages, usually French but possibly also Latin, German, Spanish, Italian, or Dutch. This expertise permitted some women to engage in translation work, such as the translations completed by Margaret Beaufort. Texts were not meant to be read silently, and medieval people commonly consumed the written word aurally, as a reader read the text aloud even privately. In monasteries mealtimes were accompanied by a sister reading aloud from a devotional or didactic text. In the home or even in social settings, reading aloud from a literary text, a collection of saints' lives, or a devotional text to a group was a common pastime. In this way a woman who could not read even in the vernacular, such as Margery Kempe, still had an intimate knowledge of many texts.

Writing was a separate skill from reading, and even those who could read a text might hire a scribe to write for them. Margery Kempe employed a number of different scribes and then finally a priest to write her book as she dictated it. This was common for holy women, to dictate their experiences to men who set them down, with the male authority and the women's holy experiences lending legitimacy to one another.

Other women could write for themselves and engaged in a world of letters to handle their family business, sending messages to children, husbands, friends, potential allies, and even business colleagues. There are a number of family letter collections, such as those of the Paston, Cely, and Stoner families, that show the clear involvement of women in pursuing family interests through letter writing.

Finding sources for the history of women in medieval England can be a challenge, since texts recording basic demographic information, such as tax records, do not always include women. While churches in England were required to record births, baptisms, marriages, and deaths after 1538, they did not do so in a systematic way earlier. Married women could not write wills, tombstones were rare for both sexes, husbands typically spoke for their wives in court, and even medical experts like midwives tended to be illiterate. Elite women did write letters and literature, but sources for the daily lives of non-elites are limited. These women are not invisible in the historical record, but finding them requires careful, sophisticated, and sometimes creative analysis. Historians are working with scholars of literature, archaeologists, statisticians, linguists, and biologists to learn new techniques and unearth new sources to be able to study women's lives in the past.

When evaluating primary sources, those texts or items created at the time under study, historians consider author, goal, audience, and context. The point of view of the source's author depends on his or her social status, level of education, location, occupation, faith, and so on. In the Middle Ages, most authors, although not all, were male elites. The majority of literate people in the Middle Ages were associated with the church: monks, nuns, and clerics. Although literacy improved over the course of the period, and noblemen and noblewomen increasingly became literate, the royal apparatus depended more and more heavily on written records, and commerce increased the literacy of the merchant and artisanal classes. Historians have excavated more and more female voices as part of the focus on women's history from the 1970s forward, but women authors and artists still account for a small portion of the sources extant from medieval England. Some scholars have pointed out the sexism of assuming that anonymous authors are all or usually male, since women are the ones who were most likely to mask their authorship, as we have seen with other female authors in later but still patriarchal periods. Some of the many anonymous texts from this period, such as *A Revelation of Purgatory*, can confidently be attributed to female authors.

Once we have a handle on knowing the author of a source, historians try to understand the author's goal: why the author created this document. This can mean determining the source's genre, as noting down a bawdy song can have a very different goal from writing a priest's penitential, a confessor's guide to sin and assigning penance, and both differ greatly from a letter or a coroners' roll. Historians want to understand what the author was trying to achieve, their purpose in creating the source.

The audience of a source refers to the author's intended or actual readers. Determining a medieval source's audience can be a challenge, but there can be clues in the source itself, in its transmission record—a history of who owned a manuscript containing the source—or in references to the source in other texts. Knowing, for example, that most medieval letters were written for a public audience can affect how historians read the more intimate details they contain. Examining the source's audience is important for understanding how significant the source was at the time, how medieval people reacted to it, and what meanings medieval audiences attached to the source.

Last, historians locate their sources in context, the time and place and situation in which the source was created. Knowing that a will was made during the Black Death can help a historian understand the way property was distributed in that source; knowing that a historical chronicle about fourteenth-century England was written in fifteenth-century France can help a historian determine how much weight to put on its description of events, particularly those that conflict with documents written closer to the places and events.

Sources for the fourteenth and fifteenth centuries in England were primarily in Middle English, Latin, or French, depending on author, goal, or audience. Several of them were filtered through notaries or scribes as they were set down in manuscripts and then recopied and distributed. Most modern students who read a medieval source, such as *The Book of Margery Kempe*, read a version that has been transcribed from its handwritten manuscript, edited, and translated into modern English. It is worth keeping in mind the number of interventions between us and the source, even when reading the source itself.

There is an important distinction between prescriptive and descriptive sources. Prescriptive sources lay out rules that people should follow or detail ideals for society, such as laws and religious treatises. Descriptive sources, as one might imagine from the name, are those that describe society and culture as it is in the author's perception, such as memoirs, letters, or court records. England in the late Middle Ages was unusually litigious and, while sources are not complete, legal documents provide an extraordinary amount of information about England and women's lives. While there were some informal customs that discouraged women from testifying in court, there appears to have been no legal bar for their testimony, and women testified quite a lot in the Yorkshire courts. Both types of sources have their place: prescriptive sources depict expectations and guidelines, even as we cannot assume that these matched actual practice; nonfiction descriptive sources depict life as it happened, but cannot always demonstrate whether that was a unique or common experience. Works of literature such as Geoffrey Chaucer's *The Canterbury Tales* offer more colorful illustrations of life as Chaucer imagined it, but it is not clear how well that matched reality, particularly when authors worked in metaphor and allegory. This is further complicated by medieval authors' conformity to genre and comfort with recycling examples to fit an expected model. By using a range of sources, historians can present a fuller picture of medieval life in its expectations, lived reality, and cultural vision.

MONEY

English money in this period was based in coinage, which was divided into units of pence, shillings, and pounds. Pence, the smallest unit, was also known as a penny and represented with a d. for the Latin *denarius* that was the smallest unit in the older Roman system. Shillings were worth twelve pence and abbreviated with an s., while the pound was worth twenty shillings and abbreviated with £. Pence might be cut down into halfpennies and even quarter-pennies, known as a farthing (Amt and Smith 2018, xix). Many transactions were conducted based on transfer of goods or services, but England, by the fourteenth century, was increasingly operating in a monetary system with cash paid for wages, goods, and even some rents.

Conversions between medieval amounts and modern currency are challenging, but it is possible to assess the value of these coins. In the 1350 London Wage and Price Regulations, a mason or a carpenter earned five to six pence per day, while a laborer earned three to three and a half pence per day. A fine cloth or silk dress for a woman cost two shillings and six pence, with another four pence for sleeves. A pair of leather shoes cost six pence, while a bottle of wine was at least sixteen pence (Amt and Smith 2018, 322–323).

FOR FURTHER READING

For more information about studying race in the Middle Ages, consult *Race and Medieval Studies: A Partial Bibliography*, compiled by Jonathan Hsy and Julie Orlemanski, https://docs.google.com/document/d/18JClsma1BMKYCxvgeWqwPej3ZSCrQXlAlXbL0C dqWmE/edit, and the Teaching Association for Medieval Studies

Featured Lesson Resource Page on Race, Racism and the Middle Ages, compiled by Carol L. Robinson, https://teams-medieval.org/?page_id=76.

Amt, Emilie, and Katherine Allen Smith, eds. 2018. *Medieval England 500–1500: A Reader*. 2nd ed. Toronto: University of Toronto Press.

Bennett, Judith M. 2007. *History Matters: Patriarchy and the Challenge of Feminism*. Philadelphia: University of Pennsylvania Press.

Blamires, Alcuin, ed. 1992. *Woman Defamed and Woman Defended: An Anthology of Medieval Texts*. Oxford: Clarendon Press.

Feminae: Medieval Women and Gender Index. University of Iowa Libraries. https://inpress.lib.uiowa.edu/feminae/.

Goldberg, P. J. P. 1995. *Women in England c. 1275–1525: Documentary Sources*. Manchester: Manchester University Press.

Goldberg, P. J. P. 2007. "Gender and Matrimonial Litigation in the Church Courts in the Later Middle Ages: The Evidence of the Court of York." *Gender & History* 19, no. 1: 43–59.

Grauer, Anne L. 2002. "Where Were the Women?" In *Human Biologists in the Archives: Demography, Health, Nutrition and Genetics in Historical Populations*, edited by D. Ann Herring and Alan C. Swedlund, 266–288. Cambridge: Cambridge University Press.

Green, Monica H. 2014. "Pandemic Disease in the Medieval World: Rethinking the Black Death." Special Issue of the *Medieval Globe* 1.

Karras, Ruth Mazo. 2005. *Sexuality in Medieval Europe: Doing unto Others*. New York: Routledge.

Partner, Nancy F., ed. 1993. *Studying Medieval Women: Sex, Gender, Feminism*. Cambridge, MA: Medieval Academy of America.

Salisbury, Eve, ed. 2002. *The Trials and Joys of Marriage*. Kalamazoo, MI: Medieval Institute Publications. https://d.lib.rochester.edu/teams/publication/salisbury-trials-and-joys-of-marriage.

Schaus, Margaret, ed. 2006. *Women and Gender in Medieval Europe: An Encyclopedia*. New York: Routledge.

Ward, Jennifer. 2006. *Women in England in the Middle Ages*. New York: Hambledon Continuum.

Waymack, Anna Fore, ed. *De raptu meo*. A Website for Documents Related to Cecily Chaumpaigne. https://chaumpaigne.org/.

Wilson, Katharina M., and Nadia Margolis, eds. 2004. *Women in the Middle Ages: An Encyclopedia*. Westport, CT: Greenwood Press.

TIMELINE

1066	Norman conquest of England.
1128	Marriage of Empress Matilda to Geoffrey of Anjou.
1135	Death of Henry I.
1154	Accession of Henry II and Eleanor of Aquitaine.
1170	Death of Thomas Becket.
1215	Fourth Lateran Council.
1218	Edict of the Badge.
1236	Statute of Merton, barred the legitimization of children born to unwed parents who later married.
1253	Statute of Jewry.
1272	Accession of Edward I.
1284	Statutes of Wales, giving England control over Wales.
1286	Death of King Alexander III of Scotland.
1290	Death of Margaret, the Maid of Norway.
1290	Death of Eleanor of Castile.
1290	Expulsion of the Jews from England.

1294	Foundation of Waterbeach Abbey by Denise de Montchensy.
1297	Birth of Cecilia Penifader in Brigstock.
1298	*Periculoso* issued by Boniface VIII.
1303	Death of Boniface VIII; election of Clement V.
1307	Death of Edward I; accession of Edward II.
1308	Marriage of Edward II and Isabella of France.
1309	Beginning of Avignon Papacy, when Clement V moved the Curia to Avignon.
1314	Battle of Bannockburn, leaving Scotland independent.
1315–1317	Great Famine.
1325–1326	Drought.
1327	Death of Edward II; accession of Edward III.
1328	Wedding of Edward III to Philippa of Hainault.
1330	Coronation of Philippa of Hainault as queen; birth of Edward, Black Prince of Wales.
1337–1453	The Hundred Years War.
1339	Foundation of Denny by Marie de St.-Pol.
1344	Cecilia Penifader died.
1346	Battle of Crécy during the Hundred Years War.
1348–1350	Black Death in England.
1349	Ordinance of Laborers.
1351	Statute of Laborers.
1351	Sumptuary legislation regarding prostitutes
1356	Battle of Poitiers/Tours.
1358	Jacquerie rebellion in France.
1358	Death of Queen Isabella of France.
1363	Sumptuary legislation limited clothing of women.
1364	Foundation of Bruisyard Abbey by Lionel, duke of Clarence.
1369	Death of Queen Philippa of Hainault.

c. 1373	Birth of Margery Kempe.
c. 1373	Julian of Norwich entered her anchor-hold.
1376	Death of Edward, Black Prince.
1377	Death of Edward III; accession of Richard II.
1377	Condemnation of John Wycliffe.
1378	Death of Gregory XI in Rome; election of Urban VI and Clement VII; beginning of the Great Schism.
1380	Cecily Chaumpaigne released Geoffrey Chaucer from her charge of *raptus*.
1381	English Peasants' Revolt.
1382	Statute of Rapes.
1384	Death of John Wycliffe.
1390	Statute of Pardons.
1394	Death of Queen Anne of Bohemia.
1394	Arrest of Eleanor/John Rykener.
1399	Deposition of Richard II; accession of Henry IV.
1400	Death of Richard II; death of Geoffrey Chaucer.
1403	Wedding of Joan of Navarre and Henry IV.
1413	Death of Henry IV; accession of Henry V.
1413	Visit of Margery Kempe to Julian of Norwich.
1415	Battle of Agincourt.
1415	Great Schism resolved by the Council of Constance and election of Martin V.
1415	Foundation of Syon Abbey by Henry V.
1416	Death of Julian of Norwich.
1420	Treaty of Troyes, marriage of Henry V to Catherine of Valois, signed by Queen Isabeau of France.
1422	Death of Henry V and Charles VI; accession of Henry VI.
1428	Decree of Parliament requiring consent for a dowager queen's remarriage after the marriage of Catherine of Valois to Owen Tudor.

1429	Joan of Arc lifts siege at Orléans.
1429	Charles VII crowned king of France.
1430	Joan of Arc captured.
1431	Joan of Arc burned at the stake.
1437	Death of Catherine of Valois.
1438	Death of Margery Kempe.
1445	Marriage of Henry VI to Margaret of Anjou.
1450	Jack Cade's Rebellion.
1453	Birth of Edward, prince of Wales to Henry VI and Margaret of Anjou. Henry VI suffered from a mental breakdown for a year.
1457	Birth of Henry Tudor to Margaret Beaufort.
1461	Deposition of Henry VI; accession of Edward IV.
1464	Marriage of Elizabeth Woodville and Edward IV.
1470	Deposition of Edward IV; reaccession of Henry VI.
1471	Second deposition of Henry VI; reaccession of Edward IV; death of Henry VI.
1471	Death of Edward, prince of Wales, son of Henry VI and Margaret of Anjou.
1482	Death of Margaret of Anjou.
1483	Death of Edward IV; accession of Edward V, never crowned; accession of Richard III; coronation of Anne Neville.
1484	Death of Edward, prince of Wales.
1485	Battle of Bosworth Field; accession of Henry VII, his marriage to Elizabeth of York; death of Anne Neville.
1487	Coronation of Elizabeth of York.
1491	Birth of Henry, future Henry VIII.
1492	Death of Elizabeth Woodville.
1502	Death of Arthur, prince of Wales.
1503	Death of Elizabeth of York.
1509	Death of Henry VII; accession of Henry VIII.

GLOSSARY

Abbess: the female superior of an abbey.

Abbey: a monastery housing either monks or nuns.

Abortifacient: a remedy that induces a woman to abort a fetus. Can be ingested, inhaled, or applied through vaginal fumigation.

Advowson: the privilege to appoint a parish priest.

Almoner: a church officer responsible for distributing donated alms to the poor.

Anchoress: a female hermit who lives in a cell.

Anchor-hold: the cell of an anchoress.

Apprentice: typically, a child from about age seven contracted to learn a craft from a guild member or other expert in the craft.

Assart: new land such as a forest or swampland cleared for farming.

Bailiff: an official on a manor who collected fines and rents.

Baptism: one of the seven sacraments, a Christian rite involving holy water and oil.

Bawd: a woman who employed prostitutes and connected them with clients.

Beguine: a lay religious woman devoted to a life of charity and chastity, but not enclosed in a monastery.

Bellatores: in Latin, "those who fight," indicating the second estate, made up of the aristocracy that governed England and devoted themselves to its wars.

Black Death: the major outbreak of plague caused by *yersinia pestis* that lasted in England from 1348 to 1350.

Brewster: a female brewer of ale.

Carthusian: an eleventh-century monastic order founded by Bruno of Cologne, as a community of hermits with individual cells but communal prayers.

Cellaress: a monastic office responsible for the abbey's stores and supplies.

Chevage: a fee for a serf to live away from the manor.

Churching: a religious ritual purifying Christian women about forty days after childbirth.

Cloister: a covered portico enclosing an open-air garden in a monastery, also used as a term for the monastery itself.

Concubinage: a heterosexual relationship that might involve a financial transaction (prostitution) as part of an ongoing relationship. Since clergymen were required to be celibate, domestic partnerships with women were described as "concubinage."

Conjugal debt: marital partners were obliged to have sexual intercourse with their spouse, a "debt" they were required to pay on demand, sometimes call the "marital debt."

Consanguinity: a familial relationship, sharing blood kinship.

Contraception: a remedy that prevents conception, often ingested or used as a barrier.

Court Rolls: records from judicial courts of various kinds written on parchment and then stitched together and kept rolled.

Cucking Stool: a wooden pole with a seat on the end that could be levered into and out of water, as a punishment for women strapped into the chair.

Demesne: the lord's arable fields on a manor, which serfs were obliged to work.

Distaff: a stick used for spinning thread or yarn, sometimes used as a metaphor for women.

Dower: the material goods, property, or cash a husband set aside for his wife's support during her widowhood should he predecease her. Typically, property was only in her use for her lifetime and then reverted to her husband's family or heirs.

Dowry: the material goods, property, or cash a bride's family contributed to the marriage.

Feme Covert: a married woman.

Feme Sole: an unmarried woman, either one who has never married or a widow.

Fief: a piece of land given by a lord to his vassal in exchange for an oath and military service.

Flagellants: a group of penitents who processed wearing long loincloths, singing hymns, and whipping themselves in an effort to atone for the sins they believed had caused the fourteenth-century Black Death.

Gleaning: the process of picking over a harvested field for grain that was left behind, typically a process reserved for poor women and children.

Great Famine: a time of starvation 1315–1322 when heavy rains caused crops to fail several years in a row.

Guild: the organization that oversaw a craft in a town.

Herbalist: a medical expert in the use of herbs for remedies, with a collection of necessary herbs, able to make medicines and advise treatment. Lower-status medical worker than an apothecary.

Infirmarian: a monastic office responsible for caring for the sick and injured in an abbey.

Journeyman: a day laborer who received wages for his craft work in a guild workshop.

Laboratores: in Latin, "those who work," the third and lowest estate made up of the peasants who farmed the land.

Leprosarium: a hospital devoted to the care of patients with leprosy.

Leyrwite: a fine charged to serfs who had premarital sex, typically imposed only on female serfs.

Lord: title for the person who controlled a manor or held homage from a vassal.

Manor: a rural estate that included a village, arable fields, pastureland, a parish church, mill, oven, winepress, and a manor house where the manor's lord might live.

Manorialism: the system of manors that organized and encouraged farming and pastoralism.

Merchet: a license serfs needed to buy in order to marry.

Midwife: a female medical worker specializing in obstetrics and gynecology, particularly expert at childbirth.

Novice: a monastic candidate in training to take holy orders, a period known as their novitiate.

Novice-mistress: a monastic office responsible for training novices during their novitiate.

Oblation: a payment to a priest for his services.

Oratores: in Latin, "those who pray," or the first estate, indicating monks and nuns as well as the secular clergy.

Pax: a decorated board passed around during mass to share the kiss of peace.

Periculoso: papal decretal from 1298 requiring female monasteries to be enclosed.

Pillory: a public shaming device made of a wooden frame with spaces for the head and hands.

Precentress: a monastic office with responsibility for the music and readings for the canonical office.

Prioress: a monastic office responsible for governing a priory or for assisting an abbess in governing an abbey.

Procuress: a woman who encouraged women into prostitution and found them clients.

Prostitute: a woman who sold sex.

Reeve: chief magistrate in a town or on a manor.

Relic: a fragment of a saint's body.

Reliquary: a case, often heavily decorated with luxurious materials, for a relic.

Rood Screen: a barrier separating the chancel from the nave and blocking view of the priest during mass.

Sacrist: a monastic office with responsibility for maintaining the abbey church.

Serf: an unfree peasant obliged to remain on a manor and perform labor in the lord's demesne lands as well as pay certain fees.

Simony: the buying or selling of church offices.

Singlewoman: an unmarried woman, or in some definitions, a never-married woman.

Stocks: a punishment device made of a wooden frame with space to bind the wrists and placed in a public place such as a market.

Tallage: tax imposed on serfs at the lord's whim.

Tertiary: member of the third order of the mendicant monastic groups.

Thewe: a pillory designed for punishing women.

Three-field system: a process of field rotation that divided arable land into thirds and left one-third fallow, used one-third for planting grain, and used the last third for planting a legume.

Ward: someone placed under the guardianship of another. A ward was typically a child, but it may also be a widow from an aristocratic family.

1

MARRIAGE

EXPECTATIONS

Most women in medieval England married and started a new household with their husbands. Marriage was a strategy for medieval families to secure alliances, ensure smooth transitions to heirs for family property, and promote social stability. Families used marriage to bring in new property, wealth, and connections; artisans married for a partner with complementary duties to support the shop; peasants married for help running the agricultural household. Yet medieval women and men also expected to find affection and love in their marriages, and love matches certainly took place. Even elites who arranged marriages for their children expected the matches to be harmonious and to become affectionate. Not all marriages could achieve these goals, however; while dissolving a marriage was difficult and challenged by the church, it was possible in some cases.

Paul had advised Christians to marry if they could not remain celibate in his first letter to the Corinthians. Paul wished that "all of you were as I am" but recognized that since "sexual immorality is occurring, each man should have sexual relations with his own wife, and each woman with her own husband" (1 Corinthians 7:2–9). Paul advised the Corinthians that to have sex within marriage was not a sin; even if it was better to remain a virgin and unmarried like Paul, he recognized this was not possible for all Christians. Chaucer's Wife of Bath expressed familiarity with this idea in a long passage of her prologue, using a metaphor of fine and lesser quality bread to describe the difference between the celibate and married life. She declared herself comfortable being made of the lesser, coarser bread if it meant she could enjoy sex both for procreation and recreation.

By the time of Chaucer, marriage was governed by canon law in medieval England. Marriage was not permitted within four degrees of consanguinity or blood relationship—so those who shared great-great-grandparents were too closely related to marry. In previous centuries the limit had been for seven degrees of consanguinity, but that restriction proved to be too challenging to enforce, and the 1215 Fourth Lateran Council changed the limitation to four degrees. There were also restrictions based on affinity, prohibiting marriage to one's former sister-in-law, one's own child's godparents, and the relative of a previous sexual partner. Any of these too-close relationships—for consanguinity, godparents, or other affinity—could be solved by a special dispensation from the church, but for most people, these were unenforceable restrictions that were largely ignored unless another reason to dissolve the marriage arose, as most famously for Henry VIII in the sixteenth century or Eleanor of Aquitaine and her first husband, Louis VII, in the twelfth. Canon law governed marriage, and documents from the church courts do contain numerous cases attempting to dissolve marriages or resolve issues related to consanguinity and affinity.

After the twelfth century, the Christian church considered marriage to be one of the seven sacraments. This set up a conflict in how the church and some members of the laity understood marriage. On the one hand, parents expected to arrange marriages for their children, which ensured a stable society with legitimate heirs to inherit property. On the other hand, the church stressed the consent of marital partners alone, without reference to the permission of the parents, a model that threatened patriarchal control of children and family. Tension between these models led to court cases disputing the validity of marriages where consent had been given in private, unwillingly, or not at all, with fathers occasionally accusing a new son-in-law of *raptus*—a legal term used to describe abduction, seduction, elopement, and rape—in seducing or abducting his daughter. Canon law governed marriage, marital relations, and possible marital dissolutions. Adultery was prohibited for both partners.

Peasants who lived on manors were not required to receive the lord's consent to marry after 1234, but elites still interfered in marriages, with particular interest in keeping peasants on the manor and not marrying someone from far away. Marriages on the estate would ensure a lasting workforce, and it was more common for families who knew each other well to encourage marriage within subsequent generations. The strong intervention of lords and families perhaps encouraged couples to cohabitate instead, or to engage in trothplight, exchanging vows before witnesses but without the church. Couples in such informal unions opened themselves up to charges of fornication, which typically fell on the woman.

In the thirteenth century, an English synod created a mechanism to force marriage on repeat fornicators—once warned, having sex again would formalize the marriage. For example, in July 1363 William Trumpour and Joan de Gyldesum were charged with fornication and swore that if they were to have sex again they would have to marry (Goldberg 1995, 117). This case demonstrates the church's interest in curtailing fornication and in pressing recidivist fornicators into marriage where their sexual activity would no longer be a problem. It also displays the sort of miscommunications between men and women around sex and marriage: Joan believed William had already promised marriage, while William denied any betrothal, not willing to take on a wife, even for a woman he bedded. The message was clear, however, that future sexual activity between them would come with a wedding, and with a court record documenting William's word, he could not in the future pretend Joan misunderstood him. It is also of note that the confession reduced the penalty, but Joan still suffered three whippings. It was possible to avoid this penalty altogether by marrying before the court date, as in 1399 John Esyngwald and Elizabeth Snawe did when they were caught fornicating. John took an oath on the Bible that he would marry Elizabeth when unmentioned obstacles to their wedding were removed and gave a deadline of the feast of St. Mark the Evangelist for the celebration.

In late medieval England, marriage was legal at puberty, twelve for girls and fourteen for boys, but betrothal could be as early as age seven. Mary Percy was married to John de Southeray in 1377 when she was only eight or nine, probably because Alice Perrers, John's mother and Mary's guardian, wanted to make the marriage official because wardship was at risk. Alison, Chaucer's Wife of Bath, notes that she was married at age twelve. A betrothal could include future consent, but both parties had to grant consent again at a legal age for the marriage. Marriage for the lower-status groups was later, late teens or early twenties, particularly for those groups that moved to the cities for work that typically delayed marriage.

Present-tense consent, or future-tense consent followed by consummation, was sufficient to make a marriage legal in the eyes of the church court. The large amount of matrimonial litigation demonstrates that marriage was more complicated than simple consent suggests, however, as various parties challenged the legality of the union, or one part of the couple remembered events differently. Witnesses testified to demonstrate that both parties were of age, were free to consent, did consent, or that the marriage was consummated, and their testimony shows how little privacy there was in the Middle Ages for even the most intimate of moments. A York woman named Maud Katersouth testified in 1355 on behalf of Maud de Bradelay, who claimed to be the wife of John de Walkyngton after he offered future-tense consent and they consummated the marriage. Maud Katersouth explained that John called for Maud de Bradelay from his bed, but she declined. She claimed that he then called out, "[Y]ou are mine and I am yours. . . . I refuse to seek permission from you to do my will with you," and that Maud had demanded a formal proposal, which he gave, and Maud responded, "[N]ow you can do your will with me" (Goldberg 2013, 37).

Bound up in these cases is concern about extra- or premarital sex. Chastity before marriage remained an expectation for elite girls, but leyrwite fines, manor fines on sexual relations before marriage, were common enough among the peasantry to suggest chastity was not a regular expectation. Sex before marriage could lead to pregnancy, which was a concern both for the reputation and future prospects of the woman and for the legitimacy and inheritance of the child. In order for a child to be legitimate, and thus a legal heir, the parents had to be married before its birth. The 1236 Statute of Merton prohibited the legitimization of children whose parents later married. There were exceptions such as the children of John of Gaunt and Katharine Swynford; John of Gaunt's elevated status as the son of Edward III brought him privileges not available to most people.

Marriages were expected to be consummated, although there might be a delay for a young bride. Both husband and wife were expected to pay the conjugal or marital debt, to have sex with their partner when requested. There were occasions of spiritual marriages that remained chaste by both parties' agreement. Margery

Kempe negotiated long and forcefully with her husband for the right to live a chaste life; while he refused, she was forced to pay the conjugal debt. He finally agreed to live in chastity with Margery, to her great happiness.

Legally, once women married, they became known as "femes covert," whose husbands were responsible for their property, business, and legal dealings, with the law treating them as a single person and dealing exclusively with the husband. Wives did not control their own property or inheritances, could not transact legal business independently, and required their husband's permission to make a will. Women could still conduct business, but their husbands were responsible legally for them.

In the thirteenth century, peasants were beginning to use surnames and pass them on to the next generation. Practice was not standard, however, and a woman might remain known under her father's surname, as Cecilia Penifader did since she remained a singlewoman, but married women might do the same or become known as "Cecilia, wife of" her husband after marriage.

PROPERTY AND NEGOTIATIONS

In the fourteenth-century conduct poem "How the Good Wife Taught Her Daughter," girls learn how to behave when approached by a suitor, with the wife telling them to report any suitors to their family for assessment regardless of her feelings (Furnivall 1908). The poem's advice acknowledges that the selection of a husband will not be the girl's decision, or at least not hers alone, but will be a negotiation between her suitor and her parents, or perhaps between both sets of parents. The warning not to hide the suitor reflected medieval fears of children eloping, since consent could be given legally without parental approval or knowledge. Yet the significance of marriage to the family, as an opportunity to rise in status, to secure titles or property, and as a way to ensure that children were well placed and well cared for, meant that parents were eager to control this process. Negotiations over marriages, dowers, and dowries were extensive and complicated. Indeed, the Good Wife advised her daughter to take good care of her own daughters from birth but to also quickly marry them off when they came of age (Furnivall 1908).

While canon law governed many aspects of marriage, secular courts had jurisdiction over marital property issues and inheritance. While at this time the law was increasingly recognizing primogeniture, the rights of the firstborn to inherit the core of a parent's estate, girls were still permitted to inherit, especially in the absence of a brother. Coheiresses, such as Isabelle and Anne Neville, could receive a division of land between them. It was occasionally custom, however, to recognize the superior claim of the elder sister and grant her a larger or more choice portion of the estate, as the Neville sisters' husbands, each a brother of Edward IV, disputed.

Husbands and wives began to practice joint tenure of their property, or jointure, in the thirteenth century. As a result there was some reduction in the size of the dower, as the wife had less need of specially designated dower income when she controlled the lot. Entailment, which forced estates to be settled on a male heir across generations regardless of the will of individual holders, was a fifteenth-century effort to both curtail dowers and limit the widow's power through jointure.

Families with wealth and status typically arranged marriages for their children, and this might even be true among the more well-off members of the peasantry. Marriage was a way to build alliances or end hostilities, such as the marriage of William de Bohun, Earl of Northampton, one of Edward III's allies, to Elizabeth de Badlesmere, daughter-in-law to one of Edward's opponents. It was also a way for a family to expand its reach, wealth, and power. As Judith Bennett quipped about the Stoner and Cely families, "[T]hese merchant families were as attuned to making a good deal in the marriage market as they were in the wool trade" (Hanawalt 2007, 82). When William Paston married Agnes Berry in 1420, and their son John married Margaret Mautby c. 1440, the Pastons chose women from wealthy families. Agnes brought with her a large dowry, and she also inherited wealth from her father, Sir Edmund Berry. Similarly, Margaret Mautby inherited properties as her father's sole heir and had extensive social connections.

Women in the families executed many of these negotiations, as the Paston letters demonstrate. Women relied on gossip within their familial and social networks to identify acceptable marriage partners for their children, paying special attention to information about children in their networks as well as to information about their financial status and inheritance prospects. News that a young woman's husband had left her widowed and wealthy was of great interest as was news that an only daughter's parents had died and left her an heiress. Letters can give hints to how this news was shared as a letter in the Stoner family documents Elizabeth Ryche

Stoner learning of a likely candidate for one of her daughters from a dinner companion while visiting London (Kingsford 1919, 19).

Status was also an important consideration, with some families hoping to marry into the peerage or others looking to maintain living standards by bringing in more wealth. Chaucer's Wife of Bath bragged that each of her first three husbands was a wealthy man of good standing. The Pastons and the Cleres, both important families in fifteenth-century Norfolk, negotiated several times to arrange marriages between their families. The negotiations are preserved in letters and demonstrate the careful consideration given to these arrangements as well as the power women such as Elizabeth Clere and Margaret Paston wielded in their families. Several of these attempted matches failed, such as that between John Paston III (d. 1504) and Margaret Clere, who instead married Ralph Shelton, one of the Clere's neighbors; that between Anne Paston and Robert Clere, who instead married Anne Hopton; and that between William Paston IV and either Audrey or Dorothy Clere, who appear never to have married while William married Bridget Heydon. The families finally arranged a match between them with William's sister Elizabeth, who married Elizabeth Clere's grandson William in 1498. Even in this we see Elizabeth Clere's great control over the family property, as in her 1493 will she made William's inheritance conditional upon his continued good behavior. Both families were large landholders in the area, and arranging these matches was a way to hold onto their properties, and women were deeply involved in both the arrangements and the administration of the family's wealth.

Elizabeth Woodville's efforts to place her many siblings into good marriages after becoming Edward IV's queen demonstrate how she and her family used her position and access to raise her family's status considerably. She helped to arrange marriages for at least eight of her siblings to earls, dukes, barons, counts, baronesses, and duchesses. Because Elizabeth's father, Sir Richard Woodville, was not a nobleman, these efforts to connect her kin to such prestigious families was not popular among her opponents, especially when she arranged the marriage of her brother John, aged nineteen, to Catherine Neville, Dowager Duchess of Norfolk, aged sixty-five and aunt to Elizabeth's greatest critic in Edward's circle, Richard Neville, Earl of Warwick.

When considering a match, families typically negotiated a marriage contract specifying what the bride might bring into the marriage with her dowry and what resources the groom would settle on her from his property as a dower. The dower would provide land or income for his widow should her husband predecease her. A widow held her dower for life, and then it reverted to her husband's heirs; she could not reassign that property herself without their permission. The dowry came from the bride's father and could be used by her husband during the marriage. Wealthy fathers made arrangements for a suitable dowry for their daughters in their wills, such as Richard, Earl of Arundel (d. 1397), who left his daughter Margaret 1,000 marks for her dowry (Ward 2006, 28). There was an expectation that the dowry and dower would be about equal, and they varied according to the wealth of the families. Dower had been regularized in the thirteenth century to constitute one-third of the husband's lands.

In London the marriage contract could be negotiated between the prospective brides and grooms, often by an older male go-between who could also determine if they were truly free to wed. For artisans and merchants, negotiations of a match especially considered movable wealth a wife might bring into the marriage as well as connections that might assist in establishing or growing a business, both of which made wealthy widows of men in similar fields very attractive. The negotiation resembled a courtship, with gift exchanges as well as notes and terms. Such gifts might be jewelry and other small items that indicated affection and suggested intent. Thomas Betson sent his future bride Katherine Ryche a ring, and she sent him a token as well (Kingsford 1919, 7).

The king's vassals were expected to consult with him about the marriage of their female relatives and children, especially their heirs, although possibly less so after the time of Edward III. English kings also held guardianship over the minor heirs and widows of their vassals and could determine the marriages of these wards. Brides and grooms still had to consent to the marriages, but they did not have many alternatives. Wardship rights could also be sold to other lords at a great profit. In London the mayor had the right to oversee the marriages of orphans and benefited financially from that privilege. He could charge a fee for a license to marry an orphan as well as fine those who married without his permission. In the case of John Hurlebatie, who married Joan, daughter of an alderman, without license, the mayor punished not only John but also the two witnesses, who were imprisoned and fined; one of the witnesses lost his citizenship (Hanawalt 2007, 72–73).

Lords held complicated rights over peasants who lived on their manors. Serfs needed a license to marry, known as *merchet*. There is some evidence that merchet declined in the wake of the Black Death and further declined during the fifteenth century. The manor court rolls of Ingoldmells included these payments, with at least one freewoman paying for a license:

> [1303] From Elena Turs for licence to marry within the manor with five acres of bond land 10s., pledge William Abald pledge. . . .
> [1387] Joan Brok, a free woman, holding bond land, has licence to marry William Osmound, and gives to the lord for license, 40d. . . .
> [1401] Alice daughter of John Polayn, a bondwoman of the lord, has licence to marry Robert de Lancaster. (Massingberd 1902, 24, 185)

As these payments suggest, the crucial issues were permission to marry at all, whether the marriage was within or beyond the manor, and payment of the fine to the lord. Peasants paid other fines—for example, *childwite*, a fine demanded from a father whose unmarried daughter bore a child, or *leyrwite*, charged on women having premarital sex.

Townspeople had more freedom in marrying, depending on the town's charter, but generally they owed no merchet and needed no license. Guilds had a strong interest in the marriages of members' widows, and their statutes increasingly limited how long a widow could continue in the guild if she remarried outside the guild. In London marriage contracts, a bride's father might promise financial support for the household as part of the dowry. Court documents include cases of men complaining that their fathers-in-law had not paid the promised money, however. These might be quite small amounts, as in the case of the London clerk Richard Dryffeld, whose father-in-law, a scrivener, had promised one hundred marks for the household but had only paid twenty-six shillings (Hanawalt 2007, 80). Richard Cely's mother Agnes promised to give her son and his bride her London house from her dower property and made good on that promise in her will (Hanawalt 2007, 91).

WARDSHIP

The king of England had the right of wardship, or custody of the child and control over their estate, over minor noble heirs. As guardian, the king could arrange his ward's marriage and manage their lands as he liked, although the marriage partners still had to consent in the ceremony to make it legal in the eyes of the church. The king could also grant wardship to another lord or lady.

Wardships were supposed to be granted to the ward's close friend or relatives not in line to inherit the ward's property, but the king could reward his favorites as he liked. Wardships were politically important, as guardians might arrange marriages to suit their own interests, although they were required to select partners for their wards who were appropriate in terms of physical, legal, and social status. The age of majority in late medieval England was twenty-one for boys and fourteen for girls who married, sixteen for those who did not. These ages are different from those of canonical consent for marriage, which were twelve for girls and fourteen for boys, so it sometimes happened that wards married but remained under wardship. To finally inherit, a "proof-of-age" case might be required, in which the court investigated when a person was born based on the memories of neighbors, family, and friends. Male wards could also fall victim to abduction and forced marriage, when someone tried to force an underage ward into marriage without the guardian's consent.

Edward III became the guardian of Mary Percy when her mother died in 1369 and left her in control of extensive and valuable property. Edward granted her wardship to a supporter, but by May 1370, Edward's mistress Alice Perrers had acquired wardship of Mary. The most profitable element of wardship for Alice was the ability to arrange Mary's marriage. There was a market for selling the marriage rights to another, but Alice chose to arrange a marriage for Mary to Alice's own illegitimate son with Edward III, John de Southeray, keeping Mary's enormous lands in the family and bringing John more power. Alice probably rushed the marriage when Mary was too young, only about eight or nine, because Edward III's health was failing and Alice's position was uncertain. Her wardship over Mary may even have been the cause for Mary's brother, Henry, Lord Percy and later Earl of Northumberland, to oppose Edward III in the 1370s. Alice lost her wardship over Mary and control of her estates anyway when Edward died, and Alice was banished under Richard II.

CEREMONY

Church control of marriage after the Fourth Lateran Council in 1215 emphasized the importance of consent and publicity, with the emphasis on consent. In an ideal ceremony, the banns would be announced in public before the ceremony—the priest would announce three times in public that the marriage would take place. Reading the banns gave the public the opportunity to register opposition to the marriage, because of bigamy, consanguinity, or another bar to the match. In Ely's 122 marriage cases in court records between 1374 and 1382, twelve registered objections to the marriage (Sheehan 1996, 46–47). A priest could choose not to publicize the banns, however. In 1491 the archbishop of York, Thomas of Rotherham, allowed a couple who had lived together for a long time to marry without publishing the banns so their neighbors would not realize they had lived together unmarried, and he allowed, in 1495, a couple to marry without publishing the banns because the bride was visibly pregnant.

The ceremony itself could happen anywhere since it only required consent, but it was typically conducted at the church door, a place where there could be many witnesses to the words the couple spoke. In her prologue, the Wife of Bath mentions that she was five times married at the church door. According to John Fische, testifying in a 1365 York case disputing his sister's marriage, he saw his sister, Alice de Rouclif, and John marry in the room of Richard Bernard near St. Mary's Abbey. He was careful to quote the words they spoke, with John saying, "Here I take you Alice to my wife to have and to hold and to this I plight you my troth," and Alice responding, "And I take you John to my husband to have and to hold until the end of my life and to this I plight you my troth," followed by a kiss (Goldberg 1995, 68). The present-tense consent was crucial. After the vows, the priest blessed rings, which the couple exchanged. Priests preferred for a mass to follow, but not all weddings included the mass in the ceremony.

The bride and groom might wear special clothes for the occasion. In her 1377 marriage to John de Southeray, Mary Percy wore "a long mantle with a train lined with pured miniver," while John wore "a lined gown of cloth of silver [and] a hood of scarlet" (Tompkins 2018, 141). A mantle was a formal sleeveless garment fastened at the chest that lay over other clothes; this may have been made of silk. The pured miniver was all-white fur from Baltic squirrels. The cloth of silver that John wore was silk with silver thread.

The ceremony was followed by feasting, both in celebration and as a demonstration of the prestige and wealth of the families. The wedding of Elizabeth, daughter of Richard, Earl of Arundel, to Thomas de Mowbray, duke of Norfolk, was celebrated with a week of feasting in 1384 and counted even the king and queen among its guests. London merchants complained about elaborate celebrations thrown by fathers who could not cover the expenses for the wedding clothes, food, gifts, and entertainments. Celebrations for the merchant George Cely's wedding in London lasted ten days in May 1485 and included luxurious foods in large quantities as well as live rabbits released at the party. Most weddings took place at times that were already filled with celebrations, particularly because the church prohibited weddings during Advent, Rogation-tide, and Lent. That left January, the summer, and harvest time, all of which were popular times for parties.

At its heart, the crucial element of the wedding ceremony that constituted legal marriage in the eyes of the church was the couple's consent to marry. Consent had to be given by both parties, preferably in front of a priest and witnesses, followed by consummation, but consent alone was enough to make a marriage. The specific words used in the ceremony were important: consent in the present tense, "I take you as mine," was binding on its own whether or not the couple ever consummated the marriage; consent given in the future tense only constituted betrothal, unless it was followed by consummation, which constituted marriage. Late medieval English synods and councils emphasized that priests should only marry couples who gave present-tense consent, after the publication of the banns, who had a public ceremony, and when the priest knew both parties, in order to avoid a legally problematic secret marriage. They also expected betrothals to be made in front of a priest so that there would not be questions later about the words spoken and whether the betrothal was actually a marriage.

Because consent was sufficient to make a marriage, and publicizing the ceremony was desirable but not required, there were a number of clandestine marriages. Some of these later led to problems in the courts, with one party denying the marriage. Sometimes this was a way to cancel an unhappy marriage to clear the way for a new wedding; at other times, this was a way to seduce someone whose family would not approve of the match. In Chaucer's "Troilus and Criseyde," the title characters may have been in a clandestine marriage, after they exchanged consent and rings, but one that might not have stood up in court.

While betrothals were possible for underage parties, the wedding was supposed to wait until both had reached puberty, the age of consent. There were examples of underage marriages despite the church's prohibition, however. In 1354, the pope wrote the bishop of London, for example, to allow Roger Germany and Cicely le Haute to stay in the marriage they began at about age ten or eleven.

Because the parents' role in marriage negotiations was so strong but in reality marriage only required the consent of the bride and groom, there was a strong tradition of elopement, particularly for daughters who wanted their own choices or for men who wanted to improve their situation through attachment to a wealthy heiress. However, it was difficult to distinguish elopement or seduction with the woman's consent from abduction; since all were termed *raptus* in medieval law, the understanding and prosecution of rape was quite difficult, and it is still challenging for scholars to separate cases in which women sought to make their own choices against their parents' consent and those in which men abducted them. *Raptus* was seen as theft, a crime against the father's or husband's property, taking something of value from the men, not the woman.

Marie of Berry marries Philip of Artois in Paris, 1393, as depicted in Jean Froissart, Chroniques, British Library Harley ms 4380, f. 6r. While the marriage ceremony only required consent, families preferred public weddings with many witnesses. (The British Library)

LOVE AND AFFECTION

While love was not the primary driver of medieval marriages for all status levels, love matches did happen. Margery Paston eloped with a lover, Richard Calle, her family's bailiff, to the great distress of her parents. Margery's mother, Margaret, met with the bishop of Norwich to urge him to annul the marriage, but he decided that the marriage was legal and binding. Margaret's description of her meeting with the bishop in a letter to her husband demonstrates the depth of the parental dissatisfaction with the church's stance that the consenting words made marriage legal: "My mother and I informed him that we could never accept, from what she said, from the words that she had spoken with him [Calle] that either of them were committed to the other" (Watt 2004, 96–98). Richard did continue to work for the Pastons, however, and Margaret left twenty pounds to Margery's sons, John, William, and Richard, in her will.

Love could also dictate the marital choices of artisans. An apprentice, Anthony Pontisbury, had married during his apprenticeship despite a contract provision that he had to remain unmarried until his apprenticeship term was complete. The artisan who was his master had him arrested and imprisoned for violating this contract. Antony admitted he understood the contract's terms but that its restrictions on marriage were "contrary to the laws of God" because he had "an inward love to a young woman dwelling in [London] and the young wom[a]n having the same unto him, intending that both were to love under the laws of God . . . he has lately married and taken to wife the said young woman" (Hanawalt 2007, 72). Love for Anthony could not be stopped by contract.

Although the arrangement of marriages focused on the property negotiations, families also hoped their children's marriages would include affection and even love. Negotiations could take time and could include a courtship, with moments for the couple to meet, send tokens, and develop emotional connections. Thomas Betson's letters, preserved in the Stoner letter collection, demonstrate his affection for his fiancé, Katherine Ryche, daughter of Elizabeth Stoner from her first marriage, even while she was too young to marry him. In 1476, two years before their wedding and when Katherine was perhaps thirteen years old, Thomas wrote her that, "I recommend me unto you with all the inwardness of mine heart. And now lately you shall understand that I received a token from you, the which was and is to me right heartily welcome and with glad will I received it." And he expressed his eagerness for her to reach marrying age, giving her the advice to eat well: "And if you would be a good eater of your meat always, that you might wax and grow fast to be a woman, you should make me the gladdest man of the world, by my troth, for when I remember your favor and your sad loving dealing to me wards, for sooth you make me even very glad and joyous in my heart" (Kingsford 1919, 7). Thomas included a ring as a token of his affection.

MARITAL RELATIONS

Medieval English sermons emphasized companionate, faithful, and loving marriages, and late medieval romances celebrated courtly love, a literary game in which a lover idolized a pure and inspiring woman popular in stories of King Arthur and Robin Hood. The tomb of Richard II and Anne of Bohemia depicts them holding hands. Margery Brewes wrote to her husband John Paston III with affection. According to Anthony Fitzherbert's *The Book of Husbandry*, the couple should look to one another for their joy: "First and principally the wife is bound of right to love her husband, above father and mother, and above all other men. . . . A man should leave father and mother, and draw to his wife: and the same wise a wife should do to her husband. And are made by the virtue of the sacrament of holy scripture one flesh, one blood, one body, and two souls. Wherefore their hearts, their minds, their works, and occupations, should be all one, never to sever nor change during their natural lives, by any man's act or deed" (Fitzherbert 1534, 145).

While some young couples lived with their parents or other extended family, the nuclear family was the norm in late medieval England, particularly after the Black Death. Rather than moving into their husband's family's home, as some medieval women did elsewhere, in England, the couple typically started their own new household.

The bride's mother or guardian was responsible for helping her daughter to prepare a trousseau, the bride's clothes to bring with her into the marriage. Katherine Ryche's mother Elizabeth Stoner had asked Katherine's fiancé, Thomas Betson, to do the shopping, as he lived in London while they were in the country, but he confessed ignorance about what to purchase or how to ask for items to be prepared and asked Elizabeth for greater help. The trousseau Edward III provided to Mary Percy when she married his illegitimate son John de Southeray in 1377 included four silk gowns with fur collars and ermine cuffs, two scarlet and miniver mantles, and two embroidered blood-red mantles trimmed with gray fur. The groom's responsibility was to prepare the house for the couple, with furniture: bed, table, benches. In addition to his gift of a trousseau for Mary, Edward III gifted his son and daughter-in-law a bed of silk cloth.

Women were expected to run the household while the husband ran the estate, tended the farm, or ran the business. He was responsible for maintaining the marital property but could trust his wife to manage property during his absence or after his death. John Paston I frequently relied on his wife, Margaret, to run the estate in his absence, which was frequent, and her letters to him demonstrate that she did this ably. Husbands frequently named their wives the executors of their wills. With the growing practice of joint tenure, wives comfortably took over shared property after their husbands' deaths.

Sex was such an important component of the marriage that marital partners were obliged to pay the "marital debt," to have sex with their partner upon request regardless of circumstances. After many children together, Margery Kempe begged her husband to take a vow of chastity with her and stop obliging her to have sex with him, but he refused for many years. Margery did eventually have her way, but only after agreeing to resume dining with her husband. The marital debt even took precedence over a religious vow, so this consent to suspending marital sex was necessary on both sides.

Violence and Abuse

Historians have had mixed opinions on how well the ideal of a companionate marriage matched the reality of medieval marital relations. Women did take oaths to obey their husbands, and husbands had legal control over their wives, with religious sanction, as Paul's letter to the Ephesians commanded: "Wives, submit yourselves to your own husbands as you do to the Lord. For the husband is the head of the wife as Christ is the head of the church. . . . Now as the church submits to Christ, so also wives should submit to their husbands in everything" (Ephesians 5:22–23). Violence within marriage was likely common, as husbands were responsible for the public activities of their wives and were responsible for their obedience. Canon law placed wives *sub virga et potestate,* under the rod and power of their husbands, which meant husbands could discipline wives physically, within reason. This was justified as a husband's responsibility to "chastise his wife and beat her for her own correction; for she is of his household, and therefore the lord may chastise his own" (Coulton 1931, 3:119). Husbands were expected to govern their wives, and they were held responsible for their wives' misdeeds even if the husbands were not present at the time. Benedicta le Blunt attacked Joan Sprot, who complained that Richard had failed "to chastise his wife" (Butler 2007, 32). Wives might expect this as well as husbands, which complicates understanding from a modern perspective what medieval women saw as abuse and domestic violence. In her prologue, Chaucer's Wife of Bath describes a violent encounter between her and her much younger fifth husband, in which they assault each other, but he hits her to the point of hurting her ribs. Afterward, they make up, and their marriage is improved.

There were limits to the amount of corporal punishment a husband might employ, as the case of Thomas Louchard, a man who appeared in Droitwich before a church court in 1300, shows: Thomas confessed that he "[i]ll treated his wife with a rod," and he was sentenced to be "whipped in the usual manner once through the market" (Goldberg 1995, 140). Corporal discipline was not seen as problematic by itself, as Thomas's punishment was whipping, but its excessive or inappropriate use. Legally, husbands should respect their wives and "treat and govern her well and honestly, and to do no injury or ill to her body other than that permitted lawfully and reasonably to a husband for the purpose of control and punishment of his wife" (Pollock and Maitland 1968, 2: 436).

Husbands were responsible for governing their wives and took seriously the wife's vow to obey him. Christine de Pisan advised women to be obedient in public and save criticism for when the couple was alone. Nevertheless, some historians have seen the relationship between husband and wife in the Middle Ages as a partnership, and one in which women, especially wealthy women, might have a good deal of autonomy. The wife in "How the Good Wife Taught Her Daughter" warned the girl to protect herself by ensuring that she behaved well enough to avoid comment, especially by obeying her husband "meekly" (Furnivall 1908). Literature portrayed women as rebellious and violent toward their husbands or as nags, shrews, scolds, and gossips who needed correction, and legal records demonstrate this was not just a concern of fiction. When Henry Cook of Kent was accused of abandonment in 1347, he claimed he had left his wife because she was a scold. In 1488 Richard Styward of London justified his abuse of his wife by blaming her nagging and hostile language.

Lawmakers also were not specific in explaining what the limits were between acceptable discipline of wives and unacceptable spousal violence. Family members and neighbors might intervene with couples where violence seemed out of hand and even present inappropriate couples to manorial courts. It is possible that such community-based regulation of marital violence reduced the number of cases that made it to higher courts.

Causes of spousal assault included adultery, poverty, and mental illness. Some medieval clerics suggested that husbands beat their wives out of a crisis of masculinity when the power dynamic was upset by a wealthier, nobler, or otherwise more dominant wife. In order to reclaim their expected male dominance, such men turned to violence. Such a turn conflicted with the late medieval idea of the husband as protector and provider, but both these narratives conformed with ideas of patriarchy kept in force through the male domination of women.

The laws of coverture made it financially and legally difficult for a wife to leave her husband, and there were few avenues for support if she chose to do so since a husband could claim gifts others offered his wife for her support away from him. Even the wealthy and experienced Wife of Bath was irritated when her fifth husband took control of her property, which was his legal right. Spousal abuse was grounds for separation "from table and bed" in ecclesiastical courts, but not for divorce. While the church permitted separations, courts had an incentive to reconcile spouses, with pressure that may have made it more challenging for women to leave an abusive situation. Under common law, a woman could ask for a divorce if assaulted by her husband, but this did not happen often. The church considered abandonment or deprivation of a wife to be abuse and stepped in to prevent women from becoming sex workers or beggars, by pressing husbands to support them properly. In 1373 the ecclesiastical court in York required Thomas Waralynton to provide his wife Maud Tripp with food and other necessities after he had abandoned her (Butler 2007, 109).

Some husbands and wives were unhappy enough with their marriage to murder their spouse. Alison, the Wife of Bath, even suggested that she had plotted her fourth husband's murder with her fifth. Juliana de Murdak was found guilty of pressing her servants to murder her husband, Thomas, perhaps with the aid of the man she then married, and she was burned in 1321. The church considered spouse murder enough of an issue to prohibit adulterers from marrying their lover if they promised marriage while the wronged spouse still lived, or if there was any inkling that the adulterer had a role in their spouse's death. Abandonment and deprivation might also drive a wife to commit murder. In 1290 Dame Christian Meynell made a plot to murder her husband Sir Nicholas de Meynell because he had turned her out of the house and refused to support her. Nicholas accused Christian of the attempted murder as well as of adultery, but the archbishop of York described her as "blameless" and "fragile" because of her husband's abuse and neglect (Butler 2007, 112–113).

Common problems in a marriage included neglect, abuse, illness, conflict with in-laws, and debt, but adultery is significantly represented in court cases and literature. Married people expected their partners to be faithful, which was an absolute necessity for women to ensure correct paternity for their children. While adultery was a sin punished in church courts, some cases in the king's court suggest that adultery was an accepted justification for homicide when husbands killed their wives' lovers or even their wives. On the other hand, the church courts perceived a husband's adultery as one reason to free a wife from her responsibility to pay the conjugal debt.

CONCUBINAGE

Concubinage, or nonmarital cohabitating and sexual relationships, might also have been considered marriage, based on the consent of both parties. The church did try to press couples repeatedly accused of fornication into marriage, as noted above. Concubinage could not become marriage when one of the parties had some other impediment to marriage, such as a previous marriage or status as a cleric.

While monks and nuns had taken oaths of celibacy since the beginnings of monasticism, celibacy was not a formal requirement for the secular clergy—priests, bishops, cardinals, and so on. Clerical celibacy was reaffirmed as a goal repeatedly over the Middle Ages, but enforcement of that goal became formal when twelfth-century church councils prohibited clerical marriage and dissolved any existing marriages involving the clergy. In England, priests before this time had wives and even children. As the church hierarchy increasingly expected celibacy for all clerics, priests constructed a new understanding of masculinity that linked manliness with celibacy. Since masculinity was tightly associated with marriage, sex, and fatherhood, clerics shifted ideas of manliness to emphasize "virile chastity" that required strong wills, control of the body, and devotion to God (Thibodeaux 2015).

Even with formal standards of celibacy enforced by the church, clerical concubinage continued to be a problem still in late medieval England. English statutes were lenient for clerical fornication, but harsher for concubinage, and covered both the priest and his lover. Concubinage was a more significant problem because it was

so public, with hypocrisy that challenged a priest's role in dispensing penance, and because any children might expect to inherit
church property.

As with any sexual activity, children were a likely outcome of
these sexual relationships, and priests, as much as any father,
wished to see their children settled well. Priests often encouraged
their sons to look to the church and ensured they had an education
that would let them enter the clergy, a sensible career for someone
unlikely to inherit much property but with strong connections in
the church. Some men did pass on family property to their sons,
such as William Penifader, a man from a wealthy peasant family
in Brigstock, who left property in 1326 to a son, John, he had with
Alice Perse.

DISSOLUTION

Dissolution of a marriage was difficult under canon law. Paul,
so influential on the church's sense of marriage, had left little room
for interpretation on the question of divorce: "To the married I give
this command (not I, but the Lord): A wife must not separate from
her husband. But if she does, she must remain unmarried or else
be reconciled to her husband. And a husband must not divorce his
wife" (1 Corinthians 7:10–11). If the two parties had given present
consent and consummated the marriage, they had few options for
dissolution.

Divorce, as we know it today, was not an option in late medieval England; instead, couples who wished to separate had to
seek an annulment, which voided the marriage entirely. Attempts
to dissolve a marriage typically rested on disputing consent and
consummation or on demonstrating affinity or consanguinity that
should have prevented the match altogether. Annulment was possible if one party's consent had not been given freely; if one partner
was underage; in cases of consanguinity, impotence, and marriages
proven illegitimate because of bigamy; or when the husband was
convicted of a crime.

Demonstrating that a marriage had taken place when one of
the parties was underage is one method that appears frequently
in the extant records. Witnesses testified to the age of the marital
partners by remembering moments in their own lives, such as the
birth of a child, death of a husband, or marriage of a child. They
might remember the person's birth, their baptism, or their mother's
churching. Fixing these moments in the memories of neighbors is

one reason that families threw parties or gave gifts, as discussed in chapter 2. While time consuming and subject to mistakes, this sort of testimony, relying on memories, took the place of birth certificates or regular practice of noting births in the parish register.

Proving that consent had not been given freely was another method and sometimes points to troubling stories of quite young girls sought for their inheritance. In 1364 a young York girl was engaged, but she was seized by a different man against her will:

> [Isabel de Scarsbrok,] who in her tenth year was espoused to Henry Molineux, and was carried off with knowledge thereof, by John de Yorke, citizen of York, more desirous of patrimony than of matrimony, and was terrified by him into a clandestine contract of marriage. Afterwards, being freed from the said John by her relations, she remained with them until she became of marriageable age, and, keeping to her first espousals, publicly married Henry. John then, falsely asserting that she was contracted to him first, brought an action against her as his lawful wife, before the official of York, and so treated her advocates and proctors that no one dared to defend her, nor did dare to appear in person before the archbishop, being in fear of John, who, with a multitude of armed men, lay in wait for her. (Bliss and Twemlow 1902, 36–47)

In this case, John was able to insist on his desire for Isabel as a local strongman even if he had not kept possession of her person the entire time.

Failure to consummate the marriage or impotence was grounds for annulment, as each spouse was obligated to pay the marital debt. The claim of impotence had to be proven, and such investigations demonstrate an array of interesting techniques, from witnesses observing the couple attempting to have sex, to women (sometimes sex workers) attempting to entice the supposedly impotent man into an erection. Men as well as women might even inspect and handle the man's penis as part of their investigation. In 1370 John Saundirson's wife Tedia Lambhird claimed he was impotent and cited as witnesses John's brother and a man named Thomas, both of whom had witnessed the couple's failed attempts at sex. The physician Guy de Chauliac suggested that a man claiming or accused of impotence should lie in bed with a woman with sexual expertise who could assess and report back afterward. In 1433 three men investigated William Barton's penis when his wife Katherine Barlay claimed he was impotent; their report was favorable.

Spouses might also petition for a separation a mensa et thoro, "from table and bed," when both parties entered a religious institution and in cases of heresy, adultery, or excessive violence, but this did not dissolve the marriage or permit either party to remarry. A number of the women abducted in cases of *raptus* were married, and several were cases of adultery that the husband reported as abduction to demand recompense.

Even extreme violence could not always yield a separation. In 1396 York, Thomas Nesfeld's wife Margery sought a separation because of his violence. Two women testified as witnesses, Joan White and Margery Speight, that he had used a club against her, beat her, and broke her arm and that she was afraid for her life. Witnesses observed that Margery left their home, and when she eventually returned, Thomas hit her in the face. Joan and Margery were joined in their testimony by John Semer, a servant, while a sixty-year-old man named Richard Hanley, presumably a more established person in York, testified in Thomas's favor. Margery's petition was rejected (Goldberg 1995, 41–42).

Church courts governed marriage, and since marriages only required consent, which might happen in private, several cases focused on proving that one party had been forced or had not properly given consent in the present tense. If one party was below the age of consent (twelve for girls and fourteen for boys) or declared insane, they could not give consent under canon law. Those below the age of consent could marry, but they reserved the ability to annul the marriage later by withdrawing consent after they reached canonical age. This withdrawal of consent had to be stated publicly. Proving the marriage was invalid would make it possible to marry again, for a more fertile spouse or a more advantageous match.

Dissolution might involve negotiation once again. When Joan Hart went to court for the dissolution of her marriage to Robert Cely, she demanded to take her property and all the gifts Robert had given her before and during the marriage. The Celys eventually agreed to Joan's demands with the exception of a few high-value items: a gold girdle, a silver and gold pendant, a diamond ring, and some damask.

Even when force or inappropriate action was clear, dissolution was challenging and focused on other issues, such as illegitimacy. Mary Percy, daughter of Henry, Lord Percy of Alnwick, sought a divorce from John de Southeray, illegitimate son of Edward III and his mistress Alice Perrers, who was also Mary's guardian, as discussed earlier. The two had married in 1377 when Alice was at the height of her power, but within months Edward III had died, and Alice had been convicted of corruption and banished from England. The Percy family submitted in 1380 a petition to the pope for annulment, citing John's illegitimate ("defective") birth as grounds for a dissolution of their marriage. Pope Urban VI granted the annulment: "[S]ince she is now close to puberty and wishes to beget children, but in no way wishes to have the said John, who is not noble but plebeian, as her husband, but instead some other honest man of those parts, that we should deign by apostolic grace that this marriage should be declared to be annulled" (Tompkins 2018, 145) Urban appointed the bishop of Ely, at the time Mary's cousin Thomas Arundel, to oversee the case from there, probably giving John an opportunity to present his side. Mary remarried in 1382.

FEME SOLE

Some women, however, did not marry, or delayed marriage, or refused to remarry. Historians have referred to such women as "singlewomen," and they appear in the records of late medieval England as a "sengle woman" or *feme sole* or *femina sola* in French and then Latin. These terms included women who were unmarried, not yet married, or widows. Medieval texts suggest that respectable women who were not wives were expected to be virgins or widows, and there was a tendency to describe any sexually active singlewoman as a prostitute. Some singlewomen joined a monastery, but that was typically an option only for elite or wealthy women. We will examine such lifelong virgins committed to the church in chapter 6 and discuss widows in the next section of this chapter. The work of singlewomen is an important part of chapter 4 and sex work an important part of chapter 5. Here we will examine the impact of remaining single on women's roles in late medieval society.

In late medieval England, particularly after the plague in the mid-fourteenth century, both men and women from non-elite families delayed marriage until their mid to late twenties, a demographic reality that led to a greater appearance of singlewomen in records from this time. English poll-tax records from the late fourteenth century suggest as much as 30–40 percent of women above the age of fourteen were still single (Kowaleski 1999, 46, 50–51). This trend was especially strong among urban women from middle- or lower-status groups. These demographics meant that even for women whose life cycle would include marriage, there could be an extended period of single adulthood before marriage, in addition to periods of widowhood. For some single people, virginity and widowhood were parts of the life cycle that included marriage, the maid, wife, widow cycle, with periods of chastity for part but not all of a woman's life. These marital patterns were different for elites, who married younger, in their teens, and among whom singlewomen were rare.

Theologically, the single state was the ideal of the early church fathers who, along with Paul, praised virginity and chastity (for widows) above the sexually active wife and far above the sins of unmarried fornication. According to an influential reading by Jerome, the parable of the sower in the Gospel of Matthew (Matthew 13:3–23) demonstrates this hierarchy through a reward: hundredfold to the virgin, sixtyfold to the widow, and thirtyfold to the wife (Jerome, *Against Jovinianus*). Legally, the status of an unmarried woman, a *feme sole*, contrasted with the status of a *feme covert*, the married woman whose husband was responsible for the management of her land and property. An adult unmarried woman could own and manage her own property, including land, and hold responsibility for her own transactions and debts.

Some singlewomen sought work in service until they married and after the plague found greater opportunities for work as servants in urban households. Towns also offered more opportunities to find marital partners without family interference. Since contracts for service work prohibited marriage, the high rates of service work—as much as 11 percent of the urban population—and delayed marriage explain the lower birth rate in late medieval England (Kowaleski 1999, 48).

Others could find places in the homes of their siblings. Women with means might set up their own households in late medieval England. The peasant Cecilia Penifader of Brigstock had the wealth to live alone based on property she inherited from her parents and properties she acquired herself. Cecilia also had a large kin network, and she wisely acquired property adjacent to that of relatives. Cecilia did require a man to serve as her pledge when she did business in court, and she typically relied on her brother-in-law Henry Kroyl, his brother John, or her own brother Henry. Cecilia's kin helped her to thrive, but she appears to have lived alone or with only a servant.

Since coverture prevented married women from making wills of their own, we have more examples of wills from singlewomen, especially widows with some property to dispose of after their death. But even low-status servants might make a will, such as the 1390 one Emmota Page left in York, stating, "I Emmota Page, servant of Katherine Lakensnyder of York, being of good remembrance, make and ordain my will in this manner" (Goldberg 1995, 96). The status and its legal opportunities were attractive, though, to married women, some of whom in late medieval England occasionally received permission to use the category of *feme sole* to handle legal business.

WIDOWHOOD

As one might expect, given the young age of marriage for women and the later age of marriage for men, many medieval women outlived their husbands. This was true despite the high rates of death for women during childbirth; indeed, a large number of widowers selected young brides, increasing the disparity in ages. While married women were known as "femes covert," widows under the law were once again "femes sole." Widows could conduct their own business, make a will and testament, determine for themselves whether to remarry or remain a vowess—one who vowed to remain single after her husband's death. The stiff negotiations for dower and dowry in a marriage contract recognized the reality that medieval women frequently outlived their husbands and required some property to support themselves once widowed. Dower lands supported a widow for her life and then typically reverted to her husband's heir's estate.

Nonetheless, widows frequently had to resort to the courts to secure the dower that had been promised to them by their late husbands. For property, there might be a dispute over whether the husband had really had the deed to promise; the husband might have alienated the property during the marriage—although he was required to have her permission for this—or another heir might challenge all or part of the dower settlement. Recognizing that children sometimes contested their father's will, Robert Hardy of Lyddington added to his will that his wife Joan should have his property for the remainder of her life, but "if any of my children be obstinate and cause trouble towards their mother against my will, he that so troubles is to have nothing other than at his mother's will. . . . The residue of my goods not bequeathed, I give to the disposition of my wife whom I make my sole executrix to dispose for me as is most expedient for the health of my soul" (Goldberg 1995, 149). Legally, his wife would have control of a portion of his land, but by giving her total control as well as power to serve as executor sent a message to his children that they should not cause a fuss.

Another way to solve this problem was to make clear that the widow was only caretaker of her husband's lands until her child came of age, which the manor court of Tottenham did in the 1395 case of Alice, wife of Thomas Ederych, to whom the court granted "the tenure of five acres and three roods of land to hold to herself until the legal age of John, the youngest son of the aforesaid Thomas, who, according to the custom of the manor, will inherit the land in bondage, and the aforesaid Alice is to keep the said John, who is now six years of age, in food and clothing well and competently until his legal age." If Alice did well, she would receive a reward: "And after the full age of the said heir, if she shall have kept herself sole and in good repute without husband, then she shall have the said tenement and lands for her whole life, and if she shall not, then it is to be taken into the lord's hands according to the custom of the manor" (Goldberg 1995, 148).

In London widows pursued claims to their dowers in the Husting court of common pleas with a writ of dower. In her study of cases in this court's rolls between 1301 and 1433, Barbara Hanawalt found 299 dower cases, about one to sixteen cases per year. She suggests that this number is so low because further disputes were likely either settled out of court or abandoned by widows unable to pursue them. The majority of widows' dower disputes in London were with tenants on the property promised in the dower, while dower disputes in the countryside were typically between the widow and one of her husband's kin; in London such cases only made up 10 percent of the disputes (Hanawalt 2007, 98–100). These cases might be with a stepson, brother-in-law, or sister-in-law.

The pursuit of a dower case could take almost a year or more, and only about half of widows used attorneys to pursue their dower, either relying on male relatives, their craft's guild, or their own knowledge of the law. Success hung on the availability of written records and the testimony of witnesses, especially of other heirs. A common argument used against a widow's claim on a dower property was that her husband did not own the property when they married, and his other heirs could explain whether that was true or not. If the husband did not have title to the property at the time of the marriage, he could not legally include it in the dower, and it was the responsibility of the bride and her family to determine true ownership at the time of the marriage negotiations. The widow of Thomas de Lincoln, Matilda, claimed a property, but its tenant, a fishmonger named Adam Pykemann, proved that Thomas had not held the property when he married Matilda. Widows claiming their dowers in court faced arguments that their writ was incomplete or inaccurate, that she had alienated the property herself, or that her marriage was never valid.

Since dower properties were held by widows for the rest of their lives, a long widowhood could create financial difficulties for the son's management of his estate. This was a problem for both John Paston I, when his mother Agnes Berry lived long after his father William's death, and for John II, who had to manage his estate while both Agnes and John's mother Margaret both lived on their extensive dower lands. This might be one disadvantage to finding dower lands approximate to the dowry of a wealthy bride.

A widow and her new husband might also make claims beyond their share against her dead husband's estate. Legally, in London, a widow was guaranteed a third of her husband's property to use for the rest of her life, while another third went directly to his heirs. The last third covered his burial and donations for his soul. King Henry III had also confirmed that London's widows were free from certain taxes. Recognizing this trouble, some husbands left property to their widows on condition that they did not marry. Thomas Wod of York's 1484 will stipulated that "I leave to Margaret my wife my terms in my fulling mill if she keeps herself sole after my death, if not then I will that my son William shall have them" (Goldberg 1995, 198). This protected Margaret against the claims of her son William, assuming she remained a widow, and protected Thomas's property against the interference of an unknown man, by requiring his wife to remain unmarried.

The wealth and opportunities for widows in London who appear in these records, and similarly successful women in England's second city of York, may not have been available for widows in other cities. Records for other English cities like Exeter and Shrewsbury show women were primarily in low-paying occupations without greater opportunities.

Remarriage

Medieval society encouraged widows to remarry. This advice is rooted, like so much about medieval marriage, in the Bible, with Paul's advice: "Now to the unmarried and the widows I say: It is good for them to stay unmarried, as I do. But if they cannot control themselves, they should marry, for it is better to marry than to burn with passion" (1 Corinthians 7:8–9). Concerns about women's independent control of wealth and property and about their potential sexual freedom had a simple solution: remarriage. To protect their reputations as well as their souls, medieval thinkers urged young widows to marry again and older widows to remain chaste.

Chaucer's Wife of Bath, Alison, defended her five marriages as though sensitive to the idea that she should have remained chaste: "Here's to the sixth, whenever he turns up. I won't stay chaste forever, that's a fact" (Blamires 1992, 200). While three of her marriages were to much wealthier and older men, by her fifth marriage, Alison was the more senior spouse: she was forty years old while her husband was only twenty.

Among elites, more than 50 percent of widows remarried, often multiple times. Records do not offer as clear a picture of urban or lower-status women's remarriage rates, but documents suggest this rate was high as well. Women also appear to have remarried quickly, most within the same year. Remarriage rates were especially high for widows with young children according to data in the court of orphans (Hanawalt 2007, 107). Medieval canon law did not require a mourning period, and medieval society did not appear to judge a man or a woman for remarrying too soon after a spouse's death, regardless of the Wife of Bath's sensitivity about her number of husbands. A new husband might assist his wife in securing her dower in court.

Widows were attractive marriage partners because of the property and wealth they could bring into the marriage as well as their demonstration of fertility if their first marriage had issue. Some men searched for prospective wives whose wealth, property, and experience complemented their own: in 1375 Sir William Stoner, a propertied gentleman whose estates held sheep, married Elizabeth Ryche, widow of a London merchant dealing in wool. William approved the marriage arrangement Elizabeth and her first husband had made for their daughter, Katherine, and became friendly with Katherine's husband, Thomas. When Thomas died and left Katherine a widow with five children, Katherine also remarried. When Joan Gedney died, a widow four times over, her will contained cash bequests of over £500 (Erler 1994, 176).

Widows with movable wealth and connections in the same fields made especially attractive marriage partners for merchants and craftsmen and helped them gain the capital they needed for newer and bolder endeavors. Margaret Stodeye, daughter of John Stodeye, a successful vintner, married four times, first in 1370 to a mercer John Berlingham; in 1376 to Sir John Philipot, a wealthy grocer; after 1384 to a financier John Fitznichol; and by 1392 to Adam Bamme, a goldsmith; each of her marriages shifted large amounts of capital around London to help these men grow and expand their businesses and influence (Rawcliffe 1994, 93). Widows in London had no guardian and could conduct their own business and negotiate their own marriages as well as those of their children. If they remarried, widows' subsequent husbands could manage not only the property she brought into the marriage but the property her minor children had inherited, until they came of age. Since London law specified that one-third of a man's estate went to his widow and one-third to his heirs, a widow with minor children could offer a new husband access to two-thirds of her late husband's wealth and property until her children reached their majority.

This might mean incredible pressure on a widow to remarry, especially if she was wealthy and well connected. Elizabeth de Burgh, lady of Clare, widow of John de Burgh and coheiress to the estate of her father Gilbert de Clare, Earl of Gloucester and Hertford, initially avoided pressures to remarry by eloping, but when she was widowed again a year later, the king convinced her to marry again, to Roger Damory in 1317. This marriage brought her into the turmoil of Edward II's reign, especially after Damory's death in rebellion in 1322. She remained a widow after this point, using her influence to support the coup of Isabella and earning royal favor under Edward III. For Margaret Stodeye, her sister's husband, Nicholas Brembre, had a vested interest in Margaret's marriages and the connections they might bring to him, placing his own pressure on his sister-in-law. Nonetheless, after four marriages, Margaret lived as a wealthy widow and managed her own properties for thirty-four years.

Queen Elizabeth Woodville's mother, Jacquetta of Luxembourg, had married King Henry V's brother, the duke of Bedford, but after his death two years later, she chose, at age seventeen, to marry the duke's servant, Richard Woodville without the king's permission. The king at the time, Henry VI, likely would not have granted permission for the match, given the difference in rank, but they satisfied the king by paying a fine.

Vowess

A widow was not required to remarry, however, and if she was wealthy enough to support herself and any minor children in her care, she might remain single for the rest of her life. Such a woman was known as a vowess, a woman who had vowed perpetual chastity. Typically, she remained in the world, conducted business, and protected her property, although she might also include religious devotions. Margery de Nerford was a vowess who had a private chapel for her devotions before her death in 1417.

While a vowess might not enter a monastery, she took her vow in an episcopal ceremony in which she took on a veil and dark clothing. The bishop received her vow and blessed her ring and clothes; sometimes her vow was included in the episcopal registry, along with the names of any high-status witnesses. Some husbands included in their wills extra benefits if their wives became vowesses: In 1421 William Lynne left his wife Alice extensive property in London, including lands, houses, a quay and business, if she did not remarry. She took the vow of chastity soon after his death, before the archbishop of Canterbury. A decision to become a vowess might come after a long career as a wife. Margaret Stodeye was married four times before she was able to free herself from the pressures to marry and take a vow to chastity in St. Paul's Cathedral before Bishop Braybrook.

The vow was intended to be for life, but it was possible to receive a papal dispensation to end the vow. Women who request such a dispensation might have wanted to marry or have children; some had already given birth. Joan Gedney became a vowess after her third marriage, to Robert Large, mayor of London, when he willed her a much larger portion of his estate after his 1441 death. She decided a few years later to end her vow and marry a fourth time, to John Gedney, which meant the loss of this larger portion of Robert Large's estate as well as social disapproval.

FOR FURTHER READING

Barron, Caroline M., and Anne F. Sutton, eds. 1994. *Medieval London Widows, 1300–1500*. London: Hambledon Press.

Bennett, Judith M. 1999. *A Medieval Life: Cecilia Penifader of Brigstock, c. 1295–1344*. Boston: McGraw-Hill.

Bennett, Judith M. 2003. "Writing Fornication: Medieval Leyrwite and Its Historians." *Transactions of the Royal Historical Society*, 6th series. 13: 131–162.

Benson, Larry D., ed. 2008. *The Riverside Chaucer*. Oxford: Oxford University Press.

Blamires, Alcuin, ed. 1992. *Woman Defamed and Woman Defended: An Anthology of Medieval Texts*. Oxford: Clarendon Press.

Bliss, W. H., and J. A. Twemlow. 1902. *Calendar of Papers Relating to Great Britain and Ireland: Volume 4, 1362–1404*. London. https://www.british-history.ac.uk/cal-papal-registers/brit-ie/vol4/pp36-47.

Butler, Sara M. 2007. *The Language of Abuse: Marital Violence in Later Medieval England*. Leiden: Brill.

Clayton, Jane. 2019. "Elizabeth Clere and Marriage between the Clere and Paston Families in the Late Fifteenth Century." *Notes and Queries* (June): 214–216.

Coulton, G., ed. 1931. *Life in the Middle Ages*. Cambridge: Cambridge University Press.

Duby, Georges. 1983. *The Knight, the Lady, and the Priest: The Making of Modern Marriage in Medieval France*. Translated by Barbara Bray. New York: Pantheon.

Dunn, Caroline. 2013. *Stolen Women in Medieval England: Rape, Abduction, and Adultery, 1100–1500*. Cambridge: Cambridge University Press.

Elliott, Dyan. 1993. *Spiritual Marriage: Sexual Abstinence in Medieval Wedlock*. Princeton, NJ: Princeton University Press.

Elliott, Dyan. 1999. *Fallen Bodies: Pollution, Sexuality, and Demonology in the Middle Ages*. Philadelphia: University of Pennsylvania Press.

Erler, Mary C. 1994. "Three Fifteenth-Century Vowesses." In *Medieval London Wives, 1300–1500*, edited by Caroline M. Barron and Anne F. Sutton. London: Hambledon Press.

Fitzherbert, Anthony. 1534. "The Book of Husbandry." Project Gutenberg. https://www.gutenberg.org/files/57457/57457-h/57457-h.htm.

Furnivall, Frederick James. 1908. "How the Good Wife Taught Her Daughter." In *The Babees' Book: Medieval Manners for the Young: Done into Modern English*, edited by Edith Rickert. London: Duffield & Co. Project Gutenberg.

Goldberg, Jeremy. 2013. "Echoes, Whispers, Ventriloquisms: On Recovering Women's Voices from the Court of York in the Later Middle Ages." In *Women, Agency and the Law, 1300–1700*, edited by Bronach Kane and Fiona Williamson, 31–41, 169–171. London: Pickering and Chatto.

Goldberg, P. J. P. 1995. *Women in England c. 1275–1525: Documentary Sources*. Manchester: Manchester University Press.

Hanawalt, Barbara. 2007. *The Wealth of Wives: Women, Law, and Economy in Late Medieval London*. Oxford: Oxford University Press.

Harris, Carissa. 2020. "The Distinguished Medieval Penis Investigators." *Narratively.com*, November 12.

Helmholz, Richard H. 1974. *Marriage Litigation in Medieval England*. Cambridge: Cambridge University Press.

Kingsford, Charles Lethbridge, ed. 1919. *The Stoner Letters and Papers, 1290–1483*. Vol. 2. London: London Royal Historical Society.

Kowaleski, Maryanne. 1999. "Singlewomen in Medieval and Early Modern Europe: The Demographic Perspective." In *Singlewomen in the*

European Past, 1250–1800, edited by Judith M. Bennett and Amy M. Froide. Philadelphia: University of Pennsylvania Press.

Massingberd, W. O., ed. 1902. *Court Rolls of the Manor of Ingoldmells in the County of Lincoln*. London: Spottiswoode.

McCarthy, Conor. 2004. *Marriage in Medieval England: Law, Literature, and Practice*. Woodbridge: Boydell and Brewer.

Pollock, Frederick, and F. W. Maitland. 1968. *The History of English Law before the Time of Edward I*. 2nd ed. 2 vols. Cambridge: Cambridge University Press.

Rawcliffe, Carole. 1994. "Margaret Stodeye, Lady Philipot (d. 1431)." In *Medieval London Widows, 1300–1500*, edited by Caroline M. Barron and Anne F. Sutton. London: Hambledon Press.

Sheehan, Michael M. 1996. *Marriage, Family, and Law in Medieval Europe: Collected Studies*. Edited by James K. Farge. Toronto: University of Toronto Press.

Thibodeaux, Jennifer D. 2015. *The Manly Priest: Clerical Celibacy, Masculinity, and Reform in England and Normandy, 1066–1300*. Philadelphia: University of Pennsylvania Press.

Tompkins, Laura. 2018. "Mary Percy and John de Southeray: Wardship, Marriage, and Divorce in Fourteenth-Century England." In *Fourteenth Century England*, edited by Gwilym Dodd. Cambridge: Boydell & Brewer.

Ward, Jennifer C. 1994. "Elizabeth de Burgh, Lady of Clare (d. 1360)." In *Medieval London Widows, 1300–1500*, edited by Caroline M. Barron and Anne F. Sutton. London: Hambledon Press.

Ward, Jennifer C. 2006. *Women in England in the Middle Ages*. New York: Hambledon Continuum.

Watt, Diane, ed. 2004. *The Paston Women*. Woodbridge: D. S. Brewer.

2

MOTHERHOOD

Women's primary role in a marriage was to bear and raise children, and they tended to start as soon as possible after a wedding, although a couple might delay consummating their marriage if the bride was especially young. Children completed the alliance sealed with a marriage; they continued the family name, could take over a family shop or business, or maintain the family claim on land and title. For these reasons, couples were eager to have male children, but girls were also valued by their parents. Daughters were important family members whose future marriages could seal alliances and bring security and wealth to their natal family. Children of either sex could help in the shop, on the farm, or in the home from a young age. Parents also took joy in their children. Fertility was an important element of both masculine and feminine identities for married people in the Middle Ages, especially because only legitimate children could inherit or seek high-status positions in the community, and marriage was for most an indissoluble union.

The importance of bearing children was strongly communicated to Anne of Bohemia at her coronation when she was met at Westminster Abbey with the prayer that "with Sarah, Rebecca and Rachel and other blessed and honorable women, she may multiply and rejoice in the fruits of her womb" (Legg 1901, 266). The fate of the kingdom rested on queens' wombs, but other families felt just as strongly about the fertility of wives and daughters-in-law. The stakes for legitimate children for a family's survival at least partially explain the double standard that penalized extramarital sex so harshly for women but not men. The pressure was also high for men: in some English families, in the late Middle Ages, a husband might not have full control of a wife's dowry until she bore a live child.

High rates of miscarriage and infant and childhood mortality meant that women needed many pregnancies in order to provide heirs who lived to adulthood. Miscarriage rates are difficult to report because so many went unreported, but they were probably similar to today's rate of about 20 percent or higher due to poorer nutrition in the Middle Ages. Perhaps 20–30 percent of live-born infants died in their first year, while only 50 percent reached age five. Children remained at risk of early mortality until about age ten (Shahar 1990). This high rate of infant mortality did not, as many scholars have thought, mean that medieval parents cared less for their children. There is evidence of parents, especially mothers, making strong and fierce bonds with their babies early on.

As a result, medieval women who married spent most years between marriage at about twelve and their early thirties being pregnant, breastfeeding, or attempting to become pregnant again. Having many pregnancies in quick succession was dangerous and exhausting, and women may have attempted to space out their pregnancies, particularly if they had already borne a male heir. There were some known abortifacients and contraceptives, but none with the accuracy of modern pharmacology. Many women also struggled with infertility.

Motherhood is an area where women educated other women, girls learning from their mothers and other relatives, women consulting a midwife or a wise woman. As a result, many of women's quotidian experiences were not written down in records that remain to us. We can, however, study medical treatises, advice manuals, records of baptisms and churchings, chronicles, court records, and even skeletal evidence to understand women's roles as mothers.

WOMEN'S HEALTH

Medieval medical thinking relied on ancient Greek medical writers such as Hippocrates, Soranus, and Galen as well as on Arabic medical texts. Salerno, in Sicily, became a major medieval center for medical education, and ideas from Greek and Arabic texts formed the heart of medical learning for the Latin West. Both men and women trained in Salerno, and Trota of Salerno was a significant female medical author. The Hippocratic Corpus of texts included two texts on the *Diseases of Women*, and it contrasted with a Soranic tradition on women's health based on the writings of the Greek physician Soranus. The writings of the Greek physician Galen became influential in Arabic texts on women's health. Fundamentally, medieval medicine theorized that there were four humors in the human body: blood, yellow or red bile, black bile, and phlegm. The balance of these humors in each body affected that individual's health and even his or her personality. A person's temperament could be dominated by the imbalance of the humors: becoming sanguine (blood), choleric (yellow/red bile), melancholic (black bile), or phlegmatic (phlegm). Many medical interventions were attempts to rebalance the humors. There were four qualities that shaped the body: hot, dry, cold, and wet.

There were further differences between women and men, with men remaining hot and dry and woman cold and wet. The "one sex" theory of the body held that there was one form of the body with inverted genitalia based on its experience in utero. If a fetus was hosted in utero long and well enough, the child would be dry and born a boy. If the fetus was born too early or had not been hosted well enough, it would be moist and female, one explanation for menstruation.

There has been a debate in scholarship on women, sex, and sexuality about the dichotomy between males and females based on this medical theory. It has been common for scholars to argue that a binary division of sex or gender did not exist in medieval thinking about either sex (biological male/female) or gender (cultural identities man/woman). Some have argued that there was only one sex in medieval thought and that males and females operated on a single spectrum, with females seen as defective males, while some have argued for a third gender to include monks, nuns, and others who remained celibate, in neither the man or woman category. Ruth Mazo Karras has persuasively demonstrated, however, that "[o]n the contrary, the binary opposition between men and women was extraordinarily strong in medieval society." Medieval people recognized real differences between men and women, just as they understood medieval monks to be men and nuns to be women. Rather than throwing off their gender, transgressive women or men were labeled "deviants," and sometimes "hyperfeminine" or "hypermasculine" (Karras 2005, 6).

In Greek ideas about gynecology, as Monica Green explains, "menstruation was a necessary purgation, needed to keep the whole female organism healthy," since women's warm bodies could not process nutrients as well as men, who expelled polluting substances through body hair and nocturnal emissions (Green 2002, 19). A woman who did not menstruate regularly, however, was susceptible to disease. Pregnancy and breastfeeding paused menstruation in normal ways, but other menstrual abnormalities signaled disease because it meant that waste material was building up in the body without release. Treatment focused on forcing menstruation to resume. While these were ancient ideas, they continued to be the founding ideas of medieval medicine, and we see this understanding in the Trotula, a widely influential collection of texts on women's health sometimes associated with the twelfth-century female healer Trota, who lived and practiced in Salerno, Italy. A fifteenth-century English version of these texts continued this ancient Greek understanding of women's bodies:

> Therefore you shall understand that women have less heat in their bodies than men and have more moistness for default of heat that should dry their moistness and their humours, but nevertheless [they have] bleeding to make their bodies clean and whole from sickness.... And they have this purgation once in every month unless they are women that are with child or else women that are of dry complexion and work a great deal. For women, after they are with child until they are delivered, they do not have this purgation at all for the child in the womb is nourished with the blood that they should be purged of. (Goldberg 1995, 57)

Hippocrates taught that one possible consequence of retention of menses was the shifting of the uterus to another part of the body, which could also result from "excessive fatigue, lack of food, lack of (hetero)sexual activity, and dryness or lightness of the womb (particularly in older women)" (Green 2002, 22). The uterus's movements could cause the woman to suffocate to death, a condition known as uterine suffocation. Regular heterosexual sex could alleviate this issue because semen was thought to moisten the uterus, stopping it from hunting for moister organs such as the liver, which meant that those women who abstained from sex were at greatest risk of uterine suffocation. The treatment advised for uterine suffocation was using smells, unpleasant ones on the nose and sweeter ones on genitalia, to convince the uterus to move back into its proper position. Soranus disagreed with Hippocrates and argued that the uterus stayed in place and that sexual activity was not required for women's health. Instead, Soranus argued, uterine suffocation resulted from tension, and treatment focused on encouraging the body to relax. Galen was also skeptical that the womb moved, but not that it caused uterine suffocation. He suggested that the symptoms could be caused not by the womb's movement, but by a retention of the woman's own semen. Galen's recommended treatment followed Hippocrates's but added bloodletting. Ultimately, Galen and Hippocrates became influential on the medieval practice of medicine for women as well as on ideas about female sexuality.

While it did not necessarily confuse medieval people in their binary classifications of sex and gender, the medical idea that female bodies were inverted males had important implications for reproduction, as it encouraged the notion that women ejaculated the same way men did, creating a "two-seed" theory for conception. If both the male and female partners needed to contribute a seed toward conception, then female ejaculation to release the seed was necessary during sex. Since male ejaculation was a pleasurable act, if a woman released a seed, she must also have experienced pleasure. This was not universally believed in the Middle Ages and was the subject of some debate, but it was accepted enough to complicate accusations of sexual assault when the woman was pregnant following the assault. If the woman ejaculated, so legal arguments went, then she must have consented.

Medieval physicians employed bloodletting to help rebalance humors and resolve tumors, constipation, and menstrual retention. The goal was to force blood to flow in a new direction. Alternatively, physicians could use cupping, or the application of small glasses to the skin, creating a suction within the glass that drew blood to the surface with the same purpose of directing the flow. Physicians also sought ways of introducing medicine to the vagina and uterus, relying on both fumigation, a technique of pushing medicine to the womb through steam that required special chairs, and pessaries, a sort of medicated tampon.

By the late Middle Ages, medicine was a regulated field with licensing for physicians based on their university educations, which were exclusively limited to men. Male physicians read medical treatises on gynecology, such as the *Book on Womanly Matters*, *Conditions of Women*, *Treatments for Women* and *Women's Cosmetics*, important Salernitan texts that developed new notions on gynecology based on Arabic texts more than on Greek ones. The academic discipline of medicine in European universities did not turn to the study of gynecology until fairly late, but by the fourteenth century several gynecological treatises appeared in Europe, such as *The Knowing of Woman's Kind in Childing*. Physicians both diagnosed gynecological issues and prescribed treatments and medicine for them. It is unlikely, however, that such physicians ever touched their female patients or even visually inspected their genitalia. As historian Monica Green notes, this opened space for female medical practitioners to be able to treat and care for women, especially their obstetrical and gynecological needs (Green 2002, 14).

Midwives were experts in women's health, pregnancy, and childbirth, and while they may not have been formally licensed, these practitioners had more hands-on experience with women than physicians did. The field of gynecology continued to have male and female practitioners, but over the course of the medieval and early modern period, women were excluded from positions of authority over women's health that they had previous enjoyed. While possibly illiterate midwives and wise women retained low-status roles in women's reproductive health, literate and educated male physicians claimed high-status roles and control of gynecology.

The oral transmission of knowledge between midwives makes the historian's job in understanding medieval medical practice challenging. Midwifery manuals appeared late, midway into the fifteenth century. Midwives' wisdom was relevant in court, where they testified about women's pregnancy. This separation between male writing about gynecology and women's practice of it transmitted only orally means that there is a significant amount of practical knowledge about midwifery we still do not know.

Despite this male authority over high-status healing, there were a number of female practitioners of medicine during the medieval period. In addition to midwives, women were engaged in nursing care; they served as herbalists, apothecaries, surgeons, barbers, and even physicians. Regulation increasingly limited medical practice to licensed, educated, or otherwise formally sanctioned practitioners, which limited the diversity of women's medical roles. And yet, medical men tended to select wives from the daughters of fellow practitioners, and guilds permitted widows to not only continue operating their late husband's business but teach his son the skills of the trade, suggesting that women worked in medicine alongside their fathers and husbands and that their skills and labor were welcome in this practical way if not deemed authoritative theoretically. Licensing was also not systematic across regions, and women may have continued to operate in medical fields in places where there was not a group of licensed, university-educated male physicians to organize their exclusion. Women also continued to be the main person dispensing medicine within a household, caring for children, providing for the poor, and nursing older or dying relatives.

Women could also consult guidebooks with selected English translations of gynecological and obstetrical medical information created for their use if they were uncomfortable with consulting a physician directly. They might also rely on prayer rolls and collections of saints' lives in order to appeal to divine assistance in fertility and childbirth. These texts could comfort women through their faith, but saints' lives also contained a great deal of medical information since saints specialized in healing.

PREGNANCY

The typical onset of menstruation, the age of menarche, fourteen, was slightly later in the Middle Ages than it is today, about twelve to fourteen, and medieval women hit their peak fertility around their late teens (Kowaleski 2013, 189). Women could theoretically continue to have children until menopause, about age fifty, but women had difficulty bearing children after their early thirties. Over their fifteen or so fertile years, women could have a dozen or more pregnancies, although several factors reduced that number. Philippa of Hainault, who became wife to Edward III at age fourteen, had twelve live births, with further possibly unsuccessful pregnancies, and seven of her children lived to adulthood. The wealthy peasant woman Alice Penifader had eight children, six of whom survived beyond childhood, which was rare in her community. Despite her pleas to her husband that they remain chaste, Margery Kempe had fourteen children before he finally agreed to a chaste marriage.

Married pregnant women were treated with respect in the Middle Ages, especially in the fourteenth and fifteenth centuries when the Virgin Mary and her mother Saint Anne came under intense veneration. Ideal femininity prized either virginity or motherhood, without many positive images for a sexually active singlewoman. Mary combined these ideals in her virgin motherhood, a pure vessel to bear the son of God. Saint Anne offered a less complex vision of the holy mother devoted to her child and her faith. Saint Margaret of Antioch was known to be a friend to pregnant women. Indeed, there was even a notion of Christ as a mother who fed his children at his altar, and the mystic Julian of Norwich compared

Jesus to a mother, each feeding with their bodies: "The mother may give her child suck of her milk, but our precious Mother, Jesus, He may feed us with Himself, and doeth it, full courteously and tenderly, with the Blessed Sacrament that is precious food of my life" (Julian 1901, 150). The picture was less rosy for singlewomen who were pregnant, as discussed later.

Medieval people also recognized that childbirth was dangerous; the average age at death for adult women surveyed in eleventh-century Norwich was only thirty-three. To give a sense of the significance of the danger, studies of female skeletons suggest that medieval women had a higher mortality than men during their midtwenties and midthirties (Grauer 2002, 277). While skeletal evidence cannot give us the full picture, this statistic does correlate with the time when women were most likely on a second, third, or subsequent pregnancy and thus most at risk of death in childbirth.

The frequency of medieval women's pregnancies made the condition dangerous for all women, but even more so for poorer women more likely to also suffer from malnutrition and poor hygiene. Given the discomforts and dangers of medieval travel, whether by horse, cart, or boat, pregnancy was reason to postpone or skip a trip. Pregnancy and childbirth were recognized as perilous, as well as uncomfortable, times. Miracle tales depict families trying to ease the pain of their pregnant relatives, and medical texts offered suggestions on how to make pregnancy more comfortable.

Medical thinking about pregnancy in the Middle Ages insisted that a woman's thoughts and the things she saw could affect the embryo. Elizabeth of York's bedroom during her 1489 pregnancy for her daughter Margaret, future queen of Scotland, was covered in tapestries with only subjects suitable for a pregnant woman (Rawcliffe 2003, 103–104). Beyond the physical discomforts and dangers of travel late in pregnancy, confinement offered an opportunity to ensure that only positive sights would confront her.

Quickening

Women recognized their pregnancy after missing one or two of their monthly cycles, but would be able to go about their regular lives without much issue throughout their pregnancy. Christian lawyers in the Middle Ages marked the moment when the soul entered the fetus, between forty and eighty days of gestation, about seven to twelve weeks. There is such a broad range because physicians proposed different models and timelines for the gestation of a boy and girl fetus. Twelve weeks is about the time that a fetus acquires a more human shape as well as the beginning of the time that a mother might start to feel fetal movements. These movements, combined with ensoulment, thought to be the time when the fetus was joined with a soul, were known as the quickening.

A woman's termination of a pregnancy after ensoulment was a violation of canon law and could be considered both homicide and infanticide, although English legal ideas about ensoulment changed over time. In early medieval England, women who lost a pregnancy through violence could press a felony charge of miscarriage by assault, with a possible death penalty, against the perpetrator. However, in early fourteenth-century England, legal understandings shifted to understand a baby as human at birth, instead of at the fetus's quickening. By 1348, England had removed miscarriage by assault from the list of felonies.

CHILDBIRTH

When possible, women birthed their babies at home in the company of female relatives, friends, and a midwife, a practiced medical worker expert in obstetrics. Late in pregnancy, maybe six weeks before the expected birth, wealthy elite women might begin their "confinement" on the estate and in the rooms where they expected to give birth, suspending their regular duties. Medieval hospitals were generally devoted to the poor and not a place for childbirth, but there were facilities for helping women in childbirth at St. Paul's Hospital in Norwich and St. John's in Oxford. For the poor mothers who died in childbirth, hospitals such as St. Bartholomew's in Smithfield and St. Mary's in Bishopsgate in London offered support to orphaned infants up until age seven.

A pregnant woman's time in confinement could continue six or seven weeks after birth, usually to the time of her churching. During her time in her rooms, she might be visited by a priest who performed services for her using a portable altar, but she was mostly surrounded by women during this time. Women's shared expertise was passed down orally and experientially as they attended the births of their neighbors and kin and then had their own children. Female attendants comforted the pregnant woman, prayed for her and the baby, and cared for the baby by washing and swaddling it after birth.

During childbirth, the pregnant woman sat on a birthing stool supported by an attendant while she pushed, and the midwife stood or kneeled in front to monitor the birth's progress. Medieval images of childbirth show the mother sitting for her labor, surrounded by women. Some images show a woman sitting behind her to support the pregnant woman in her labors; others show the woman holding onto something. Midwives might use scents to attract the fetus as well as baths to comfort and relax the pregnant woman. Once the baby was delivered, the midwife cut the umbilical cord so that the baby could be washed and swaddled and then attended to the afterbirth, extracting the placenta.

Once swaddled, the baby would be presented to his or her father, who had waited beyond the birthing room. Sometimes fathers were not present for the birth, and journeys were required to notify him, and these notifications were so significant that men who took them could remember their timing well enough later to give testimony in court for the child's proof of age. Wealthier men might give a gift to the person who brought them the good news of a healthy baby, especially for a first son. When Edward III's first son was born in 1330, he gave the man who brought him the news a pension for life.

Men were not entirely excluded from the birthing chamber, as a male medical worker such as a surgeon might be called in for an emergency, but for the most part, this was a female-only space. Some men found this female control of childbirth—an event that was crucial to the legitimacy of their heirs, control of their property, and continuation of their families—problematic and worrying. Among other concerns was that women would trick men by substituting another's child for their own. That was a particular concern of existing heirs, concerned that a fraud committed by a scheming stepmother could threaten their inheritance. In the later Middle Ages a shift began to bring men more control over obstetrics and childbirth. Hearing the baby's cry became important proof that a child had been born alive, since women were the only witnesses and they did not usually testify in court; this was later significant in proving the child's age, a relevant issue for a marriage's legality or claiming inheritance, as we saw in chapter 1. Fathers and their other heirs were not the only men concerned about the female-controlled space of the birthing chamber. Clerics also feared that heretical activities might take place there. Agnes Marshall was accused in Yorkshire in 1481 of using "incantations" instead of proper Christian prayers.

The *Treatments for Women* treatise based on work by Trota of Salerno, a twelfth-century female physician, describes interventions for problems that might arise during childbirth, such as a retained placenta, excessive bleeding, or stillbirth. This guidance includes emetics, poultices, and tossing the pregnant woman up and down on a sheet. Midwives were able to handle more common issues, such as turning breech fetuses into the proper birthing position and performing and repairing episiotomies, small incisions that allowed the baby to pass out of the vagina. Childbirth was dangerous, and it was recognized that a woman could die, as did Mary de Bohun, Henry Bolingbroke's wife, in 1394. Some held that a woman who died in childbirth could not be buried inside a church because their body was still polluted by the blood and instead would have to settle for the church graveyard. Even a successful birth might have consequences: Margaret Beaufort's labor at age thirteen produced a healthy Henry Tudor, future Henry VII, but the experience left her unable to have any further children.

Midwives were also trained by the later Middle Ages to assist a barber or surgeon during a Caesarean section, also known as a C-section, by cutting a live fetus from the corpse of a mother who had died in childbirth. The procedure was named for Julius Caesar under the assumption that he was born via this method, but his mother was known to survive his birth, not a possible outcome for a woman during the premodern period. As depicted in artwork, the barber or surgeon made an incision that allowed the midwife to extract the fetus, while an attendant opened the woman's mouth, theoretically, to allow the fetus to breathe. The Caesarean section was often performed not with an expectation that the child would survive, but so that he or she might be baptized.

If the birth did not go well for the fetus and it resulted in a stillbirth or a child who would not long survive, the midwife was responsible for baptizing the baby. For this reason, the church increasingly encouraged Christians to have a midwife attend all births; this also meant that Christian families required a Christian midwife, which was less of an issue in England after the 1290 expulsion of the Jews but was a concern in other areas.

Christian women were encouraged to pray during childbirth, to ask the Virgin Mary for an easy labor. Mary was an intensely popular figure in the late Middle Ages, closely associated with her pregnancy and motherhood. By this time, belief in Mary's immaculate conception and her virginity were well established as was an idea that she labored in childbirth without suffering, since her pain was deferred to mourning at the Crucifixion. Girdles, a long and thin belt women wore at the waist, associated with the Virgin Mary, became prized relics used by women in childbirth. According to a legend well known by the fourteenth century, Mary dropped her girdle to St. Thomas to prove her Assumption, and it became a symbol of faith and Mary's fertility. Elite women could borrow or rent girdles worn by statues of female saints from the churches or monasteries where they stood. Westminster Abbey had a relic of the Blessed Virgin Mary's girdle that elite women, primarily queens, might borrow during their confinement and labor. Some birth girdles contained prayers offering a pregnant woman hope that she and the baby would survive to be churched and christened. Women without such access and status might instead buy a pilgrim badge depicting the Virgin Mary's girdle relic. After the birth of a child, some women donated their own jewel-encrusted girdles for churches to place on statues of the Virgin Mary as well as candles offered in thanks for a safe delivery. While the Virgin Mary, or saints Dorothy and Margaret, make logical recipients for prayers, thanks, and gifts for surviving childbirth, there were also girdles associated with male saints such as Gilbert of Sempringham and Saint Francis who were known to protect women against death in childbirth or against miscarriage.

Margaret of Antioch was also known to pay special attention to women in childbirth, likely because she had delivered herself from the belly of a dragon, and could be invoked during the pains of labor. In a fifteenth-century poem, Margaret prayed to God for women in labor to console them and keep them from dying in childbirth, "Let them, Lord, not perish in their childing" (Reames 2003). In addition to Christian protection, women relied on amulets and talismans, but the church hoped to discourage that practice through access to more approved relics and devotional items. Women might wear images of St. Margaret, the Virgin, or Saint Anne, as a brooch, admire their images in a manuscript, or carry a small image with them. At Walsingham, pilgrims could buy badges of the Annunciation or the Nativity. Or women might visit churches to admire images there of these saints and pray for their assistance with fertility, pregnancy, and labor. Some such images were funded by gifts from female patrons, such as Anne, daughter of Sir Robert Harling, a wealthy heiress who remained childless through three marriages and who paid for images of the Virgin Mary in windows at East Harling, Norfolk (Rawcliffe 2003, 102–103).

Whether or not the birth was a success, Christians with means might mark the occasion with a gift to the church. Such a gift could be made out of gratitude to God for a successful and safe delivery or out of recognition that childbirth was dangerous for both baby and mother, or a husband might mark the loss of his wife in childbirth with a donation for a church chantry that said prayers for her soul.

After childbirth, the woman had a choice to make about breastfeeding. Babies require milk for the first several months of their lives, and mothers' bodies typically produce milk after birth. Breastfeeding has a contraceptive effect on the body, and medieval women who breastfed tended to do so for about eighteen months. It takes several months for women to ovulate again after breastfeeding, so mothers who breastfed could expect about two or two-and-a-half years between births without any other impediment. Some wealthy women used nursemaids, who breastfed their children, and could return to bear-

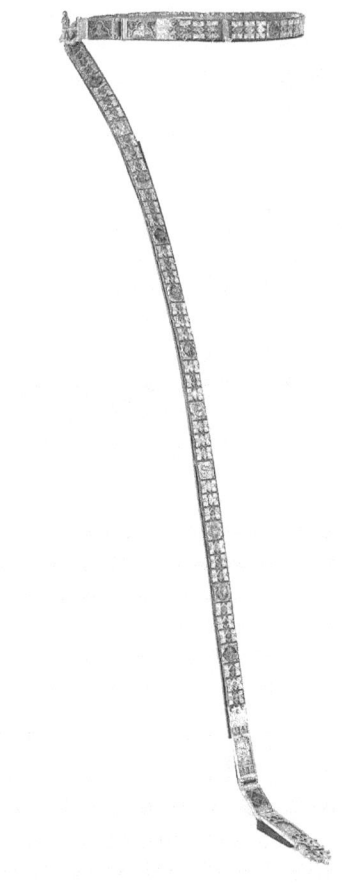

A girdle, or belt, was an important accessory for women's clothing. Objects such as a purse, keys, a knife, and a book could be attached and demonstrated a woman's wealth, status, and devotion. Girdles also played an important role in childbirth. (Gift of the John Huntington Art and Polytechnic Trust, The Cleveland Museum of Art)

ing children more quickly. It was often the midwife's role to select a wet nurse. Not all wealthy women opted to use a wet nurse, preferring instead to breastfeed, both for connection with their children and to space out their pregnancies. As childbirth was a risky endeavor, more frequent pregnancies and greater menstruation risked everything from anemia to death.

Wet-nurse, from "De arte medica infantium libri quatuor," Ferrarius 1577. Hiring a nurse to feed an infant allowed women to become pregnant again more quickly. (Wellcome Collection)

BAPTISM

A baby was baptized as soon as possible, by the midwife if it seemed like the baby would not thrive, otherwise by a priest at the parish church. Even a healthy newborn would be baptized within a day of their birth, brought to the church by the midwife and the baby's godparents. Baptism made the baby Christian and offered the hope of salvation if they died young, while unbaptized babies had an uncertain spiritual future. During the baptism the baby formally acquired his or her name. Girl babies were also exorcised during their baptism. The midwife's presence at the baptism was crucial, since she had to confirm that a baptism had not yet taken place, or, if one had begun, whether or not the words of the ritual had been spoken. Although the mother was not present during the baptism, women had key roles, as the midwife, godmother(s), or witnesses.

The baby was carried to the church by a woman, possibly the midwife, with a procession of people carrying candles. Baptism rituals at the parish church focused on a font, a permanent basin of water on a pedestal in the west part of the church. In English tradition, it was typical for a girl child to have two godmothers and a godfather and for a boy to have two godfathers and a godmother, who gave gifts to the baby such as silver goblets, jewelry, or money.

Many children were then named after their godparents. Godparents were chosen from among family, friends, or influential figures such as members of the local aristocracy or royalty. John Swafham testified that he saw a duke give his godson Thomas Montague a "golden reliquary with precious stones and a picture of the Trinity," in church on his baptism (Deller 2010, 6). Selection of godfathers for girls could be complicated since rules of consanguinity prohibited marriage between godparents and godchildren, and families close enough to offer godparents might also desire marital ties when this daughter was of age.

During the ceremony (one of) the godmother(s) held the baby while the priest performed the baptism, which included saying the words of the ritual in either Latin or English: "I christen thee N, in the name of the Father and of the Son and of the Holy Ghost. Amen" (Clarke and Hicks 2016, 168). Water, salt, chrism all played important roles in the ritual. The godparents washed their hands in a basin; for wealthy families a silver basin was brought to the church along with towels. The priest poured water over the child's head, or dipped him/her in the font three times, and anointed him with oil. After the ceremony, the procession carried lit candles or torches home again for a feast. The details of the baptism might be recorded by the parish clerk or the rector. Celebrations might even begin in the church, with wine passed around in great quantities.

Since the timing of a child's birth is unpredictable and baptism took place within a day, these ceremonies were often arranged quite quickly without much time for godparents, family members, or other witnesses to travel for the ritual. Parents likely planned ahead by arranging gifts, candles, and decorations in anticipation of the child's birth. For elite ceremonies the church might be decorated, as for the 1406 baptism of Thomas, son of William Lord Roos, when St. Mary's Church was decorated with silk and gold cloth, with gold and red cloth for the font. Bottles of wine and silver basins were included in such elite ceremonies. After the ceremony, the procession brought the child home with lit candles, and the celebration may have included a feast once there. Parents gave the witnesses gifts to help them remember the event later, and this tactic was successful, as shown in proof-of-age inquests later.

CHURCHING

A mother could not attend her baby's baptism, partially because she would still be recovering from childbirth but also because she could not yet reenter the church out of fears about pollution caused by blood from childbirth. Medieval mothers underwent the ritual of churching about forty days after childbirth, for each birth. Since the blood pollution would also be present for stillbirths and miscarriages, it is also possible that women were churched even when there was not a live birth. The ritual was important for the spiritual life of the women and also for her marital life. The eradication of blood pollution through churching also facilitated a return to marital sexual relations, which, in turn, might lead to another pregnancy. For royal women, this ritual also marked their return to court duties. Liturgical books linked churching with either baptism or marriage, acknowledging the connection between churching, a legitimate child, and marital relations.

Churching was a purification ritual that brought a woman back into the community after her pregnancy. Royal versions of the ceremony were most lavish, but scaled-down versions were available to most women. The day began by helping the queen leave an extravagantly decorated bed wearing expensive new clothes. For the churching of her first son in 1330, Philippa of Hainault wore a rich robe of purple velvet, trimmed in fur, and embroidered with golden squirrels. Even the royal bed might be richly dressed, as for Philippa's churching following the birth of her daughter Isabella in 1332, when the bed was draped in green silk embroidered with mermaids, with a green velvet canopy embroidered with birds (Shenton 2003, 106–109). Queen Elizabeth Woodville's churching began with a procession to the church. During the procession, the woman was normally veiled and joined with her female network, especially her child's godmother. They were met by the priest at the church door. He cleansed her with a few drops of holy water, blessed her, and led her to the church altar, holding her right hand, which is a difference from the French ritual, where the priest led the woman into the church while she held his stole, avoiding direct contact with her pollution. At the altar she gave the church a candle, and a mass followed in which she was the first to take communion. During the church ceremony, a cloth-of-gold canopy was suspended over the queen's head. A feast hosted by the woman's husband followed the ceremony, including gifts for the guests, and possibly gifts for the newly purified woman as well. A royal churching might include jousts and musicians. Women who were too ill still to be publicly churched might instead receive a private blessing from the priest.

While the ritual was supposed to be free, after a 1293 decree barring fees, it was customary to thank the priest with a financial gift and to throw a feast after the ceremony, costs that may have led some women to avoid churching. For others, this was a welcome expense and an opportunity to display wealth and status with expensive gifts, new clothes, gallons of wine, and freshly hunted game.

In the later Middle Ages, churching became a ritual primarily for married women and was denied to single mothers. The ritual thus became another way of marking the status of married women—especially through the celebration that followed—and the marginalization of unwed mothers who could not afford such festivities.

Baptism and churching were important rituals for introducing a child to the community and fixing the time of his or her birth in the memories of friends, family, and neighbors. This information would be useful later when proving age at a time before birth certificates or mandated parish registers. Witnesses were called to testify in court about the age of an heir claiming inheritance or a woman wishing to marry or shed a marriage for being contracted too early. Public celebrations helped to mark the time, particularly in relation to other events. Thomas Boure was able to remember in a 1430 inheritance case that the man in question had been baptized on the same day that his own wife was churched. Gifts given at the feast could also help set the memory. When Margery Inge was churched, guests at the following breakfast were gifted one arrow in 1355 (Clarke and Hicks 2016, 169–170). Relationships with a child's godparents were lifelong, close spiritual relationships that became a bar to marriage. Godparents were responsible for the child's religious education, to know the Lord's Prayer and the Nicene Creed, and for having them confirmed when the time came.

The study of baptism and churching by historians also points to some inventive approaches scholars have made to the sources. Liturgical texts for these two rituals only contain brief details without the other cultural practices such as gifts and feasts, while births were not recorded systematically in medieval registers, and even historical chronicles do not contain many rich details about these events, even for elites. However, proof-of-age inquests read creatively offer a great deal of insight about these two events that offered women central roles. During the hearings, witnesses testified to the time of a person's birth and noted personal details to document why and how they could remember that event. Receiving a gift at the person's baptism or a feast celebrating the child's mother's churching proved memorable many years later. The quality and quantity of these testimonies—William Dellar found over

10,000 separate testimonies between 1246 and 1432—mark the importance of feasts and gift giving, not just as a celebration and demonstration of status at the time, but as support for the child's later claims on inheritance (Deller 2010).

INFERTILITY

Infertility was a serious problem for a society that insisted on legitimate heirs and yet prohibited divorce. While it is not possible to know the share of the overall population that faced the issue, T. H. Hollingworth found that 16–17 percent of married British ducal men and women remained childless, and malnutrition among lower-status groups must have pushed infertility even higher (Hollingworth 1957, 4–26). As we will see in chapter 3, this was a major concern for the aristocracy, who were not just concerned about family, but also titles and kingdoms. Even a delay in a first pregnancy or first live birth could cause anxiety, such as the three years it took for Eleanor of Provence to birth a son for King Henry III in 1239 or the eight years it took for Margaret of Anjou to bear Henry VI's only son, Edward, in 1453.

There were even fears that women would try to fake a pregnancy in cases of infertility, an issue that made it into English law codes. A woman accused of a false pregnancy could be physically inspected by six women who assessed her breasts and abdomen; she could be taken into the king's custody and held there until she gave birth, and she could be kept from all other pregnant women so that she might not claim another's child as her own. While this seems like the flights of a legal theorist, court records show that some thirteenth-century women really did endure this treatment, including Matilda, wife of Richard, and Leticia, wife of William of Caynes, and Muriel, wife of William de Meutona. Nevertheless, if a married woman's husband accepted the child as his own, it was almost impossible for him or for others to contest the child's legitimacy later.

There were also concerns that women tried to assert legitimacy for children born after their husband's death. Legally, children born up to forty weeks after their father's death could be considered legitimate, but not beyond that point. There was concern that widows might attempt to disinherit the legitimate heir, such as her husband's brother or children from a previous marriage, by passing off another man's children as her husband's posthumous heirs.

While physicians left much of the hands-on work of pregnancy and childbirth to midwives, they did consult and treat patients for infertility, especially given the high stakes for producing legitimate heirs. Physicians were keen to encourage conception and deal with infertility. Arnald of Villanova, a thirteenth-century physician in Montpellier gave recipes to encourage menstruation and increase sexual activity (Riddle 1992, 137). Physicians, apothecaries, midwives, and women were interested in contraception and abortifacients, but infertility was a much larger issue for the majority of sexually active women and men. Physicians treated infertility as a problem for either men or women, but its weight fell primarily on the woman's shoulders unless she had children from a prior marriage. Physicians considered infertility incurable.

Medieval people dealing with infertility turned to charms, talismans, alternative medicine, prayer, and the saints for assistance. Margaret of Antioch and the Virgin Mary were saints believed to take a special interest in fertility and pregnancy and might procure the same sorts of aids for infertility that they sought for protection in labor. Cecily Neville (d. 1495), Duchess of York, visited Walsingham on pilgrimage, where she might have purchased a pilgrim's badge associated with the Virgin Mary or a vial of holy water. Margaret of Anjou also visited Walsingham in 1453 to give an expensive gem-covered gift in hopes of ending her childlessness. More modest gifts from grateful women include almost one hundred nightgowns left at Hereford's shrine to Thomas Cantelupe, who had answered their prayers for pregnancies. At the wedding of George Cely and Margery Rygon, three rabbits were released as a symbol of fertility, and indeed, Margery was pregnant within their first year of marriage.

CONTRACEPTION AND ABORTION

While married women prayed for greater fertility, singlewomen were eager to prevent conception or terminate unwanted pregnancies. Here, again, the saints might be useful, and saints' lives counseled women to pray for solutions. The late medieval lives of some Irish saints include stories about interventions into unwanted or dangerous pregnancies. Historian Maeve Callan has shown that four medieval Irish saints performed abortions, the most famous was Brigid of Kildare, joined by Ciarán of Saigir, Áed mac Bricc, and Cainnech of Aghaboe. Ciarán emptied a woman's womb after she was sexually assaulted while a member of his religious community, Áed, blessed the womb of a pregnant nun who had sinned, and the fetus disappeared; Cainnech blessed the womb of a woman who sought his help after she had secretly fornicated. Saint Brigid's interventions into pregnancy are more extensive, as she assisted with infertility, eased discomforts of pregnant and postpartum women, and cared for children after birth. Brigid also performed an abortion miracle, for which the recipient expressed grateful thanks.

Medieval women were aware of several forms of contraception beyond breastfeeding, as efforts to block conception were practiced in the ancient period. In the thirteenth century, William of Saliceto, a physician operating in Bologna and Verona, wrote a chapter titled "Those Things That Prohibit Conception and Abortion," in which he said, "Although this chapter may not be according to the strict rules of law, nevertheless for the ordinary course of medical science on account of the danger that comes to a woman because of a dangerous risk of conceiving on account of her health, debilities, or the extremity of her youth" (Riddle 1992, 136). The law he means is canon law—all contraception and abortion was prohibited by the church, as was any nonprocreative intercourse. The penalty for contraception was penance, not criminal prosecution, and thus is not well documented in legal records.

As noted earlier, in the mid-fourteenth century, English common law changed its definition of when life began, shifting from the fetus's ensoulment to birth. Previously, intentional termination by the mother and miscarriage by assault—whether by violence or poison—had been considered homicide, but after this point, homicide was a charge reserved for murder victims who had been born. Infanticide, murder of a child, was known but very rarely presented in court, since jurors were reluctant to see a woman who killed her child as guilty of murder. Historians have found fewer than five cases of infanticide in court records that include thousands of thousands of homicide cases. Coroners' rolls of accidental deaths for infants under a year old indicate that the children did not die of neglect, drowning, or exposure in the way one would expect from infanticide. The majority of these infant deaths was due to fire in their cradles or house, a dangerous accident but not an indication of intentional infanticide. There was not a higher proportion of female infants who died, which might have been another indication of infanticide in a patriarchy. Medieval families do not appear to have used infanticide in a routine way as a form of contraception, even though mothers were not likely to be legally punished for killing their own child.

Abortion was criminalized in Europe in the fourteenth century and prosecuted most in areas of Italy and Spain. Even in cases of pregnancy or childbirth, when the mother's life was at risk, the focus was on preserving the fetus, but authorities demonstrated discomfort about investigating and prosecuting abortion, or imposing penalties, especially on those who had local status. By 1500 European jurisdiction over abortion, miscarriage, and infanticide shifted from ecclesiastical to secular authority, and this shift saw an increase in the prosecution and punishment of these crimes. Protestant thought also shifted the moment of ensoulment to conception, setting the stage to make any form of miscarriage by assault or abortion into a potential homicide.

Couples intent on prohibiting conception despite these prohibitions could use coitus interruptus to avoid pregnancy. Physicians had access to a great deal of information about contraception from Greek and Arabic medical texts but had ethical quandaries about making use of that knowledge when it opposed the church's position. Some physicians advised that it was acceptable to treat women for whom childbirth or miscarriage would be dangerous. Women might use a variety of plants such as savin juniper, rue, pennyroyal, and Queen Anne's lace as contraception based on popular information or medical advice. Savin, rue, cypress, and pennyroyal were among those plants used to concoct abortifacients. The Greek doctor Hippocrates had recommended fumigants—medicines that were burned and women sat over so that the medicine could fumigate the vagina—but William advised these medicines to be inhaled instead (Riddle 1992, 136). The Trotula included fumigants of iris as a method for abortion: "Also the root of iris put up into the womb or fumigated from below with iris makes her lose her child, for its roots are hot and dry and have the virtue to open, to heat, to consume, and to waste. For when the woman is weak and the child is unable to come out, then it is better that the child is killed than the mother of the child dies as well" (Goldberg 1995, 57). While there is no limitation placed on the use of this technique, it is interesting that this last sentence hints that its purpose is to save the life of the mother when both mother and fetus are at risk.

The *Breviarium* attributed to the fourteenth-century Arnold of Naples included instructions for fumigants, suppositories, and potions that included thyme, rue, blackberry, birthwort, pepper, betony, sweet flag, opopanax, galbanum, willow leaves, fern, ivy, and scammony. The text advised women to burn a mule's hoof or use elephant dung as a suppository as well as gave instructions for the removal of a dead fetus. Peter of Spain advised on contraception for men, using hemlock on the testicles before sex. Both men and women could carry talismans or wear amulets. Court records from late medieval France demonstrate that common methods of abortion matched the ingredients and techniques contained in these literary texts. Women desperate to terminate a pregnancy could also find advice to jump from high places or have themselves beaten in the abdomen.

CHILD REARING

Historians have debated for many years about the affection medieval parents may have borne for their children. Given the high infant and childhood mortality rate, historians once suggested that parents avoided connecting with their children until they passed an age where mortality was not such a risk. Medieval historians have successfully proven this was not the case and that parents did indeed love their children a great deal. Coroners' rolls prove that parents, especially mothers, were quick to find a child who met with an accidental death, and saints' miracle tales depict parents bringing ill, injured, or disabled children across great distances to seek help from the saints. Given the high risk to children's health and the many dangers, medieval parents had to care deeply about their children, watch them quite closely, and attend carefully to their health. This suggests a high degree of affection, not emotional distancing.

Mothers were the primary caregivers for young children, especially if they breastfed them personally, which they might do up to two years. Wealthier mothers might employ a wet nurse and/or a servant to assist them, but the mother was still responsible for her child's education. Nurses might live with the family or receive payment to take the child into their own homes.

Mothers taught their children, up to age six or seven, morals and faith, perhaps some of their letters, and literature. The mother was responsible for their early religious education, although the godparents also had a role in ensuring that their godchildren knew the Lord's Prayer and the Nicene Creed. While boys commonly left home around age seven, girls usually remained their mother's responsibility until they married. Between age seven and puberty, children began to learn from others, possibly as an apprentice in a town guild's workshop or by living with another household in an elite family's network. After about age ten or twelve, children might look toward marriage and adulthood.

Girls of any status could attend school after a 1406 edict claimed that right for both boy and girl children. Girls might learn at a nunnery, or they might go to another elite household to make social connections. But more commonly, they learned from their mothers. The 1371 *Book of the Knight of La Tour* contained instructions for the education of his daughters. This proved to be a popular book, and William Caxton published an English version in 1484. It is possible that this version was made for Elizabeth Woodville and her large family. The popular depictions of saints with books and especially of the Virgin Mary learning from her mother, Saint Anne, encouraged girls in their literacy and general education.

Elite mothers taught their daughters—or arranged for them to learn—how to dance, play music, embroider, and manage their estate and servants. A lower-status mother taught her daughter to manage the household tasks as well as more profitable skills—by puberty, a girl should know how to cook, clean, spin, tend a kitchen garden, weave, make candles, and possibly, brew beer. An artisan's or merchant's daughter would assist in the shop, perhaps also in the craft. Girls could also become apprentices, although at lower rates than boys, as discussed in chapter 4.

The cult of Saint Anne in the later Middle Ages emphasized her role as a mother teaching the Virgin Mary to read. Such a holy example was inspiring, and in the fourteenth and fifteenth centuries, literacy became more common, and mothers, especially aristocratic or urban elites, may have taught daughters to read. While literacy in the Middle Ages was understood as the ability to read Latin, and it is possible that some elite women understood and could teach children to read Latin, women outside the monasteries who could read were more likely to do so in vernacular languages, English and possibly French. Women and girls might read devotional literature such as the lives of the saints or more secular literature such as histories and romances. When Eleanor Townshend was responsible for her estate during her widowhood, she had the relevant documents written in English so she might read them (Moreton 1992, 144). The ability to read did not always come with the ability to write, two different skills that were not always taught together, particularly when trained scribes were available to elite women to write what they dictated. Girls raised to work in urban crafts and shops were more likely to learn to write so that they could assist in keeping inventories, records of sale, and other relevant documents.

Children were expected to work and contribute to the household from a young age. By age four, children were performing chores around the house, and by age eight, children were performing tasks determined by their sex, girls working with their mothers and boys assisting their fathers in their work. There was a great deal of work to do around the medieval home, and girls assisted with the tending of animals, the preparation of food, the production of clothes and household textiles, and the minding of younger children. As they did so, they joined the community of women who kept their families fed, clothed, and healthy. Along with their chores, they received an education in household management, child raising, women's labor, and their future responsibilities. They also likely enjoyed joining women's networks with their fellowship and conversation.

Canon law allowed parents to physically punish their children, as it allowed husbands to discipline their wives. The wife in "How the Good Wife Taught Her Daughter" advised her daughter to deal with disobedient and disrespectful children by using a "sharp rod" on them until they begged for mercy and confessed their guilt, remarking that even beloved children needed this sort of "instruction" (Furnivall 1908). These were expectations, and parents and husbands could be called to account for wayward behavior in those they were expected to discipline. Corporal punishment was common in medieval society and would not have shocked children or other adults. Discipline was not expected to be abusive, however, and coroners did investigate suspicious deaths of children.

Children played with toys made of lead, tin, wood, or cloth. Balls, keys, puppets have all been found, and there are references to dolls. Children likely played with items they could find near their homes: sticks and rocks, wooden spoons, farming tools, and so on.

SINGLE MOTHERS

There were undeniable differences in the ways that unwed, single, and typically poor women experienced motherhood and were able to raise their children. The emphasis on virginity and chastity outside of wedlock meant that pregnancy announced unmarried mothers' sexual sins. Medieval communities valued charity highly and typically gave generously to the worthy poor. For unwed mothers, however, the notion that they had committed a sin, fornication, complicated typical Christian charity, since giving alms to a sinner encouraged that sin. While there was sympathy for women who had suffered sexual assaults, medieval understanding of conception meant that women who became pregnant had to have experienced pleasure; pregnancy thus undermined a claim of assault. Even formal charities formally excluded unwed mothers as unworthy of Christian charity. Not only were women who committed fornication on medieval estates charged a fine—the leyrwite fine—when their male partners were not, but such women who became pregnant with illegitimate children were marked as marginal and unwelcome. In the 1280s, the village of Horsham expelled four poor single mothers and their children (Bennett 2003, 155). As a result, unmarried mothers were usually poor and vulnerable, without many options. By the fifteenth century, the term "single-woman" became equivalent with "prostitute" for any woman who engaged in sex outside of marriage.

FOR FURTHER READING

Bennett, Judith M. 2003. "Writing Fornication: Medieval Leyrwite and Its Historians." *Transactions of the Royal Historical Society*, 6th series 13: 131–162.

Blumenfeld-Kosinski, Renate. 1990. *Not of Women Born: Representations of Caesarean Birth in Medieval and Renaissance Culture*. Ithaca, NY: Cornell University Press.

Cabré, Montserrat. 2008. "Women or Healers? Household Practices and the Categories of Health Care in Late Medieval Iberia." *Bulletin of the History of Medicine* 82: 18–51.

Callan, Maeve B. 2012. "Of Vanishing Fetuses and Maidens Made-Again: Abortion, Restored Virginity, and Similar Scenarios in Medieval Irish Hagiography and Penitentials." *Journal of the History of Sexuality* 21, no. 2: 282–296.

Clarke, Katie, and Michael Hicks. 2016. "What Went on in the Medieval Parish Church, 1377–1447, with Particular Reference to Churching." In *The Later Medieval Inquisitions Post Mortem: Mapping the Medieval Countryside and Rural Society*, edited by Michael Hicks. Woodbridge: Boydell Press.

Deller, William S. 2010. "The First Rite of Passage: Baptism in Medieval Memory." *Journal of Family History* 36, no. 1: 3–14.

Furnivall, Frederick James. 1908. "How the Good Wife Taught Her Daughter." In *The Babees' Book: Medieval Manners for the Young: Done into Modern English*, edited by Edith Rickert. London: Duffield & Co. Project Gutenberg.

Goldberg, P. J. P. 1995. *Women in England c. 1275–1525: Documentary Sources*. Manchester: Manchester University Press.

Grauer, Anne L. 2002. "Where Were the Women?" In *Human Biologists in the Archives: Demography, Health, Nutrition and Genetics in Historical Populations*, edited by D. Ann Herring and Alan C. Swedlund, 266–288. Cambridge: Cambridge University Press.

Green, Monica H. 1988–1989. "Women's Medical Practice and Health Care in Medieval Europe." *Signs* 14: 434–473.

Green, Monica H., ed. and trans. 2002. *The Trotula: A Medieval Compendium of Women's Medicine*. Philadelphia: University of Pennsylvania Press.

Green, Monica H. 2008a. "Gendering the History of Women's Healthcare." *Gender & History* 20: 487–518.

Green, Monica H. 2008b. *Making Women's Medicine Masculine: The Rise of Male Authority in Pre-Modern Gynaecology*. Oxford: Oxford University Press.

Green, Monica H., and Daniel Lord Smail. 2008. "The Trial of Floreta d'Ays (1403): Jews, Christians, and Obstetrics in Later Medieval Marseille." *Journal of Medieval History* 34, no. 2 (June): 185–211.

Harris-Stoertz, Fiona. 2012. "Pregnancy and Childbirth in Twelfth-and Thirteenth-Century French and English Law." *Journal of the History of Sexuality* 21, no. 2 (May): 263–281.

Hollingworth, T. H. 1957. "A Demographic Study of the British Ducal Families." *Population Studies* 11, no. 1: 4–26.

Julian of Norwich. 1901. *Revelations of Divine Love*. Edited by Grace Warrack. London: Methuen & Company. Project Gutenberg.

Karras, Ruth Mazo. 2005. *Sexuality in Medieval Europe: Doing unto Others*. New York: Routledge.

Kowaleski, Maryanne. 2013. "Gendering Demographic Change in the Middle Ages." In *The Oxford Handbook of Women & Gender in Medieval Europe*, edited by Judith M. Bennett and Ruth Mazo Karras. Oxford: Oxford University Press.

Legg, L. G. Wickham, ed. 1901. *English Coronation Records*. London: Archibald Constable and Co. Ltd.

Leyser, Henrietta. 1995. *Medieval Women: A Social History of Women in England 450–1500*. London: Orion.

Maitland, F. W., ed. 1887. *Bracton's Note Book: A Collection of Cases Decided in the King's Courts during the Reign of Henry the Third*. London: C. J. Clay & Sons.

Moreton, C. E. 1992. *The Townshend and Their World: Gentry, Law and Land in Norfolk, c. 1450–1551*. Oxford: Clarendon Press.

Mueller, Wolfgang P. 2012. *The Criminalization of Abortion in the West: Its Origins in Medieval Law*. Ithaca, NY: Cornell University Press.

Park, Katharine. 2006. *Secrets of Women: Gender, Generation, and the Origins of Human Dissection*. New York: Zone Books.

Park, Katharine. 2018. "Managing Childbirth and Fertility in Medieval Europe." In *Reproduction*, edited by Nick Hopwood, Rebecca Flemming, and Lauren Kassell, 153–166. Cambridge: Cambridge University Press.

Rawcliffe, Carole. 1995. *Medicine and Society in Later Medieval England*. Stroud: Alan Sutton.

Rawcliffe, Carole. 2003. "Women, Childbirth, and Religion in Later Medieval England." In *Women and Religion in Medieval England*, edited by Diana Wood. Oxford: Oxbow Books.

Reames, Sherry L., ed. 2003. "John Lydgate, the Lyfe of Seynt Margarete." In *Middle English Legends of Women Saints*. Kalamazoo, MI: Medieval Institute Publications.

Riddle, John M. 1992. *Contraception and Abortion from the Ancient World to the Renaissance*. Cambridge, MA: Harvard University Press.

Rieder, Paula M. 2006. *On the Purification of Women: Churching in Northern France, 1100–1500*. New York: Palgrave Macmillan.

Shahar, Shulamith. 1990. *Childhood in the Middle Ages*. New York: Routledge.

Shenton, Caroline. 2003. "Philippa of Hainault's Churchings: The Politics of Motherhood at the Court of Edward III." In *Family and Dynasty in Late Medieval England: Proceedings of the 1997 Harlaxton Symposium*, edited by Richard Eales and Shaun Tyas. Donington: Shaun Tyas.

Ward, Jennifer. 2006. *Women in England in the Middle Ages*. New York: Hambledon Continuum.

3

ROYAL AND NOBLEWOMEN

In "The Legend of Good Women," Geoffrey Chaucer recounts instruction he received from Alceste, a fictional figure of the ideal wife from Classical literature, to write stories about good women as penance for his previous tales of unfaithful women. In the *Legend*, Alceste ordered Chaucer to give his new stories to the queen, Anne of Bohemia, wife of King Richard II. The scene explains Chaucer's change in tone in this poem and suggests that the request for this new subject came not from his character Alceste but from Queen Anne herself, or perhaps from Anne's mother-in-law, Joan of Kent. Alceste demonstrates the queenly service of intercession, where she helps her subjects by intervening with the king to moderate his policies, demonstrating her charity and influence:

> You shall, while you live, year by year
> The most part of your time spend
> In making a glorious Legend
> Of Good Women, maidens and wives,
> That were true in loving all their lives
> And tell of false men that them betrayed
> That in all their life did none but assay
> How many women they may do a shame;

For in your world that is now held a game

And though you are not likely to a lover be

Speak well of love; this penance give I thee.

And to the god of love I shall so pray

That he shall charge his servants, by any way

To further you, and well your labor requite;

Go now your way, this penance is but light.

And when this book is made, give it to the queen

On my behalf, at Eltham or at Sheen.

(Chaucer 1889, 36–37)

The exchange also references the interest of English noblewomen in literary patronage and Chaucer's ability to attract royal patrons whose attention could shape his work. Chaucer's Alceste introduces us to some of these crucial aspects of aristocratic women's lives in late medieval England.

LADIES

While it can be challenging to uncover the history of women during the Middle Ages, female members of the aristocracy in England left a number of sources that permit us to know much about their lives. Even so, until fairly recently, historians have focused on the lives of kings and their barons in England and ignored or downplayed the stories of the queens and noblewomen. These women had important roles in England's political world, however, and had a great deal of influence on its economy, culture, and society as well. As this chapter suggests, the study of politics that has long suggested that only men held power has truly only told half the story, or less. Women, their actions, their property, their claims to thrones, their interventions, and their models have all been incredibly influential on medieval politics.

Medieval historians describe the aristocracy as the "second estate," known to medieval authors as *bellatores*, or "those who fight." We might expand that category, when thinking about women, to "those who fight, and the women who love them." Noblewomen were medieval elites who lived off land; noble families made up about 1 percent of the English population but controlled about 10–20 percent of England's cultivated land (Harris 2002, 7). Nobles received titles and land in a system of vassalage, in which they swore oaths to provide military service in support of a lord who granted them control over part of his territory. The king of England, for example, served as a lord to the Duke of York, his vassal who controlled the duchy of York, and in return for control of that duchy and the revenue it provided, the duke was responsible for supporting his king and providing troops for his armies. This system of obligations, land, and service is sometimes called "feudalism," but that term is used in so many other confusing ways that historians have stopped relying on it.

In exchange for military service and an oath of loyalty, kings bestowed on their vassals—those who swore these oaths—a title and a "fief," a parcel of land the vassal could control for his or her lifetime. At their death, the vassal's heir could swear a new oath to the lord and receive the fief and title for their own lifetime and so on. The fief could be of any size, but many were quite large, such as the duchy of York given to the Duke of York. The duke could then bestow smaller fiefs from his territory, along with lesser titles for service to him. Typically, the lords and vassals were men, since a vassal's obligation was to provide troops and other military support to protect their lord, but there were occasions when women or even institutions swore oaths of vassalage and controlled these fiefs.

Control of these properties could bring families who managed their estates well enormous wealth and great power. A fief often included a number of manors—large estates that included a manor house, village of peasants (some of whom were "unfree" serfs who legally owed their labor to the lord and could not leave the manor without permission), orchards, hunting forests, arable fields, pastures, and so on. Lords could live in one of their manor houses full time or travel between them as they wished. On each manor there were a number of money-making tools that contributed to the lord's income. The lord controlled the demesne, a portion of the fields and their produce, for which he typically did not have to pay for labor; he charged rents to the villagers; he charged fees for their use of his ovens, winepress, and mill; he charged them a number of customary annual fees; and he extracted fines as penalties for crimes and violations discovered in his manor court. Tallage was a fine the lord could charge his serfs on a whim.

Peasants had little recourse to fight their exploitation, which meant there were few restraints on the lord's ability to exploit them. Even kindly lords were known to raise rents and demand the most labor possible from their serfs, a situation that provoked rebellion in the late fourteenth century. And if lords were not interested in exploiting their manors directly, they could lease them to those who would or make money from further leases. The king owned the manor of Brigstock, but he leased it to Margery de Farendraght for thirteen pounds a year. Margery then subleased the manor directly to the villagers in 1318 for forty-six pounds. The tenants of Brigstock likely enjoyed having control of the manor they lived on, but they paid handsomely for the privilege, to the benefit of those with existing wealth and status.

Nobles were also the commanders of troops, including knights, infantrymen, and yeomen, and while their armies were meant to serve the king and keep the peace, by the fourteenth century, these had become personal armies nobles might use to solve their personal conflicts or even to rise up against the king as shown in the Introduction. Noblewomen were thrust into the world of politics based on the loyalties of their fathers, husbands, and brothers, but they often also pursued political negotiations in their own battlefields: court, the marriage negotiation, and with their patronage. They were partners with their male family members, seeking advancement for their relatives and themselves.

As we will see in chapter 4, there is some evidence that women were involved in the artists' workshops of the later Middle Ages, but we unfortunately have little evidence to document what paintings, statues, tapestries, or other artworks may have had female creators. This is similarly true for medieval literature, where scholars are forced today to refer to the "Pearl Poet," rather than use a known name, for example. Since much medieval artwork and writing went unsigned, it is possible to consider that many "anonymous" works had female creators, especially since women were the ones most likely to complete their work without credit. We do have another way to observe women's involvement with important cultural artifacts from the Middle Ages, however: their patronage. Women are well documented as donors for literature, paintings, illuminated manuscripts, and church decoration. This patronage demonstrates that women had a significant impact on the content and focus of late medieval culture.

Noblewomen generally had two options that shaped their lives: they could marry, or they could enter a monastery. We will examine those who chose the church in chapter 6, while this chapter focuses on noblewomen who chose marriage. Barbara Harris found that this group was the majority of noblewomen: 94 percent of Yorkist or early Tudor aristocratic women married, most before age twenty-one (Harris 2002, 18). Chapters 1 and 2 have already examined the institution of marriage and the experience of motherhood generally in medieval England, so now we will turn to experiences particular to royal and noblewomen of the fourteenth and fifteenth centuries. These women's private lives were essential to the public affairs of England. Their homes were places where political, economic, social, and cultural work took place, and they were not bystanders. Noblewomen frequently took care of the family estate while their husbands were away at court, at war, or in Parliament, and their work included overseeing their children and home as well as taking care of the property, supervising servants, and keeping the peace. A number of letters and other documents from the fourteenth and fifteenth centuries—such as from the Paston and Plumpton families—demonstrate that aristocratic wives proved able administrators of these estates.

England's elites knew well which families were noble (titled families and their relatives) and which were members of the gentry (the families of knights), but there was both upward and downward mobility between these two groups, particularly through marriage. A poor nobleman's family and a wealthy gentleman's family might have similar lives. It was still noteworthy, however, when a member of the gentry married a noblewoman, such as Richard Woodville's marriage to Jacquetta of Luxembourg or Catherine of Valois's marriage to Owen Tudor. More acceptable was when a gentleman's daughter was able to use her inherited wealth to marry into a noble family.

In England the nobility typically lived in the countryside, and one family might control many manor houses, moving between them throughout the year (see chapter 4). They also likely spent some time at court, the group of people surrounding the king and his queen. Court was an expensive prospect, requiring luxurious clothes, adornments, and gifts as well as time away from one's own family. Time at court could also be profitable for authors, artists, scholars, and other talented people seeking patrons, ambitious people seeking advantage and position, or nobles trying to protect their property and interests. Women might offer financial assistance, but even more important was promoting them to other allies or offering them an opportunity to showcase their talents. Wealthy medieval women were important book patrons and book owners. Women spent time at court as part of the queen's household, and that close association with the queen allowed them to benefit from royal patronage, gain influence in securing the best marriage arrangements for their family members, or gain access to valuable information. Ladies-in-waiting and maids-of-honor also earned annual incomes for their service in the queen's household.

The late medieval English "court" included the royal household and the bureaucratic operations of the monarchy. At its core were the king and his entourage of family, friends, and officers. The court was not fixed in a certain place; instead, it followed the king. The bureaucracy, the ceremonial ritual, the diplomacy and statecraft, and palace patronage formed the core of the court. Courtiers looked to the king for position, office, and support and helped him to administrate the country. Their wives served as the queen's ladies, and together they used their funds to enhance the court's grandeur with celebrations and support for musicians, dancers, artists, and authors. Spectacle and pageantry were important opportunities for court celebration as well as forms of communication between king and people. Among these diversions, noblewomen participated in riding and hunting with bows, dogs, or birds of prey.

During the fourteenth and fifteenth centuries, England's kings made great efforts to centralize their rule and shift the center of power from aristocratic families rooted in the countryside and into their own hands at the center of the court. It was a period of turmoil that brought some individual women opportunities to increase the status of their families while overall reinforcing England's patriarchal royal rule.

These women were certainly aware of their privilege and of the limitations society put on them. They were bound by patriarchy as much as they themselves reinforced it through expectations on the women around them. Women were subordinate to men in medieval England, but noblewomen had access to wealth and privilege that permitted them greater influence over their lives and greater personal comfort than other contemporaries might expect. At the same time, even aristocratic women faced limitations in their access to property and the law.

The English practiced primogeniture, which meant that titles and estates passed on to the oldest male heir, but women could still inherit wealth. If they married, women brought with them dowries from their own families and could expect a husband to give them dower lands when they wed, lands whose wealth would support them if widowed. Coverture, the legal concept placing married women under the authority and protection of their husbands, meant that even noblewomen could not legally sign contracts or create wills without their husbands' (rarely granted) consent, which impeded their legal ability to deal with property. Women could

inherit wealth from their fathers, mothers, siblings, or other relatives such as cash or properties that were not part of the patrimo-
nial estate, but that property was legally under the control of their
husbands, unless the couple had signed a prenuptial agreement.
Noblewomen who married or married multiple times could build
great wealth through their dower lands, which they could use to
shape their worlds or to attract even more influential husbands.
This made widows enticing to men without great properties, as can
be seen in the marriage Elizabeth Woodville arranged between her
brother John and Catherine Neville, Dowager Duchess of Norfolk.

Even after their marriage women remained members of their
natal families, and aristocratic fathers took a keen interest in their
daughters' lives, often continuing to protect their legal rights, especially around property. After her father's death, a noblewoman's
brother or other male member of her natal family would assist them
in dealing with economic or legal issues. Married sisters, cousins,
and nieces might themselves, in turn, assist male relatives by facili-
tating marriages, promoting them to patrons, or otherwise drawing
on their now expanded network to their family members' advantage. Elizabeth Woodville' success at placing her siblings and cousins in advantageous positions once she married King Edward IV
demonstrates that access to power relied on securing it for future
generations.

Mothers also maintained an interest in their married daughters'
lives, traveling to assist with childbirth, sending gifts, writing with
advice for running their new households, and helping to arrange
the marriages of their grandchildren. Sisters might fill similar roles
for one another after marriage; childless women tended to leave
their property to a sister's child, often a daughter. Elizabeth Neville
had no surviving children after her two marriages and so named
her sister's daughter Lucy as her heir, but she offered no bequest
for either of Lucy's brothers. Noblewomen also developed close ties
with their daughters-in-law, often remembering them in their wills
with objects that held sentimental value for the two women. And
women also invested time in the positions of their husbands' siblings. Margaret Paston took a role in arranging her sister-in-law's
marriage to Sir Robert Poynings in 1458.

Aristocratic widows, discussed in more detail in chapter 1, did
often find themselves in vulnerable positions, needing to defend
their property against their husbands' collateral male relatives,
against their own children, or against stepchildren. Sons or step-
sons were especially keen to limit their mother's ability to bestow

property from their fathers onto subsequent husbands or new half-siblings, which might happen if their mothers were executors of their fathers' estates. Lawsuits and petitions from the children suggest the possible interests these subsequent husbands had in marrying widows and the benefits they believed would come to them from their control of property and wealth. Widows also defended their wealth from inheriting sons as a way of ensuring that they could properly bestow dowries on daughters and arrange preferments, positions, for their younger sons.

The noble household likely included more than the natal family, a difference from other status levels in this period, but one likely due to the younger age at marriage, the larger size of the homes, and the concentration of wealth into fewer and fewer hands. Often, young couples lived with their parents, which could complicate a young wife's ability to assert herself in the presence of an influential mother-in-law. Extended family, particularly unmarried siblings, widowed parents, allies' children they were supervising "in service," and a number of servants might live with the couple and their children. Most noble families had children—over 90 percent of the families Barbara Harris studied in the Yorkist and early Tudor period had children, and 40 percent of the women she studied had five or more children, a number she notes could be low because medieval record-keepers did not note down all births (Harris 2002, 99).

Chapter 2 delves more deeply into motherhood, but it is worth noting here some maternal experiences that were particular to aristocratic women. Servants such as nursemaids and governesses raised noble children, and noblewomen often attended to other duties rather than spending much time during the day with them. That should not suggest that aristocratic women did not love their children; they often showed great affection for and connection with their children; they were just not intimately involved in the minutiae of their day. By avoiding breastfeeding, noblewomen could more quickly begin a new pregnancy and increase the likelihood of some children reaching adulthood. Aristocratic women took a careful role in their children's education, in arranging their marriages, and in nurturing their connections to a crucial support network, tasks that prioritized the status of the larger family as well as the individual child.

Wardship was also an important feature of aristocratic women's lives. Selection of a guardian for a minor child whose father had died was the king's privilege. While mothers or stepfathers might petition the king for the wardship of their own children or step-children, the king had no obligation to grant the petition. Margaret Beaufort, for example, lost the wardship of her son Henry to his uncle Jasper Tudor and, upon her remarriage, was not even able to see her son often. Mothers could write to their children, however, and often wrote their guardians with advice as well.

Serving at court was another way that aristocratic women could support their families. As noted above, these women earned an income from their service in the queen's household and had access to the central networks of power and culture in the kingdom. Families hoped to place their daughters in the court in order to position them for excellent marriages and close personal connections to the royal family. The queen's maids and ladies typically came from families currently in favor with the king, from among the queen's own relatives, or from the extended network of royal allies. Current ladies had some influence over the selection of new maids, and families hoping to rise in status might solicit support for a daughter or niece from one of the queen's ladies.

Unmarried aristocratic girls could join the queen's household at age sixteen, when they could become maids-of-honor. Among their qualifications was an expectation of beauty, a knack for fashion, good manners, talents in dance and music, knowledge of French, and an ability to please the queen. After their marriage, which might be arranged or even paid for by the king and queen, former maids could continue their service as ladies-in-waiting. It was also not unusual for well-placed married women to serve as one of the queen's ladies after their marriage to one of the king's powerful supporters.

It is worth noting that serving as one of the queen's ladies also put these women in the path of the king, and several kings selected their mistresses from this group. The most notorious example of a royal mistress in this period was Alice Perrers, mistress of Edward III. This sort of experience for their daughters was not a disadvantage for many families. While chastity before marriage was ideal, the king's favor had many benefits, as Edward's affection for Alice and his many extravagant gifts for her show. Men were not afraid to marry a king's mistress, as they too could benefit from the king's generosity.

There might be many opportunities for service: Elizabeth Woodville had seven maids-of-honor and five ladies-in-waiting. Women might serve for short periods of time before returning home to take care of children, or they might offer lifelong service to the royal family, moving between positions as the queen's lady to serve in her daughter's household. The queen's ladies might also serve a subsequent queen and thus show her the ropes of her new royal position. Women who formally served in these positions mingled with other women present in the court, such as wives of the king's advisors and noblewomen who visited the court temporarily.

Barbara Harris has demonstrated that these women's service to the court constituted careers that "were essential for the court to perform its central social, ceremonial, political, and diplomatic functions," and so historians should not overlook the importance of these women. As she argues, women who offered lifelong service to the king and his family should be considered "career servants of the crown as accurately as men in comparable positions" (Harris 2002, 211, 217). They shaped the culture of the court and had an impact on the art, literature, fashion, and discourse of the kingdom as well as its economic, social, and political life.

The significance of the queen's household was especially clear during ceremonial events, particularly those having to do with diplomacy. A large contingent of beautifully dressed ladies helped to display the majesty of the king to visiting dignitaries, and their well-developed skills in conversation helped to develop positive relationships with foreign officials. Their display of beauty and luxury during ceremonial events—weddings, christenings, churchings, holidays, tournaments—contributed to a narrative of the court's magnificence and also positioned the ladies well for patronage, advancement, and marriage. The ladies also had quieter duties: serving the queen while she dined or helping her pass time by playing games such as chess, dice, and cards or dancing and playing music together or joining her in creating beautiful items for the court and palace with their needlework. These were, at times, displayed to visitors to give them a simpler but equally powerful glimpse of the queen and her ladies.

The fourteenth and fifteenth centuries were a time of turmoil for the monarchy, and women supported their families by aligning themselves with the king or with his political opponents through support, marital arrangements, or even advice. Factional strife was present within the court, where power brokers fought for access and connection through the king's favor. Women participated in these negotiations, and a privileged position at the court gave them great advantage in these struggles. Margaret Beaufort served as a lady-in-waiting to multiple queens on various sides of the Wars of the Roses, which eventually proved useful for her son's rise to power as Henry VII.

While the Black Death pandemic affected all segments of English society, including wealthy elites, the relatively superior health and nutrition, as well as the more sanitary and spacious living conditions of their homes, provided nobles with better protection against the disease than their poorer counterparts. The devastation of the pandemic on economic life also affected the nobility. The fourteenth-century noblewoman Elizabeth de Burgh, for example, saw her annual income of £3,500 in the 1340s drop to £2,300 in 1349–1350 (Davis 2012, 365). Such a significant change in circumstances is part of what led nobles to demand that the king freeze prices and wages at pre-plague levels as well as to enforce the price and wage legislation once ordered. Women who controlled estates and seigneurial towns, such as Elizabeth de Burgh and her control of Clare, were the ones responsible for this enforcement, and their income depended on it.

CHARITY AND SPIRITUALITY

Devotion to their faith is a common virtue attributed to Christian ladies in late medieval England. This is clear in their charity, in their support of the church, and in their roles as advocates for the Christian needs of the community with their husbands. They are often remembered as patrons or inspirations for new church decoration, new chapels, or spiritual manuscripts. Aristocratic homes sometimes included a private chapel where a chaplain could say a weekly mass, and noblewomen's household goods sometimes included a portable altar, a recognition that their lives were not settled in one home and that their religious needs continued even during an active life. The church still expected these women to attend services at a regular church on significant holidays and to take communion at Easter.

Private devotional objects such as rosaries could be quite luxurious. The elaborate rosary beads made of boxwood with intricate carvings on them, such as the early-sixteenth-century one on display at the Cloisters division of the Metropolitan Museum of Art in New York City. There was a vibrant medieval trade in saints' relics, which could be placed into decorated reliquaries, luxury objects in their own right. These could be set in a place of honor at home or, more likely, carried as a frequently held personal item, perhaps has a necklace.

Wealthy women could also own devotional books such as breviaries, books of hours, psalters, collections of saints' lives, mystical

works such as anchoress Julian of Norwich's *Revelations*. Collections of these texts in English and/or French were popular reading for women. Such manuscripts might also be illuminated, with
images on which women might focus their devotions. While manuscripts for the altar were often large, these texts could be quite small,
sized to fit into a hand, or even smaller, to fit into a pocket. Girdle
books were small devotional manuscripts with hooks that could be
attached to a belt and quickly accessed for reading and consulta-
tion. While many of the extant girdle books appear to have been
intended for the clergy, fifteenth-century images of noblewomen
and female saints include girdle books. These may have operated
like reliquaries, rosary beads, or a talisman, a devotional object to
keep close and provide a tactile experience for devotion and prayer.

Noblewomen were well placed to be able to fulfill the Christian
good work of charity. They both had more funds than most other
women and tied into influence networks where their example and
attention might benefit a recipient of charity much further than her
donation itself. These ladies' patronage might be considered an act
of charity, but medieval Christians emphasized the works of mercy
identified in the Gospel of Matthew: to feed the hungry, give drink
to the thirsty, give hospitality to strangers, clothe the naked, care
for the sick, and visit prisoners (Matthew 25:35–37). These were all
areas of charitable giving for Christian women, and especially for
noblewomen. They fed poor people at their gates, donated to hospitals and almshouses, supported pilgrims, and gave generously to
religious houses. Household accounts show that noblewomen gave
to the poor, hungry, sick, and needy throughout their lives, but
their wills also document significant bequests upon their deaths.
Noble widows, who were able to make their own wills, typically
remembered their servants and gave to local institutions for the
poor and sick such as hospitals, almshouses, and leprosaria. They
often gave to the church, but sometimes earmarked that money for
further distribution to the needy. See chapter 6 for further discussion of charity.

It was common enough for noble ladies to desire to retire to a
monastery in their widowhood, sometimes taking holy orders and
joining the community, sometimes renting a house or rooms within
the abbey enclosure. Such a place of retirement for their final years
fit with ideas about noblewomen's devotional lives, but monasteries also provided a place for such women to find care and community without standing in the way of the next generation's use of
resources.

QUEENSHIP

The royal family was the center of the court, and they too moved frequently from place to place. Such movement allowed the sovereign to display himself to his people and to make them feel connected to him. People could present the king with petitions while meeting him in public, often as he traveled the country, or bring a petition to his court. They might also ask the queen or members of his court to bring their petition to the king for them, since members of the court might attract his attention. Noblewomen could petition the king for assistance with grievances or for his patronage. They asked for positions in the court, for wardships, for protection against cruel family members or spouses, and for help securing their property. Elizabeth Woodville petitioned King Edward IV in person for help regaining her husband's lands for her sons after he died fighting against the king. Others might petition him in writing or through an ally close to the king. This was an informal use of power that relied on reputation, network, and influence. Having connections at court obliged noblewomen and men to act as advocates for their broader network of relatives, friends, and allies. Wealthy and well-connected families thus became patrons for their less fortunate connections.

The king's wife could become queen, but only as a queen consort. While medieval women ruled elsewhere, such as Melisende of Jerusalem and Isabel of Castile, queens did not rule in medieval England until the sixteenth century. As in much of Europe, male primogeniture, the custom of passing the entire property or kingdom on to the oldest son, became the norm by the eleventh century, definitively limiting female access to many thrones and titles. Eleanor of Aquitaine inherited her duchy as her father's only surviving child, but she could not govern there for long; instead she transmitted control to her husbands, first King Louis VII of France and then Henry II of England. There was a brief moment in the twelfth century when English nobles promised to support a female claim to rule, when King Henry I asked his nobles to swear that his daughter Matilda would inherit the throne at his death. Matilda was already empress, married to the Holy Roman Emperor Henry V until his death in 1125, and she fought ferociously to make good her claim on the throne. The English nobles betrayed their promise to her father, however, and supported her cousin Stephen instead. Matilda persevered, challenging Stephen militarily and assuming duties such as minting coins and collecting taxes, but she was never crowned queen.

The English did not go so far as the French, who in the fourteenth and fifteenth centuries created political theories to explain why women could not rule or transmit claims on the French throne. In theory, England could have a ruling queen, but the nobles who determined the succession of each new monarch refused to permit a queen to rule in practice during the Middle Ages. The English had no problem asserting that claims to power could descend through the female, however. Stephen kept the throne, but he did agree to allow Matilda to pass her claim on to her son, the future Henry II. Claims descending through the female line were also the basis for continuing the Hundred Years War, as noted above.

The wedding ceremony and the coronation ritual were not the same, and sometimes, as in the case of Philippa of Hainault who waited two years after her wedding to be coronated queen, there might be a long delay between them, although one would usually follow the other. For a typical late medieval coronation, the queen spent the evening before at the Tower of London and then processed on the morning of her coronation to Westminster Abbey where the ritual took place. This was an opportunity for her to present herself to the people of London and for the people to greet her, perhaps with small pageants or speeches. The *Liber Regalis* that detailed the requirements of the ceremony dictated that the queen wear only a plain purple garment, but some women, like Philippa, embellished the garment, demonstrating the enormous wealth that her arrival, and alliance with the house of Hainault, brought to Edward. The ceremony was followed by feasting and celebrations that likely involved jousting, tournaments, and performances. After an official coronation, the queen had greater access to the dower lands and household income associated with her office, moving out of her husband's household accounts and establishing her own.

The role of the queen consort was essential to the continuation of the monarchy: it was her responsibility to provide a healthy male heir and, according to the medieval notion of the "marital debt," she was required to be sexually available to her husband. Her obligation did not stop at the production of a single male heir, as subsequent children would provide the heir with brothers to support him or join the church and sisters who could marry and thereby build important alliances to protect the throne; brothers would also take the heir's place should he die young—the sad idea of an heir and a spare. Wifely fertility and fidelity were the primary expectations for married aristocrats even more than for other status groups.

Women who failed in the duty to provide heirs could be put aside in favor of a more productive queen. Infertility was typically blamed on the woman, so long as her husband performed his sexual duties and was not distracted by intimate male relationships, as was suggested for Edward II. A queen who had too many children could also create problems, as too many sons might create rivalries, a legacy of Edward III's many surviving sons. Infant and childhood mortality was still a significant enough issue in the later Middle Ages that parents wanted to have multiple sons to ensure an heir would survive to adulthood and the dynastic line could continue, but it was important to raise these children with different intentions clear so that brothers would not fight among themselves. That threat became real, for example, when Edward IV's brother George rose up against him.

English kings tended to select foreign women as wives for themselves or their heirs. Marrying a royal or noblewoman from another country was a mark of prestige and a way of marking difference from other English noble families. It was also a diplomatic tool, as a foreign woman could seal alliances between her natal and marital families. Such "peaceweavers" bridged cultural divides more intimately than any other ambassador might, and by bearing children, they could make the bridges they built permanent. Marrying foreign women also meant, however, that the queen was an outsider with foreign practices, languages, religious practices, and expectations for her role in England. English barons were occasionally unwilling to accept or respect fully foreign queens. If there were other problems that generated hostility, the queen's foreignness amplified them. Foreign marriages also brought subsequent generations' claims on foreign territory, such as the claim to France that English kings pressed in the Hundred Years War.

As informal ambassadors, queens had a political role in advising their husbands on the subject of their homeland, but also a cultural role in sharing their perspective and taste with their new people. One way that queens accomplished this was through patronage and book ownership. Women were frequent patrons of authors as well as collectors of books. Their collections spanned secular and spiritual interests, and women appear to have been frequent readers of devotional texts, some sized to fit into a pocket, as well as of poems, chronicles, treatises, and all manner of books. Their circles might exchange or circulate books, which could bring courtly attention to an aristocratic lady's favored author(s).

One of a queen consort's roles was that of the "mediatrix," an intercessor who could intervene with her husband on behalf of his people. Such power was based on the intercession of saints, who were believed to carry messages to God and do holy work to benefit petitioners, and the Virgin Mary was the ultimate model of an intercessory queen. Subjects might petition the queen to ask her help in moderating her husband's policies and decisions. Most famously, Philippa of Hainault interceded with Edward III during the Hundred Years War to spare the people of Calais, appearing before him publicly and heavy with pregnancy. Queenly intercession was built into the royal relationship, as her intervention permitted a king to have stricter policies, without alienating his people through cruel actions. Intercession allowed the king to be strong but merciful and the queen to be wise and kind. Intercession was also a way for the queen to raise funds, known as the queen's gold, a percentage—possibly as high as 10 percent—of all fines petitioners made to the king through the queen's intercession (Earenfight 2013, 146).

The queen's household and her finances were supposed to be separate from those of the king, but organized just as his were. Her household included a series of rooms, each with guards limiting access to the queen's increasingly more private chambers. She might dine in her own rooms, with or without the king, in the company of her ladies. A queen of England was expected to be able to support herself and her household with these resources and not draw on the king's funds any further.

While a queen consort did not rule, she might have short-term responsibilities to govern as regent for an absent or unavailable husband or son. Women made attractive regents because they were invested in the success of their male relatives and less likely to try to claim power for themselves. Isabella of France proved the exception to the rule when she pushed her husband Edward II aside and ruled as regent for her son, but ultimately she did yield to her son, Edward III, when he asserted himself. Regencies often came during a period of crisis. Margaret of Anjou took responsibility for governing during her husband Henry VI's illnesses, but was not an official regent. Her use of power was unpopular, particularly as a foreign French woman.

After a king's death, his wife became known as the "dowager," or widow, queen. The king gave his wife dower properties at their marriage intended to support her after his death so that she did not have to rely on the next king for a living. A dowager queen might have extraordinary influence over the young king, particularly if he was too young to rule on his own yet, and she could serve as a regent, like Isabella of France did for Edward III. Most dowager queens served as a bridge between their husband's reign and that of their son, helping to smooth the transition and transfer loyalty and respect from one man to the other. Many dowager queens would eventually retreat from court, but in the fourteenth and fifteenth centuries, England's royal transitions were chaotic, and these women facilitated the growth of a new administration.

THE QUEENS

When Chaucer was born, a powerful dynasty ruled England, the Plantagenets. They had come to power through a woman, Empress Matilda, Henry I's daughter, who had fought for the crown promised to her but finally settled on securing her son's right to the English throne. This son, the future Henry II, was the child of her second marriage, to Count Geoffrey of Anjou, nicknamed Geoffrey Plantagenet. Henry claimed the throne in 1154, shortly after his marriage to the wealthy heiress Eleanor of Aquitaine. Henry inherited his claim to England from his mother; massive holdings in northwestern France from his father; and he gained a large, powerful, and independent duchy when he married Eleanor in 1152. His Plantagenet descendants ruled England until 1399, although this end date is deceptive. The house of York that seized the throne next was made up of cousins of the Plantagenets, and indeed, the first use of the name as an actual surname was in 1460 when Richard III declared himself Richard Plantagenet.

This book focuses on the women of the fourteenth and fifteenth centuries, but it is worth noting how important wealthy, powerful queens such as Matilda and Eleanor had been to the founding of the dynasty. The chaos of the fighting between Matilda and Stephen made the English eager for a period of peace and stability, and Henry II's vigorous efforts to create a strong, centralized kingdom went a long way toward creating that stability. Rebellions from his own sons, supported by his wife Eleanor, as well as his possible role in the assassination of Archbishop Thomas Becket, made peace elusive. The large properties that Henry inherited and that Eleanor brought into his control through their marriage meant that Henry was a wealthy and powerful man. For the lands he held in France, he owed the French king, his rival and his wife's former husband King Louis VII, his vassalage. This meant that Henry owed Louis

Eleanor of Aquitaine was queen of France and then England, as well as a wealthy heiress who brought her husbands, and then her sons, great wealth and land. (Library of Congress)

his respect, cash payments, and military support. But since Henry was also the king of England, this was a complicated relationship. The rise of the Plantagenet dynasty meant that the English crown was heavily involved in France and invested in controlling French land, a cause of several military conflicts between the two kingdoms.

Eleanor of Aquitaine is also a tantalizing model for English queenship. She bore five sons and was influential over them; she witnessed hundreds of charters in support of her husband, and she was charismatic and personally charming. But Eleanor also took a role in governing her own lands, issued her own writs, and encouraged rebellion among her sons, which led to her imprisonment in one of Henry's castles. As a dowager queen after Henry's death in 1183, she served as regent when her son Richard went on Crusade, arranging his marriage and even his ransom when he was captured in Germany. Eleanor's example certainly inspired women like her granddaughter Blanche of Castile, the powerful queen of France, but her reign proved to be a cautionary tale for future English monarchs about the dangers of too many sons, of queens too personally wealthy, of women too powerful. Future queens of England were encouraged to be loving, fertile, and charitable assistants to their husbands, and chroniclers judged harshly women who sought power or influence for themselves.

The rest of this chapter focuses on the individual queens of England in this period and how they negotiated these expectations for English queenship.

Eleanor of Castile and Margaret of France, Wives of Edward I

Eleanor of Aquitaine's great-grandson Edward I (r. 1272–1307) married Eleanor of Castile (d. 1290), who was Eleanor of Aquitaine's great-great-granddaughter, and the two became what Theresa Earenfight called "the quintessential power couple of the thirteenth century" (Earenfight 2013, 145). Eleanor of Castile bore Edward sixteen children including his heir, the future Edward II, and she arranged marriages for her children that were advantageous for the kingdom and dynasty. She accompanied Edward on Crusade in 1272 but was not much involved in his governance of the kingdom.

Eleanor's foreignness threatened her people who were uncomfortable with her use of Spanish and her enjoyment of chess. Her management of her money also caused concern. Eleanor acquired extensive properties by collecting the queen's gold and through careful management of her finances. The queen's gold typically funded the queen's charitable giving, and Eleanor directed her patronage toward religious institutions, artists, and universities.

When Eleanor died of an illness in 1290, Edward had twelve "Eleanor crosses" erected to mark where her casket rested overnight along her funeral procession's route between Lincoln and Westminster Abbey, where she was interred. Three surviving crosses can still be seen at Geddington, Hardingstone, and Waltham Cross. The crosses indicate Edward's deep love for his wife and his public mourning for her.

That did not stop Edward from remarrying, and for his second wife, he looked to France. Philip IV initially agreed to betroth Edward to his sister Blanche but changed his mind and sent another sister, Margaret of France, a twenty-year-old French princess. Edward married her in 1299 but went to war with France first, a war that required papal involvement to resolve. The treaty secured Edward I's marriage to Margaret and his son Edward's marriage to Isabella, Philip IV's daughter. Margaret and Edward had three children. He seems to have loved her as well, as can be seen in his letters, and she worked as an intercessor for the people. Margaret was never crowned queen, but she also never remarried after his death.

Isabella of France, Wife of Edward II, "She-Wolf of France"

The reign of Edward II (1307–1327) and his queen Isabella of France (d. 1358) was plagued by scandal rooted in the challenges

Edward II marries Isabella of France in 1308, from Jean de Wavrin's *Anciennes et nouvelles chroniques d'Angleterre*, British Library Royal ms 15 E IV. This marriage was not a success, since Isabella took a lover and deposed Edward, but it did result in a son, Edward III, and a powerful line of kings. (The British Library)

of their marital relationship. Isabella was the daughter of Philip IV of France (d. 1314), a king with a reputation for tough negotiating and cruelty, such as expelling the Jews from France or in burning the Knights Templar for heresy. Edward I and Philip had bickered during the marriage negotiations about the English claim to Plantagenet lands in Aquitaine. But a more serious threat to the marriage was Edward II's closeness to his male friends Piers Gaveston (d. 1312) and Hugh Despenser (d. 1326), and his rumored sexual relations with these men, which led people at the time to question his manliness. Edward and Isabella did have four children, including the heir, Edward III (r. 1327–1377). Edward II's reputation with his people was challenged further by his ineptitude at war and especially his failure at the Battle of Bannockburn.

Like her predecessors, Isabella drew on intercession to win the hearts of her people and increase her household wealth. She attempted to build a positive relationship with the people of England. She remained deeply involved in England's politics until her son sent her away from his court.

Isabella opposed her husband's favorite, Hugh Despenser, which caused a rift with her husband and a conflict with the influential Despenser family. She had an affair, with Roger Mortimer (d. 1330), who also opposed the Despensers. Mortimer was a borderland lord from the Welsh Marches. With his assistance and wealth she gained from the dowry her son Edward's betrothal to Philippa of Hainault secured, she hired troops to fight against her husband. Mortimer and Isabella captured and killed Hugh Despenser and forced Edward to abdicate the throne. They crowned the young heir Edward III, and Isabella ruled England as regent for her son. Edward II was murdered in 1327 at Isabella's order or with her knowledge. Mortimer also fell out of favor by 1330 when Edward III arrested and executed him, despite Isabella's pleas for mercy, a moment of queenly intercession that failed. Once Edward seized control for himself, Isabella lived on as a dowager queen. Isabella arranged for her own tomb to be built in Greyfriars Church by a female stonemason, Agnes Ramsey.

Historians have long described Isabella as a power-hungry manipulator of her husband, the "she-wolf" who tried to steal the kingdom for herself and her lover. Theresa Earenfight, however, suggests that it was Edward II's own failure to live up to medieval expectations of royal masculinity and "inept governance" as a bad king that gave Isabella the opening to assert her more competent control. Isabella nurtured an alliance with Scotland's Robert the Bruce (d. 1329) to recognize an independent Scotland, and this can be interpreted as a peacekeeping effort or selling away England's territory. Isabella's relationship with Mortimer also connected her reach for power with her sexuality, which contributed to her legend as a dangerous woman. In the end, Edward's inability to control his wife, her influence over the political life of his kingdom, his close relationships with men, and his wife's sexual relations with another man all undermined his masculinity. As a result, his compromised masculinity also delegitimated his rule in the eyes of his subjects.

Philippa of Hainault, Wife of Edward III

The engagement of Philippa of Hainault (d. 1369) to Isabella's son Edward (r. 1327–1377), and the arrival of Philippa's enormous dowry, was what brought Isabella the funds to fight the Despenser family. Edward married Philippa in 1328, but their first two years were awkward because her coronation as queen was delayed, likely because Isabella did not want to relinquish the dower lands. Edward finally decided to push Isabella aside, and he seized control of the dower lands due the queen. Philippa was finally crowned in 1330, already five months pregnant. During her coronation at Westminster Abbey, Philippa wore purple cloth of gold lined with fur and was escorted under a purple cloth-of-gold canopy embroidered in red silk (Shenton 2003, 118). Philippa bore Edward at least twelve children, including his heir Edward, the Black Prince.

Philippa was a popular queen because of her generous use of intercession for the benefit of her subjects, particularly women, a model of a motherly queen with affection for her people as opposed to Isabella's power-grab. Edward brought her with him during his campaigns in the Low Countries, Scotland, and France, where in 1347, according to the chronicler Jean Froissart, she begged for the lives of the burghers of Calais. This incident was memorable because the queen kneeled before the king while heavily pregnant, urging him to give up his anger as a favor to her. Modern historians have argued that Froissart embellished his story, since Philippa would not have been pregnant at this time, but the tale establishes important elements of the way Edward and Philippa wielded power. Edward was able to demonstrate his masculinity through his strong stance against the burghers, while Philippa demonstrated her feminine ability to protect the people by humbly begging the king for a personal favor that allowed her to modulate her husband's strong, manly governance.

Philippa was a generous patron and encouraged development of the English court. She supported Jean Froissart, the chronicler who wrote about her intercession at Calais, founded Queen's College in Oxford, gave to churches, and patronized artists and authors.

Philippa died in 1369, eight years before Edward III's death, but he did not remarry, likely because of his attachment to his mistress Alice Perrers (d. 1400), one of his wife's ladies, who dominated the court after Philippa's death and gathered enormous wealth before being run out of England at the end of Edward's life. Edward and Philippa expected that their son Edward, the Black Prince, would inherit the throne, but he died in 1376, leaving behind his young son Richard to succeed Edward to the throne at his own death in 1377. Regents governed for the ten-year-old Richard, particularly Edward III's influential other sons such as John of Gaunt.

Anne of Bohemia and Isabella of Valois, Queens of Richard II

Richard II (r. 1377–1399) married twice. His first wife Anne of Bohemia (d. 1394) arrived in England in December 1381 and was welcomed into London by a series of entrance pageants in January. Anne was a controversial figure because of her foreignness—she did not learn English—and because she brought no dowry despite promises from her father, Emperor Charles IV, and from Pope Urban VI, who had arranged the match. According to the chronicler Thomas Walsingham, the nobles felt Anne spent too much money. Her brother Wenceslaus, king of Bohemia, also sought a loan from the English, which increased financial concerns. Richard was fond of Anne, however, and was even buried with her despite his second marriage.

Anne had many strikes against her: she was expensive, she was foreign, and she did not bear a son. But Anne was still a popular queen among the people, who called her Anne the Good, because of her intercessory work. On Anne's wedding day, the people reminded her that she was a "mediatrix," whose role it was to intervene with her husband the king to protect her people with her soothing words and graceful manner. Anne got the message. The documents of Richard's monarchy include several pardons obtained through the queen's intervention, suggesting that Anne and Richard's subjects found many moments where his rule required her moderation.

Like her mother-in-law, Anne was a generous patron of the arts and even criticized Geoffrey Chaucer for his portrayal of women in "Troilus and Criseyde," which caused him to write "The Legend of Good Women," as we saw at the beginning of this chapter. It was this sort of cultural intervention that earned her the title "Anne the Wise."

Anne died, likely of plague, in 1394, having borne no child by age twenty-eight. Richard remarried, choosing a six-year-old child, Isabella of Valois, and they had no opportunity to consummate the marriage before his deposition in 1399. Richard had exiled his cousin Henry Bolingbroke, son of Edward III's fourth son, John of Gaunt, and prohibited Henry from inheriting his father's land at John's death in 1399. Henry returned to England to assert his rights to the duchy of Lancaster, but received such support that he declared himself King Henry IV. He defeated Richard, imprisoned him, and dispossessed Richard's heir Edmund. This was the beginning of a Lancastrian branch of the Plantagenet dynasty and the heart of the Wars of the Roses that would break out in a few generations. Henry ordered Isabella of Valois to stay under house arrest, initially planning for her to marry his son Henry. She repeatedly refused to marry Henry, and he eventually allowed her to return to France as her family demanded. She later married her cousin, Charles, Duke of Orléans, but died in childbirth three years later.

Mary de Bohun and Joan of Navarre, Wives of Henry IV

Henry IV (r. 1399–1413) had already been married and widowed by the time he seized the throne. His first wife, Mary de Bohun, was a descendant of Llywelyn the Great, and had borne him seven children before her death, including his heir, Henry. His second wife, Joan of Navarre, became queen consort when she married Henry in 1403; they had no children together. Joan was the daughter of King Charles II of Navarre and the princess Joan of France and had already been Duchess of Brittany before marrying Henry. She had experience as regent in Brittany for four years for her son, experience that proved helpful when Henry V continued the Hundred Years War, and she served as his regent in England. Her Breton courtiers were seen as suspicious and banned from England, likely because Joan preferred them. During the Hundred Years War, Henry V captured Joan's son and brought him back to England, and Joan was accused of opposing Henry for this reason. He accused her of witchcraft in 1419 and imprisoned her at Pevensey Castle and Leeds Castle until 1422.

Catherine of Valois, Wife of Henry V

Henry V (r. 1413–1422) pursued the Hundred Years War vigorously, as Edward III had in the mid-fourteenth century. Henry's marriage to Catherine of Valois (d. 1437), daughter of King Charles VI of France (d. 1422) and Isabeau of Bavaria (d. 1435), was part of peace treaty negotiations between the two countries in the 1420 Treaty of Troyes. Henry appeared devoted to Catherine, pursuing his claim to her as much as his claim to France. Through the treaty, Henry and Catherine were betrothed and married, and Henry was named heir to the French throne so long as he did not declare himself king of France until Charles VI's death. Even this accommodation disinherited Charles's son, the future Charles VII, an issue that became even more complicated at Henry's early death in 1422, only one year after Catherine bore a son, the future Henry VI. Catherine's father died a few months later, leaving Henry VI king of England and France before he could walk.

Catherine was only twenty-one and the dowager queen, or, rather, *a* dowager queen, since Joan of Navarre still lived and held control of the dower lands that would one day have been Catherine's, but nobody had thought that day would come so soon. When Catherine remarried, to Owen Tudor, a Welsh man without much status, it caused so much anxiety about the influence a second husband could have over a young king that Parliament passed a statute in 1428 requiring consent for marriage to a queen. Henry VI looked on Catherine's two sons with Owen Tudor, Edmund and Jasper, as siblings and gave them titles: Edmund became the Earl of Richmond and Jasper the Earl of Pembroke. Catherine's second marriage may not have seemed significant at the time, but this was the germ of the Tudor rise in the late fifteenth century.

It is worth reflecting on the role of Catherine's mother, Isabeau of Bavaria, in politics at this time. King Charles VI of France suffered some serious mental illness and was periodically incapable of governing, and he left Isabeau in charge of state affairs, with the assistance of his brother and uncle. This was at the same moment that French political theory returned to the concept of the Salic Law, a political idea that said women were excluded from ruling or passing on claims to the throne. Salic Law interested the French in the fourteenth century because it was a convenient way to dismiss the claims of Edward III and then, later, those of Henry V because they relied on claims passing through female relatives. This ignored the fact that the Valois claim to the throne also depended on female ancestors. But one of the advantages of the Salic Law was that it did not deny the basic competence of women to govern; it simply denied them access. This was crucial for a kingdom whose queens had served as capable, competent regents, women such as Blanche of Castile or, indeed, Isabeau of Bavaria.

During Charles's illnesses, Isabeau helped to keep French affairs going, with the assistance of Charles's powerful brother, the Duke of Orléans, and uncle, the Duke of Burgundy. Unfortunately, relations broke down between the two dukes, with hostilities embroiling even a second generation in the fighting, and eventually France broke out into war between the Burgundians and the Armagnacs, roughly the Orléans faction. The debacle reflected poorly on Isabeau. Worse, however, was the way her son Charles responded to the Treaty of Troyes that formally transferred the kingdom away from him and named Henry V heir to the French throne. Later historians saw Isabeau as a poor mother for her work on the treaty and for her mismanagement of the regencies, claiming she had a "Black Legend," but Historian Tracy Adams has effectively demonstrated that this is a later interpretation out of step with contemporary sentiments that were much more sympathetic to the queen's efforts to hold France together in a difficult situation.

Margaret of Anjou, Wife of Henry VI

The young Henry VI (r. 1422–1461, 1470–1471) was raised in the midst of several regencies and a series of battles to hold onto territory that his father had won. When he married Margaret of Anjou (d. 1482) in 1445, the hope was that this union would end the fighting between England and France. Unfortunately, Margaret's time as queen was rocky. First, Margaret had a difficult time conceiving a child, and the couple remained childless for their first eight years of marriage. Finally she bore a son, Edward, in 1453, but after this long period of supposed infertility, some speculated that Edward was not Henry's child.

Henry suffered from the same sort of mental illness as his grandfather Charles, which pushed Margaret into the role of regent again and again. While for Margaret the model of queenly regency was Isabeau of Bavaria, for the English, female regency meant Edward II's Queen Isabella, a model that made them anxious. Out of this fear, the English barons created a new office, the "Protectorate," which they limited to men, attempting to assert patriarchy in a delicate situation. The first protector was Henry's cousin, Richard, Duke of York, and Margaret appeared to respect his authority in 1453 when Henry needed a regent. When the king recovered, however, York was excluded from the Great Council, and Margaret was blamed for his eviction. Richard fought for his place on the council, while Margaret raised funds for the army to fight Richard and his allies. The Wars of the Roses—named for the white rose of York and the red rose of Lancaster—had begun. Henry and Margaret were pushed off the throne in 1461; Henry was later confined to the Tower of London, where he died, but Margaret continued to build allies and raise armies to press their claim. Their son, Edward, died in battle in 1471, which made things impossible for Margaret to continue. Margaret was also captured and held at the tower until her cousin King Louis IX of France ransomed her. Margaret lived the rest of her days in France.

Elizabeth Woodville, Wife of Edward IV

The Lancastrians were defeated by the sons of Richard of York: Edward, George, and Richard. Edward IV (r. 1461–1483) seized the throne, with the aid of his brothers and his cousin Richard Neville, Earl of Warwick, known as the "kingmaker." Edward's choice to marry Elizabeth Woodville (d. 1492), daughter of Richard Woodville, a gentleman, and Jacquetta of Luxembourg, Duchess of Bedford, caused a sensation, partly because he was expected to marry a wealthy and well-connected foreign woman, preferably a princess, and partly because the Earl of Warwick had already worked hard to arrange such a match for him and found this marriage offensive and unworthy.

In the fifteenth century, the distinction between the gentry, like the Woodvilles, and the nobility, like the Yorks was great, particularly for a royal marriage. While the marriages of Prince William to Kate Middleton and Prince Harry to Meghan Markle were sensational in 2011 and 2018, Edward's marriage to a gentleman's daughter in 1464 caused a scandal, one more like that surrounding the Sussexes for stepping back from the royal family in 2020. Beyond Elizabeth's status, she was already the widow of a man who had supported Henry VI against the Yorks, and the mother of two young sons, Thomas and Richard Grey. Elizabeth's mother Jacquetta's first marriage was to Henry VI's uncle. Worse, Edward kept the marriage secret in order to avoid angering Warwick, which later led to claims that the marriage was not legal.

When the marriage was revealed, Edward scuppered a treaty Warwick had planned with King Louis XI of France to marry Edward to Bona of Savoy. Most of Edward's followers disapproved of the marriage, particularly his mother, Cecily, Dowager Duchess of York, and his brothers. The Woodvilles were a large family, and they used Elizabeth's role as queen to raise their own status, particularly through advantageous marriages and state offices. Warwick increasingly worked against the Woodvilles, sponsoring rebellions against Edward, and he eventually switched to the Lancastrian side in the Wars of the Roses, giving Margaret of Anjou a new hope.

Elizabeth had ten children with Edward, including her eldest, Elizabeth of York, and the heir, Edward. She weathered many stories of her husband's infidelity, especially with a long-term mistress, Jane Shore. Her mother, Jacquetta, weathered an accusation of witchcraft.

Elizabeth was a traditional consort with extensive public charity and piety, including the foundation of the St. Erasmus chapel at Westminster Abbey, and a series of pilgrimages. She was publicly beloved because of her beauty and her devotion to Edward and their children. But the rivalry between the brothers left her uncertain and unsafe.

Edward IV died of an illness in 1483, leaving the throne to his thirteen-year-old son, immediately named Edward V, and giving his brother Richard, Duke of Gloucester, the role of lord protector. Edward IV had expected Elizabeth to serve as Edward's regent. Here the secrecy around her marriage left Elizabeth vulnerable. Richard seized Edward V while Elizabeth and her unmarried children, five daughters and her only other son with Edward, the young Richard, Duke of York, sought sanctuary. Declaring that Elizabeth's marriage to Edward IV was never legitimate, and that Edward V was illegitimate, the "lord protector" seized the throne and declared himself Richard III. He imprisoned Elizabeth's sons Edward and Richard in the Tower of London, and their fate as the "Princes in the Tower" is one of England's great mysteries; neither was seen again.

As discussed below, Elizabeth continued to be active in politics through her daughter's time as queen. She died in 1492, possibly of plague.

Anne Neville, Wife of Richard III

Richard III's (r. 1483–1485) wife, Anne Neville, daughter of the "kingmaker" Earl of Warwick, had borne Richard an heir, Edward, who died in 1484, and she followed him into death a year later. With a powerful father, Anne had played an important role in the machinations of the Wars of the Roses. She had been engaged to Henry VI's heir, Edward, until his death. It was a gambit designed to unite the houses of Lancaster and York as well as to bring the Neville family into even greater prominence. Her sister, Isabel, married Edward IV's brother George, Duke of Clarence, at a time when her father's, the Earl of Warwick, relationship with Edward was shaky, and that marriage may have been designed to allow Warwick to make a new king in George. George and Warwick allied with Margaret of Anjou in 1470, and Henry VI rewarded George by naming him his second heir, after Henry's son Edward. When Warwick betrothed Anne to Edward, George likely realized that Warwick was more interested in his own power than in supporting George's hope to the throne. Anne married Edward later that year, but he died in battle in 1471.

Later in 1471, Warwick died in battle against Edward IV, leaving Anne to find her own way. Richard, Duke of Gloucester, may have married Anne to gain a claim to her father's valuable estate, forcing George to share the estate rather than take it entirely for himself in Isabel Neville's name. Isabel died in 1476, leaving behind two children, Margaret and Edward, whom Anne raised after George's execution for treason in 1478. These children remained risks to the monarchs for the rest of their lives, and Edward died in the Tower of London under Henry VII. When Richard seized the throne for himself following his brother's death in 1483, Anne became queen. When Richard and Anne's son died the next year, Edward became the heir apparent as the king's nephew. Anne herself died in March 1485 during an eclipse that was interpreted by some as foreboding Richard's fall, which came in August at the Battle of Bosworth Field, where he was defeated by the armies of Henry Tudor. Richard was the last of the Plantagenet dynasty.

Elizabeth of York, Wife of Henry VII, and Margaret Beaufort, Queen Mother

Henry VII (r. 1485–1509), first of a new Tudor dynasty, gained the throne through his military victory, but the key to holding it was his marriage to Elizabeth of York (d. 1503), eldest daughter of Edward IV and Elizabeth Woodville. While Warwick might have hoped the marriage between Anne and Edward would unite the houses, the marriage between Henry Tudor, of the house of Lancaster, and Elizabeth, of the house of York, created that peace. The fact that most other claimants to the throne were dead certainly helped as well. Since they were cousins and Elizabeth had been declared illegitimate by Richard III, their marriage required a papal dispensation and an Act of Parliament, but Elizabeth was finally crowned queen in 1487.

Henry Tudor had been helped on his way to the throne by his mother, Margaret Beaufort. Margaret was a descendant of Edward III through John of Gaunt, the Duke of Lancaster. As her four marriages attest, she was a desirable commodity on the marriage market of fifteenth-century English noble circles because of her connection to Edward III. As a member of the house of Lancaster, she was a major supporter of Henry VI. Her marriage at age twelve to Edmund Tudor, son of Catherine of Valois's second marriage, produced her only child in 1457, two months after her husband's death in captivity. The childbirth was so difficult she never had another child.

As a thirteen-year-old widow Margaret was forced to leave the young Henry with his uncle Jasper Tudor while she went to a new marriage to Sir Henry Stafford (d. 1483), who also died fighting the Yorks. Henry was forced into exile from age fourteen, living mostly in France. Her fourth marriage, to Thomas Stanley, brought Margaret into the York court as a lady to Elizabeth Woodville and then to Anne Neville, even carrying Anne's train at her coronation as queen. During Richard's reign, Margaret schemed with Elizabeth Woodville to betroth Henry to Elizabeth of York as a way of gaining support from both houses for Henry's plan to take the throne from Richard.

Once Henry became king, Margaret rose to an important status at court as the mother of the sovereign, but she was not queen, and that relative difference in status with her daughter-in-law, the queen consort, and the dowager queen Elizabeth Woodville seemed to rankle her. She took to signing her name "Margaret R," which could stand for Richmond, referring to property she held with Stanley, or to "*regina*," the Latin for queen. Elizabeth Woodville was forced out of court in 1487, and her daughter spent much of her time in pregnancy or with her children, which allowed Margaret to preside often at court.

Elizabeth of York bore Henry ten children, five of whom survived into adulthood. They named their heir Arthur, hoping to recapture the glories of the Britain of Arthurian legend with the name. Arthur's engagement to Catherine of Aragon, the daughter of the illustrious Isabella of Castile and Ferdinand of Aragon, was intended to bring him great wealth and raise England's status on the European stage. Unfortunately, Arthur died in 1502, leaving Catherine a young widow in England. When Elizabeth died the next year, only three of her children survived her: Margaret, Mary, and her son, the future Henry VIII. Henry VII died in 1509, and Margaret was able to arrange his funeral and her grandson's coronation before her own death in June.

Margaret Beaufort and Elizabeth Woodville might have been eager to know that their granddaughters, Mary and Elizabeth, would rule England in their own rights, as queens regnant.

England's aristocratic women thus sat alongside their male relatives on the power networks of the court through their diplomatic work, their shaping of court culture, the alliances they maintained among the aristocracy, and their intercessory work with the king's subjects. Queens' positions depended on their reproductive labor and success, but they were also intimately involved in the governing of the kingdom. Women's daily labor included maintaining the royal or noble household, building and maintaining power networks, and depicting the majesty of England.

FOR FURTHER READING

Bennett, Judith M. 2002. "Queens, Whores, and Maidens: Women in Chaucer's England." Hayes Robinson Lecture. Royal Holloway, University of London.

Chaucer, Geoffrey. 1889. *The Legend of Good Women*. Edited by Walter W. Skeat. Oxford: Clarendon Press.

Davis, James. 2012. "Selling Food and Drink in the Aftermath of the Black Death." In *Town and Countryside in the Age of the Black Death: Essays in Honour of John Hatcher*, edited by Mark Bailey and Stephen Rigby, 351–406. Turnhout: Brepols Publishers.

Duggan, A. J., ed. 1997. *Queens and Queenship in Medieval Europe* Woodbridge: Boydell Press.

Duggan, A. J., ed. 2000. *Nobles and Nobility in Medieval Europe*. Woodbridge: Boydell Press.

Earenfight, Theresa. 2013. *Queenship in Medieval Europe*. London: Palgrave Macmillan.

Erler, Mary C., and Maryanne Kowaleski. 1988. *Women and Power in the Middle Ages*. Athens: University of Georgia Press.

Erler, Mary C., and Maryanne Kowaleski. 2003. *Gendering the Master Narrative: Women and Power in the Middle Ages*. Ithaca, NY: Cornell University Press.

Furnivall, Frederick James. 1908. "How the Good Wife Taught Her Daughter." In *The Babees' Book: Medieval Manners for the Young: Done into Modern English*, edited by Edith Rickert. London: Duffield & Co. Project Gutenberg.

Goldberg, P. J. P. 1995. *Women in England c. 1275–1525: Documentary Sources*. Manchester: Manchester University Press.

Harris, Barbara J. 2002. *English Aristocratic Women, 1450–1550*. Oxford: Oxford University Press.

Hector, L. C., and Barbara Harvey, eds. 1982. *The Westminster Chronicle, 1381–94*. Oxford: Clarendon Press.

Parsons, John Carmi, ed. 1993. *Medieval Queenship*. New York: St. Martin's Press.

Shenton, Caroline. 2003. "Philippa of Hainault's Churchings: The Politics of Motherhood at the Court of Edward III." In *Family and Dynasty in Late Medieval England: Proceedings of the 1997 Harlaxton Symposium*, edited by Richard Eales and Shaun Tyas, 105–121. Donington: Shaun Tyas.

Strohm, Paul. 1992. "Queens as Intercessors." In *Hochon's Arrow: The Social Imagination of Fourteenth-Century Texts*, 95–119. Princeton: Princeton University Press.

Taylor, Andrew. 1997 "Anne of Bohemia and the Making of Chaucer." *Studies in the Age of Chaucer* 19: 95–119.

Ward, Jennifer. 2006. *Women in England in the Middle Ages*. New York: Hambledon Continuum.

The White Princess, season 1, Starz, 2014, streaming. https://www.starz.com/us/en/series/the-white-princess/30887.

The White Queen, season 1, Starz, 2013, streaming. https://www.starz.com/us/en/series/the-white-queen/18124.

4

URBAN AND RURAL WOMEN

While previous chapters have examined crucial life cycle moments of marriage and motherhood, and the group of aristocratic women whose wealth and status gave them access to influence and power, this chapter focuses on the daily lives of women of lower-status groups regardless of their place in the life cycle. It details the rhythm of the year determined by major holidays and festivals and the living conditions in the countryside and town. Here is where you can find information about women's working and domestic lives, about their homes, clothes, food, and drink. This chapter also examines disease and disability as well as the way people handled death in this period.

WOMEN'S WORK

Whether rural or urban, women's labor was key to the success of the medieval economy. Women's work changed over the course of their life cycle, with younger women contributing toward their family, married women running the household, and widows carrying on the family business, but throughout their lives, women's labor supported their families and helped them survive. Adult women were responsible for clothing their family, provisioning the household, preparing food, and raising young children as well as for helping their husbands, if they were married, in their work.

Many women hired servants to help them, but it was the woman's job to oversee the servants' work and keep them on task.

Children were also put to work quite young, assisting with the cooking as young as four years old. This work could be dangerous and risky, which is one reason we know as much as we do about their participation: the coroners' rolls describe the investigations when an unnatural death occurred, and they include details about activities the deceased was performing that led to their deaths. For example, in 1340, a nine-year-old London girl named Mary died while doing household chores: "Mary, daughter of Agnes de Billingesgate, aged 9 years, lay dead of a death other than her rightful death under the wharf of Thomas de Porkele. . . . The jurors . . . say that on the preceding Sunday, after the hour of Vespers, the aforesaid Mary filled an earthen pot with water on the aforesaid wharf, the Thames being in flood, when she fell into the water and was drowned" (Sharpe 1913, 252–253). Boys tended to have accidents doing labor along with their fathers, while girls tended to have accidents while cooking or fetching water.

In addition, to make ends meet, women took on by-employment, in which women ran a number of small, temporary, occasional businesses, depending on their wealth, status, and location. Given their many duties, women were not often able to start an independent, lasting business for lack of time and lack of capital. It was easier to take on work before marriage, when their children were grown, or during their widowhood. For wives still in their childbearing years, work that meshed with their existing responsibilities was easier to fit in as ways to earn extra money. Many women sold surpluses when they brewed ale or made butter and cheese, and they might sell other food items or run a tavern or alehouse. Women took in laundry, spun, offered healing skills, worked as servants. Women's labor was consistently low status and low paid across these centuries.

Poor women might not have steady professions and live in a state of precarity. When Maud Katersouth testified in a 1355 matrimonial case in York (see chapter 1), she was living apart from her own husband and raising her fifteen-year-old son alone. She supported herself and her son by piecing together jobs running errands, milling, and fetching for her neighbors (Goldberg 2000, 60).

Brewing

Brewing ale was hot, labor-intensive work that women did and which had to be done regularly because the ale did not last long. Ale was a popular, filling beverage, given its high grain content, and it was drunk by all members of society, including children, who consumed weaker versions. Women in both town and countryside brewed ale for their families and could brew extra for sale. Brewsters, women who brewed ale, might even expand their efforts into a business, selling their ale at market or in an alehouse or even a tavern under their control. Some brewsters worked commercially, brewing ale for sale as their main occupation, although this sort of time commitment was typically more accessible for a woman with access to capital for their investment. Elizabeth Baker in Battle brewed after becoming a widow in 1460 and did so for more than twenty years, sometimes assisted by her daughter (Ward 2006, 87). In Brigstock, 311 women were known to brew ale: 273 brewsters did this work occasionally, and thirty-eight alewives brewed professionally. Brewing, as a repetitive, low-status occupation was not a lucrative industry, but it was a way that women could earn money based on their expertise and typical work.

As Judith Bennett has shown, however, when beer came into fashion, this situation changed. Beer has a longer shelf life due to the use of hops and could thus be more lucrative. Most brewers of beer were professionals, while household brewers continued to make ale. As a result, more men became interested in this industry, eventually shunting women out of a field they had controlled once it became less labor intensive and more profitable. As Bennett argues, although women's control of this industry was lost, women's status in the economy did not really change, as they remained low-status workers with lower wages working in brewing ale.

Service

Based on poll-tax data, about one-third of late medieval households had at least one servant, while two-thirds of households had none (Goldberg 2000, 60). Whether in town or in the countryside, women could most easily find positions in service, as even some peasant homes employed servants. Agnes, wife of a Lincolnshire shepherd, kept two maidservants (Goldberg 1995, 177). In towns servants were so common they made up 15–30 percent of the urban population and were employed in perhaps half of all households. Domestic servants typically signed on for one-year contracts for compensation that included room and board, possibly some clothing, and likely some small cash wages. These wages were typically low, with payments around ten shillings or less per year. Domestic servants did work such as cooking, cleaning, fetching water, making beds, washing clothes, tending fires, and running errands (Goldberg 2000, 61).

When women became servants, they joined their employer's household and came under their authority. Some servants were such integral parts of the household that they were remembered in their employers' wills, sometimes with quite generous bequests, often marked for their dowries. In "How the Good Wife Taught Her Daughter," the wife taught her daughter that she had to govern her servants without becoming too stern or too friendly and that she was responsible for making sure the work was done well and for keeping track of who was a good worker, modulating her treatment to who deserved praise or punishment (Furnivall 1908). While servants assisted with the household tasks, they did not alleviate all of them, as the wife advised her daughter to monitor them and their work closely. And yet, as *The Ballad of the Tyrannical Husband* made clear, a wife without such assistance had great difficulty: "The goodwife had much to do, and servant had she none / Many small children to keep beside herself alone / she did more than she might within her own home" (Salisbury 2002). Tasks like staying up all night with young children; rising early to tend and feed the livestock while her husband still slept; and then beginning her chores of providing food, minding children, and caring for the home all belonged to women

Some wills also made bequests to servants contingent on fulfilling their full contracts. For example, in his 1444 will, William Nunhouse, a fishmonger in York, left to his "servant Margaret a Prussian chest, a brass pot of my wife's choosing, a coverlet, and a blanket with a pair of sheets so that the aforesaid Margaret does not leave or depart from my wife Joan's service during the term of her hire and contract made between me and her" (Goldberg 1995, 94). There must have been some concern that a servant would consider their contract complete upon the man's death and not feel obliged to continue serving his widow, leaving her without assistance at a time she needed it and likely without the same finances to attract new servants. Other wills attempted to ensure the moral expectations for servants remained in place after the mistress's death. In 1401, a York merchant's wife, Emma, left in her will "to Alice Stede if she will stay and remain an honest virgin and of good repute until she shall have a husband, that then she shall have five marks to her marriage, but in the event that ignorantly or heedlessly she shall commit fornication or adultery, that she shall have only two marks and 6s 8d" (Goldberg 1995, 126).

Service helped young women save for their weddings as well as to meet new people and possibly encounter candidates for marriage. It also provided them opportunities for premarital sexual encounters. Servants were expected to remain chaste and respectable as members of their employers' households and reflections of them. In the poem "The Serving-Girl's Holiday," a young maid looks forward to her time away from work to enjoy a dalliance with her lover, but fears telling her lady about the consequences of this affair: that she has been impregnated (See Singlewomen later in this chapter).

Women in service performed a wide range of work. If employed in a household with a married couple, she could be a maid, a nanny, a wet nurse, a cook, or an assistant to the wife in her duties. If employed by a bachelor, she might take on all the household responsibilities of a wife, either alone or as part of a team of servants. This was excellent training that enhanced the education in women's work girls had obtained from their mothers.

In either situation, domestic servants were always vulnerable to abuse and harassment from their employers or their employers' children and friends. Women could be exploited for their labor, maltreated, or harassed and assaulted. Similarly, employers might be robbed or cheated by servants they trusted to live in their homes and care for their families. The Good Wife also advised her daughter regarding servants to guard the keys herself and to be careful about whom she should trust, a sense that servants were to be watched and could be dangerous to the household (Furnivall 1908).

Employers were expected to punish servants who caused problems. In 1276, William Yedrich responded to a dispute between two of his servants, William de Chiselhurst and Alice Bude, who "quarreled together and William de Chiselhurst struck her and she raised the hue. William Yedrich as a consequence guaranteed to make amercement on behalf of his [male] servant and it was judged that he may hold back the wages of his said servants" (Goldberg 1995, 93). The "hue" Alice raised was the "hue and cry," a shouting that called out her neighbors to danger and trouble, a vocal alarm that help was needed. Yedrich agreed to make restitution to Alice for William de Chiselhurst's assault, and the court also granted him the option of holding back wages from both servants because of their troublemaking.

SHAPE OF THE YEAR

Medieval people marked time quite differently from the way we do in the twenty-first century. Their reference points were typically holy days associated with the cult of the saints or important biblical moments for marking time within the year and the reigns of English kings for marking the years. Women also used significant moments in their own lives as reference points, especially the birth of a child, her own churching after a birth, and a marriage or death. For example, when Agnes Litelfayrwas called in 1316 to respond to a plea of debt by Isold Clerevaus, Isold stated that the two women were "in the town of Lynn the first day of Lent in the eighth year of the reign of King Edward" (Goldberg 1995, 90), using both religious and royal markers for the time. In another example, in 1420, William Burton complained about an event that took place "on the Tuesday next before the feast of the Ascension of our Lord in the eighth year of the reign of our sovereign lord the present King" (Baildon 1896, 119).

The Romans established the Julian calendar, named for Julius Caesar, as a twelve-month calendar with twenty-eight to thirty-one days in each month, and leap years added a day to February every fourth year. This remained the calendar until the reforms of Pope Gregory III in 1582. Larger months with thirty-one days alternate with shorter months, except for the months of July and August, which were named for the Romans Julius Caesar and Octavian Augustus, and both have thirty-one days. The leap years acknowledge the Romans' belief that the year is really 365.25 days long, requiring an extra day every fourth year. The sixteenth-century revision dropped one leap year addition to February every 400 years based on the revised math that the earth travels around the sun once every 365.2425 days.

Romans began the year on January 1, naming the month for their double-headed god Janus, who looks backward and forward over a lintel. Medieval people understood this idea, but more commonly began accounting for their year with March 25, Ladyday, marked by the feast of the Annunciation, when the Virgin Mary learned that she was pregnant with Jesus. Some account books focused on agricultural produce might start instead with September 29, Michaelmas, the feast of Saint Michael. Either way, this method of marking time demonstrates the medieval mindset about the calendar, that it was defined by Christian feasts and holy days. Sundays were always expected to be days of rest when no or very little work was done as well as feasts on which no fast should be scheduled. Christians similarly avoided work on holy days, those dedicated to the story of Christ's life or those devoted to saints significant in the church or local calendar.

Christians organized their devotional lives according to the liturgical year, which divided into seasons, often related to the life of Christ. Advent, starting four Sundays before Christmas and ending Christmas Eve, marked a time of fasting in which Christians avoided meat and other treats such as pudding, pies, or roasted meat. Christmas Eve deepened the fast, with no eggs, cheese, or meat. This fasting made the celebratory Christmas feasting on December 25 all the more delicious, but came after a candlelit mass in a dark church. Christmas celebrated the Nativity, the birth of Christ, and while it was not the most spiritually significant holiday in the Christian calendar, it was a time of feasting, celebration, and parties. Masks and dancing, ale and sweet treats defined the time. The dating of the holiday falls near to the winter solstice and co-opted some older traditions such as Yule logs, pine trees, and garlands. It was traditional on Christmas for manor lords to welcome their tenants and their servants to a feast with entertainment in their home. Such entertainments continued into the local parish, with benefit events including games and church ales. The royal court might be especially festive, decorated with garlands and greenery, and the site of plays, jesters, dancers, and parties.

Christmas might also be a time for playful reversals in status that allowed participants to let out steam and accept the hierarchical system on other days of the year. The Lord of Misrule or Abbot of Misrule or Christmas Lord was a play title bestowed on someone typically low status given the chance to "rule" during Christmas, play courts within the parties of noblemen, in towns, or in colleges, who were able to lord themselves over the actual powerful men for this one day. Some of this chaos was dangerous: the popularity of performances by masked players meant that criminals could use Christmas as an opportunity to cause mayhem undetected, which led to the prohibition of masks during Christmas in several English cities.

Christmas lasted for twelve days, as remembered in the song, and concluded with Epiphany on January 6. January 1 was acknowledged as New Year's Day and was a day for gift giving, especially among the wealthy. Twelfth Night, January 5, was the night of a final feast of celebration and revelry. Epiphany, January 6, remembered the visit of the magi, the three wise men, as they welcomed

Jesus in the manger and gave their gifts of gold, frankincense, and myrrh, and began with a church service, followed by feasting and entertainment. This ended the Christmas celebrations.

While the feasting ended with Epiphany, the season of Christmastide continued to Candlemas, February 2, a holy day that remembered the Purification of the Virgin Mary. As noted in chapter 2, women required a purification ritual after childbirth in order to reenter the church, known as churching. Celebrating the Virgin Mary's purification on February 2 placed it forty days after the birth of Jesus. This ceremony became known as Candlemas because of the large number of candles used in the mass early on a dark, cold February morning and because the congregants followed the mass with a procession holding candles blessed by the priest. The day before was a fast day, but the Candlemas service was followed with feasting. In Coventry and Cambridge, musicians processed the town streets to add to the merriment (Hutton 1994, 18). Candlemas was also considered the end of winter. In the same season, Valentine's Day, on February 14, was a time to send small gifts, marks of affection, to loved ones.

So far, these celebrations were set in time, held on fixed dates year to year. The next seasons were movable since they were based on set numbers of days before or after Easter, a feast whose date shifted. The formula for Easter used in the fourteenth and fifteenth centuries was the product of much negotiation that had caused a number of problems in earlier times, to the point that an English king had to call a council to reconcile formulas so he and his wife could celebrate Easter at the same time. This formula used in the Latin West, however, still differed from that of the Orthodox Church in Byzantium. The formula used by the churches that looked to Rome determined that Easter was the first Sunday that fell after the first full moon that fell on or after the vernal equinox, understood to be March 21. That meant that Easter might fall on any Sunday between March 22 and April 25. If March 21 was the vernal equinox, and a full moon, and a Saturday, Easter would be March 22; if it was a Sunday, Easter would be the following Sunday, March 28; if the full moon fell on March 20, Easter had to wait until the next full moon, and if that was a Sunday, another week after that, pushing the date to April 25. Medieval calendars calculated the date for Easter for many years in the future so that Christians would be able to plan the feasts that rotated from it more easily.

Lent, or Shrovetide, was a penitential season preceding Easter by forty days, not counting Sundays. During Lent, Christians fasted and avoided sex, and any art inside the church was covered up. Diets became simple through this long period, with meat, eggs, cheese all prohibited. Lives of the saints recount how simple their subjects' diets were during this time, existing on a diet of only lentils and water, but less abstemious Christians might use Lent as a time to consume more fish and less meat. Shrovetide was the time for "shriving" or confessing sins and performing penance to seek absolution.

Before the season of Lent began, Christians enjoyed a last day of feasting, where they ate these foods for the last time, on Shrove Tuesday, today called Mardi Gras or Carnival in some places. Shrovetide, Shrove Tuesday and the two preceding days, extended the period of festival and feasting, a time during which reversals of status were common in a "world turned upside down" attitude. Today, Shrove Tuesday is marked by eating pancakes—known as Pancake Day in the United Kingdom—and may similarly have been a time of baked goods in the Middle Ages, using up the products that would go to waste in the weeks of fasting. The next day was Ash Wednesday, and Lent was underway.

Holy Week punctuated the end of Lent. The last Sunday before Easter was Palm Sunday, a time when Christians brought tree branches to be blessed in church and then hung in their homes, in memory of the palms honoring Jesus when he entered Jerusalem. They carried these branches in procession behind the priest who carried the consecrated host wafer in a monstrance around the church, to honor that entrance.

Holy week was spent remembering the story of the Passion, from the Last Supper to Jesus's Crucifixion. Starting on Wednesday evening, churches held services in darkness, with no or very few candles, known as the Tenebrae service, from the Latin for shadows. Maundy Thursday marked the Last Supper between Jesus and his apostles when he washed their feet. In honor of that service, the king and queen might wash the feet of poor people and give them alms in memory of the "mandatum" or commandment Jesus issued to his followers, that they should love one another as he had loved them (John 13:34). For men this day was also called "Sheer" Thursday as a time for haircuts and beard trimming.

Good Friday, the day that commemorated the Crucifixion, when Jesus died on the cross, was a day of strict fasting when the story of Jesus's Passion was read from the gospels, often with one candle. Clergy and royalty attending services in cathedrals participated in ritualistic crawling, barefoot, toward a crucifix placed on the steps

of the church altar. Some Christians built small tombs, called sepulchers, in their churches, a commemorative scene much like the
Nativity mangers. On Good Friday a statue of Christ was placed
inside the sepulcher. While major cathedrals and abbey churches
such as Durham, York, or Lincoln might have stone versions, in a
parish church, the sepulcher was constructed annually out of wood,
probably by parishioners. At Durham, the stone sepulcher included
a crucifix with a crystal case in Christ's breast that could hold the
Eucharist wafer. On Good Friday the host was placed inside its case
and then covered with a gold-embroidered cloth of red velvet.

Late Saturday night of Holy Week, Christians attended church,
extinguished all the candles, and then relit them in a ritual of
renewal and light. They then lit the large paschal candle to mark
the start of Easter. The paschal candle could be quite large and tall,
requiring a ladder to light it. The services on Easter were a joyous occasion, celebrating the Resurrection of Jesus with lit candles,
music, and the uncovering of the church artwork. Easter sepulchers
were opened, as in Durham, the red velvet cloth of the sepulcher
was removed to reveal the crucifix with the wafer visible. Eggs,
along with rabbits, a symbol of the pagan spring celebration of the
goddess Eostre, were blessed and enjoyed again, as were the other
foods forbidden during Lent. Christians might enjoy games, dancing, singing, and other festival sports to celebrate Easter and the
days that followed. In Chester archery contests were popular. East-
ertide, the season from Easter to Pentecost, was a time of renewal,
feasting, and spring flowers. This was the time for spring cleaning,
work that housewives oversaw.

The Monday and Tuesday of the second week after Easter were
known as Hocktide, a ritual celebration that offered further opportunities for role reversals, as well as for earning money for the
church in some English parishes, usually more urban than rural
ones, starting in the fifteenth century. On Hocktide Monday, married women captured and restrained men, who had to pay for
their release. On Hocktide Tuesday, the roles reversed, and men
captured and bound the women, who had to pay for their freedom. The bounties went to benefit the church, often for a project
of interest to the parish's women. The fun of Hocktide was a major
fundraiser for the church, even more than the popular church ales.
Hocktide was also a time for manorial courts and for making rent
payments.

Christians believed that after his resurrection, Jesus walked
the earth for forty days, before ascending bodily into heaven. A

movable feast set forty days after Easter celebrated the Ascension, and since Easter was a Sunday, Ascension always fell on a Thursday. The Monday, Tuesday, and Wednesday that preceded Ascension were known as Rogation Days, and they were typically filled with processions. In larger towns, the processions had a schedule to them, with the clerics and monks of the town processing to certain churches each day and delivering a sermon there, completing a circuit of the entire town by the end of Rogation Wednesday. In many areas the residents of a village or town "beat the bounds," processing along the boundary of their jurisdiction, whether walled, marked with boundary stones, or simply remembered. Banners and a cross were carried, relics might go on display with especially precious ones carried by a barefoot bearer, and church bells rang throughout the processions. Priests accompanying the procession blessed the boundary markers. Reportedly, young boys were beaten at intervals along the procession so that the boundary was fixed in their memories, hence "beat the bounds." On Ascension Thursday the paschal candle received its last lighting for a service, followed by feasts. In some places there were further processions on this day, as at Durham, where the clergy carried their crosses and relics throughout the town (Hutton 1994, 36).

May Day, or May 1, was a more pleasure-based celebration of the beginning of summer. The day began with morning walks for flowers to decorate homes and give as gifts to loved ones. Communities came together for feasting, drinking, and Morris dancing, with young people courting and sharing flowers with one another. A maypole erected in a public place created an opportunity for boys and girls to dance together, weaving patterns in ribbons as they danced in circles around the pole. May Day initiated a season of games and ales, outdoor celebrations, often as church fundraisers. Alison, the Wife of Bath in Chaucer's *The Canterbury Tales*, talks about her pleasure drinking and dancing. In some parts of England, a king or queen was crowned sometime between May Day and Midsummer. In the South, Robin Hood also played a prominent role in these celebrations, sometimes performing for donations, or receiving his own Robin Hood ale fundraiser. These were occasionally full productions with Robin Hood and his band, including Friar Tuck, Little John, and even Maid Marian, presiding over festivities. Robin Hood was a popular story at the time, but his association with Midsummer probably came from his green garments, his connection with the forest, and his association with role reversals by robbing from the rich and giving to the poor.

Detail of a miniature of the Feast of Ahasuerus, with musicians, England, from British Library, Harley ms 2838, f. 45. Feasts were important celebrations for a community to gather and to fix events in the memories of guests. (The British Library)

On the seventh Sunday after Easter came Pentecost, a feast remembering the Holy Spirit falling on the apostles, when they spoke in tongues (Acts 2:2–4). It was known as Whitsun, or White Sunday, probably for the knowledge (wit) the apostles gained on Pentecost, but also possibly associated with white vestments and garments. Some churches released a white dove into the church or displayed a dove statue. While this feast also moved about, it tended to fall in June, and the pleasant weather allowed for outdoor celebrations. Whitsuntide was a week free from work, and Christians enjoyed church ales, games, dancing, and feasts. On Whit Monday, some parishes also held processions with statues of the apostles.

The second Thursday after Whitsun was the feast of Corpus Christi, celebrated with processions and rituals around the Eucharist. The blessed wafer was carried through the streets in a monstrance under a canopy as part of these processions, which became quite popular events. In many cities, especially York and Coventry, the feast day of Corpus Christi was celebrated with the Mystery Plays, major pageants performed on wagons that processed throughout the streets. These pageants were mounted by the town's guilds, with larger guilds performing a part of the pageant themselves, and other guilds coming together. The plays at Coventry were especially popular and drew even the monarch for a visit, while those in York were written down in clear detail. Participants wore costumes and devised elaborate sets built into wagons that could be pulled from station to station, where the performers staged their part of the pageant before processing to the next station, over and over again for up to sixteen stops on a route through the city. The Mystery Plays told biblical stories from Adam and Eve through the Last Judgment. The financial outlay for musicians, costumes, wagons, and sets could be astronomical, which encouraged guilds to come together to finance a wagon. The pageants show the strength of the guilds, the community interest in theater and pageant, and the strength of the cult of Corpus Christi in the late Middle Ages. The cult of Corpus Christi was a factor in some of the blood libel accusations discussed in chapter 6.

Midsummer was celebrated on June 24, but the parties began the night before, Saint John's Eve, the night before the feast of Saint John the Baptist. Saint John's Eve was a time of bonfires that cleared evil from the air. Medieval people considered this to be the summer solstice, which astronomers locate on June 21, another moment of Christian festivals coming as close as possible to astronomical events and earlier pagan holidays. The bonfires were set at sunset after the long day, providing a spectacle as exciting to medieval people as firework gatherings might be for us today. Midsummer was a time of revelry, with feasting, drinking, more dancing, and likely several sexual encounters. Midsummer day was a time of games and contests and feasting that could erupt with periodic celebrations according to local customs until July 31, the end of summer.

August was the beginning of autumn and the harvest time. Festivals in this season celebrated the harvest much like modern apple and pumpkin festivals do. As with Midsummer, festivals might include the crowning of a harvest queen or king. From Midsummer it was a long stretch to the next significant holy day, another fixed date, November 1, the feast of All Saints. Christians remembered the dead, said prayers, visited church and graveyards, and rang church bells. People might dress all in black as if in mourning, and churches rang bells in honor of souls in purgatory, and repeated this again on November 2, All Souls. All Saints was also considered the beginning of winter, with the harvest in and frost beginning to fall on the fields.

All these rituals and celebrations had local variations, as custom determined which holidays to stress and what sort of observations were appropriate to that community, and these changed over time.

Local communities also celebrated saints who were special to them, such as the patron of their parish church or a saint associated with the royal house. The feast of England's patron Saint George, April 23, was a popular feast in the fifteenth century. In Norwich, Saint George's day was celebrated with feasting and a procession featuring a statue of the dragon he defeated, and people processed dressed as George and Saint Margaret, herself a defeater of dragons. Christians were likely to celebrate the feast day of the saint for whom they were named rather than their own birthday, a date they may not know. In Canterbury, the most important celebration of a saint was July 6, the feast of Thomas Becket, with parades, musicians, and pageant wagons performing "The Martyrdom of Saint Thomas." Important dates in the lives of universal saints, such as Mary Magdalene, the Virgin Mary, Saint Peter, might also have significance to people, villages, or towns. As discussed in chapter 6, several communities had saints who received local veneration but did not receive formal canonization or make it into the official calendars.

Some rural celebrations were pinned to the liturgical calendar, such as Plow Monday, the Monday after Epiphany, when farmers brought their plows to the priest for blessing before the spring plowing began. As local customs, these varied by region. In Hull and Grimsby, towns more associated with fishing, statues of ships were brought through the streets for blessing on this day instead of the plow.

Christian calendars, typically found in devotional manuscripts like psalters, helped people remember, or know in the case of movable feasts, major Christian holy days, such as Christmas, Epiphany, Easter, and saints' feast days. The most important of these saints' names were written in red ink to make them stand out— creating red letter days. There were major saints' days, the evangelists, Mary Magdalene, Thomas Becket, and so on, as well as more local saints, which might help locate a manuscript. Saints' days might be celebrated as festivals, particularly those of local saints or of patron saints for a local monastery or church.

The religious organization of the year affected all medieval Christians with a rhythm to the year that was predictable and comforting. While Lent was a period of deprivation, Easter, Christmas, and Whitsun were times of celebration.

MANOR

As we have seen, medieval people organized their worlds into three orders, *oratores*, *bellatores*, and *laboratores*. The third category, those who work, indicated the peasants who lived on rural manors and made up 90 percent of the medieval English population. They lived in an economic system known as manorialism in which peasants worked land controlled by noble elites. The lord of the manor typically was a nobleman, but it might instead be a noblewoman, especially as men included estates in their wives' dowers. The royal manor of Brigstock, for example, was part of the dower lands King Henry III had granted to Eleanor of Provence and held to her death in 1292; Edward II included Brigstock in the dower lands for his wife Isabella of France who held the manor until her death in 1358. Monastic houses also controlled manors and served as their "lords."

The manors were large estates that included a manor house for the lord, a village with peasant homes, kitchen gardens, farmland, grazing and pastureland, a mill, an oven, an orchard, and a parish church. One lord might have many manors and move between them through the year, but peasants were unlikely to move far from the village for their entire lives. By the fourteenth century, about half of the peasants in England were free, but the other half were unfree "serfs" or "villeins." Serfs were not slaves, and their bodies could not be sold, but their labor was tied to the manor, and they were not permitted to leave the lord's land. Serfs had a number of obligations to the manor's lord, but most important was their obligation to farm his fields, known as the demesne. The availability of a free workforce made the manor quite profitable to the lord who controlled it, as the lord could use the produce to feed themselves and their supporters and sell surplus at market. Lords also charged rents, which peasants paid with cash or produce from the land they rented, and fees to use the manor's oven and mill. Lords also earned income from their manorial court and manorial fees. These fees included merchet, permission for peasants to marry; heriot, charged upon a tenant's death; and tallage, a tax on serfs. The manor of Brigstock earned its lady forty-one pounds and ten shillings a year (Bennett 1999, 30). The manor provided everything that peasants needed, except for trips to market towns to sell their surplus goods, and most peasants probably never ventured more than fifteen miles from the place they were born.

Some lords held only a single manor where they remained in residence, but most had multiple manors. Lords might move between these manors, spending part of the year in different estates, or they might remain in residence in only one manor, preferring that manor house to an itinerant lifestyle. Some estates could go a generation without a visit from the lord who controlled the manor. Lords relied on a network of officials to oversee their manors, particularly when the lord was not personally present. These men collected the rents, supervised the peasant farming, maintained the manor, and kept careful records for the lord. The bailiff supervised the manor in the lord's absence or on his behalf, keeping accounts and collecting rents, which meant that candidates for this position needed to be literate. The reeve assisted the bailiff and focused on more of the manor's quotidian needs, especially supervising labor on the demesne lands. The reeve might supervise haywards who oversaw maintenance on the manor's fences, checked that pastureland was used appropriately, and directed the serfs' work during harvest time.

Justice on the manor came from a number of different directions. Most immediately, the lord was responsible for a manor court and had the right to collect fines for a variety of infractions, as discussed earlier with leyrwite fines for serf women who had premarital sex. The manorial court was held predictably, about every few weeks, in a public place accessible to the entire peasant community. These were places to handle small crimes, but also to seek resolution of disputes, to register contracts, and to seek permission for special privileges. Peasants could be brought before a church court for breaking canon law, especially for fornication and marital cases. The king also relied on itinerant justices who visited the kingdom to resolve more serious cases beyond the jurisdiction of the manorial court. The king's coroner, for example, investigated deaths and kept records in his coroners' rolls of how someone died. The king had the right to collect taxes from all peasants on any estate, and his tax collectors traveled around to collect the tax.

Careful records of the manorial court were kept in court rolls, long sheets of parchment stitched together and kept rolled up. Extant versions of these records, in addition to the manor's account rolls kept by the bailiff, provide an extraordinary amount of information about the lives of peasants on villages. Accounts could record who lived on the manor, how much land they held, rents they owed, and when they were paid. While peasants were at the bottom of the system of estates, their labor provided the food that made the rest of medieval society function, which lords and their stewards were careful to track. These records also documented who was a serf, a status that was passed down through generations, and is one reason why peasants targeted these records during rebellions. Serfdom was a much-detested institution among the villagers and under serious attack during the fourteenth century. The practice had largely declined by the mid-fifteenth century.

Lords responded to this change in the labor market by introducing other methods to maintain their wealth and power. One of these was enclosure, fencing off fields once treated as common and transforming arable land into pasture for more profitable—and less labor intensive—sheep raising. To make this change, lords began shifting peasants off their land, ending leases that had lasted for generations and through centuries. These changes to the rural economy of the manors forced more and more peasants into towns, whose population started to swell again in the late fifteenth century.

There were obvious status differences between the aristocratic lord who controlled the estate and its profit-making apparatus, but there were also status differences among the peasants. The first and most obvious of these was the distinction between free and unfree peasants, but their modes of life might look very similar. Wealth provided a second and powerful difference among peasant families. Some peasant villagers might be able to rent a larger house, own several pots, and own an animal such as a horse or cow, and so on. Peasants, free or unfree, farmed the land and sold surplus produce as well as products they created such as butter, cheese, soap, and raw wool, and the more resources they had to draw on, the more profit they could derive from these products. Poorer families could have much less, such as "Joan Symkyn Woman of Rawcliffe, having almost nothing in goods save her clothing for body and bed, and a small brass pot, tenant of Sir Brian de Rouclif," who testified in a Yorkshire court (Goldberg 2013, 34).

Rural Work

The manor included the peasants' homes, often clustered together in a village but sometimes spread out across the manor, the fields, pastures, and common land where hay might grow. There might also be forests, where hunting was limited to the nobles, but peasants occasionally poached rabbits and deer. Depending on the quality of the land, some peasants might rely exclusively on farming or exclusively on animal husbandry, but many English peasants relied on a mix of both, planting in arable land and using pastures for cattle or sheep.

The manor included arable fields that peasants worked, plowing, planting, harvesting, and fertilizing. Some of the land belonged to the lord, making up his demesne that serfs were obliged to work for a certain number of days each week, called "week work," and again for several days during harvest, called "boon work." The reeve directed serfs on how to spend their obligatory workdays.

For plowing the fields, peasants in Northern Europe relied on the heavy plow, a large piece of metal that turned the rich and wet soil, drawn by a team of animals. The heavy plow lived up to its name, making it difficult to turn and pushing peasants into using strip farming. They divided their large, open fields into long strips, limiting the number of turns the plow required. This meant that the strip one family owned sat between those of other families, and peasants had to work together in deciding what and when to plant each field. Otherwise, competing crops would doom the entire field to failure. They marked the boundaries between the strips they controlled with boundary stones that were low enough to not affect the plow. Peasants used the three-field system by the fourteenth century to determine which fields to plant with a winter crop, such as wheat, which to leave fallow, and which to plant with a spring crop, such as peas or beans, and how to rotate for the next year. This permitted the fields to rest every third year, to receive benefits from nitrogen-rich spring crops, and to produce food from two-thirds of the available arable land, instead of the one-half available under the two-field system that had been in use in the early Middle Ages. Peasants who kept animals let them graze on the fields after the harvest and on the fallow field, so that their droppings further fertilized the fields.

Peasants sometimes tried to clear new land to add them to their arable land, often by encroaching on the forest. These additions were called assarts. Farmers could gain profitable new land by cutting trees, draining swamps, and generally preparing new lands to farm. They might mark these off with fencing to indicate that these were not part of the open fields the manor's peasants worked according to a common plan.

The manor also contained meadows where peasants grew and cut hay for feeding their animals through the winter, pastures where they could graze through the summer. There were orchards where peasants might have the right to collect fruit—often only the fruit that had fallen on the ground already, but long sticks might help the fruit in falling—such as apples and pears. If the manor had a pond or stream, fishing might be possible and could supplement the peasant diet. It also provided water for making ale, bathing— which often meant only face and hands but could on special occasions include the entire body—and washing clothes.

The rhythm of the year discussed here framed the work of the manor, since among the holidays and religious celebrations, the rural work year hinged on their crops and their animals. The Monday after Epiphany was known as Plow Monday, when farmers brought their plows to church for blessing and sought donations from their neighbors in a procession of plows. The plows were then put to work preparing the fields for spring planting. During Lent Christians fasted, but they were also busy with finishing the plowing, harrowing the fields, and sowing their seeds. This was the time for the birth of new lambs and new kids, requiring shepherds and goatherds to carefully monitor the ewes and does.

By Whitsun, medieval peasants were deeply engaged in their fields, plowing, sowing, weeding, and haymaking. The young animals were old enough to start putting on weight, grazing with their

Shepherds in a Round Dance, tapestry, from the Netherlands c. 1500, Cleveland Museum of Art. Dancing was a community activity for celebrations. (Gift of Leonard C. Hanna, Jr., for the Coralie Walker Hanna Memorial Collection, The Cleveland Museum of Art)

adults. The hard work of making hay wrapped up by Midsummer and freed farmers for the heavy labor of late summer, weeding and cultivating their crops. Depending on what they planted, August and September focused on the harvest, and the large amount of labor required all hands to join in the work. In the fall, with the large crops in, farmers who also participated in animal husbandry started to slaughter animals, especially the adult pigs, and gather fruit and nuts from the orchards and forest. Creating a larder full enough to allow the farmer and his community to eat during the winter was the entire focus of the time between August and November.

Both men and women were responsible for work on the manor. Men had primary responsibility for plowing and planting, but all peasants worked the fields during harvest and assisted in cutting and gathering hay. Women's work in running the household, minding the children, preparing food, and clothing the household was valuable to the family as was their work assisting their husbands in the fields. This value was recognized in Anthony Fitzherbert's *The Book of Husbandry*: "For there is an old common saying, that seldom does the husband thrive, without the leave of his wife" (Fitzherbert 1534, 143). Women assisted in the weeding, hoeing, threshing, reaping, haymaking, and in any other urgent tasks for which their family did not have enough labor to perform in a timely way, since farm labor is time sensitive. If she was a serf, a woman was also obliged to work in the lord's demesne lands according to the instructions of his reeve and could be fined in the manor court for not doing her duties as he demanded. Women also performed this work as servants, typically day or temporary laborers, for which work they were paid less than men. This was acknowledged in a thirteenth-century treatise on husbandry: "If there is a manor in which there is no dairy then it is always advisable to have a woman there for much less money than a man would take, to take care of the small stock and of all that is kept on the manor and answer for all the issues there just as the dairymaid would do" (Oschinsky 1971, 427). After the Black Death, women could seek such work for higher wages, such as Isabella, who asked for four pence to reap in Essex, when the statute of laborers limited pay to two or three pence. Meanwhile, by 1380 both men and women in Minchinhampton received the same pay, four pence, demonstrating the volatility of the post-plague labor market (Ward 2006, 85).

In addition to helping their husbands and fulfilling their week works and boon works, women fed the animals, gathered eggs from the chickens, milked the cows or sheep and turned the milk into butter and cheese, and processed wool from sheep and flax and hemp into thread and cloth. Fitzherbert's *Book of Husbandry* details the difficult process of tending the flax, from its March or April planting, when it needed to be "sown, weeded, pulled, rippled, watered, washed, dried, beaten, braked, tased, heckled, spun, wound, wrapped, and woven" so that a wife "may they make sheets, broadcloths, towels, shirts, smocks, and such other necessaries." He also advised that the distaff, the wooden stick used to spin thread or yarn, "be always ready for a pastime, that thou be not idle" (Fitzherbert 1534, 146).

Women were responsible for their kitchen gardens that produced cabbages, garlic, onions, leeks, peas, and beans. They tended the beehives, collected honey, and used combs to make wax and candles. Housewives might have assistance in these tasks from their children and/or servants, but they were still responsible for managing the work and seeing it completed well. On top of these tasks, many women took on additional labor to support their family, but in a temporary way and usually on a small scale, such as serving as laundresses, brewing ale for sale, or doing piecemeal work.

After the harvest was over, the very poorest members of society were allowed to glean, to search a harvested field for grain left behind. These were typically older women or poor women, either in the community, or travelers who tried to create their winter stores by gleaning from fields in multiple places. Although gleaning was reserved for the poor, others resorted to it as a way of supplementing their own income, even though this was considered theft.

Some women used their land to grow products they intended for sale, such as grain for brewing ale commercially or flax they intended to spin and weave into linen cloth. Any of their raw products might be sold commercially, either as surplus above their own family's needs or as a crop intended for sale.

The family was the basic economic unit in the countryside. Rural men and women married, and remarried upon a partner's death, because it was necessary to manage the large workload of a rural household. Widowers required assistance raising children, cooking, cleaning, and managing the household and without a wife had to rely on family or hired servants. Widows could not manage their usual workload and add plowing and the other traditional male activities on a farm without assistance.

The 1349 Ordinance of Laborers limited wages and movement for workers who sought to improve their lives in the demographic crisis following the Black Death as did the 1351 Statute of Laborers. The statute declared that laborers had to continue working for their pre-plague employers and threatened those who refused to serve as required with imprisonment. It prohibited employers from paying higher wages in order to take labor from other employers and barred artisans from charging more for their labor and workmanship than they had in the twentieth year of Edward III's reign.

The necessity for this is demonstrated in the court records, which show peasant laborers accepting higher wages from employers beyond their manor, with neither side respecting the statutes. For example, in 1373, "Alice, the servant of William de Scampton of North Carlton, who was assigned and charged by the constable of the vill of North Carlton to serve the abbot of Barlings in reaping his grain in the autumn in the 47th year [of Edward III], left the vill to take a higher wage and refused to serve the abbot in contempt of the king" (Goldberg 1995, 176). While Alice was caught, it was in her interests to accept work from someone who would pay her higher wages. Similarly, in 1374, Agnes, the wife of a shepherd, "was instructed . . . to stay with the aforesaid John Malteby at hoeing time to hoe his grain according to the form of the Ordinance of Labourers. Agnes, however, refused to do this and neither allowed her [two] maidservants to be judicially compelled nor to work at the aforesaid task" (Goldberg 1995, 177).

Peasant Rebellions

After the Black Death, peasants saw the opportunity for better lives, with higher wages, better working conditions, and more mobility. The Ordinance and Statute of Laborers made this opportunity more challenging, but peasants did not let go of the hope raised by the post-plague labor shortage. Serfs especially sought an end to their unfree status, the fees they had no choice but to pay, and the work they were forced to do for their lords. The right of tallage allowed lords to tax serfs for any reason, and they could demand that the tax be paid in cash or in kind, with no pattern or custom.

Peasants across Europe began to demand better conditions through rebellions. Peasants in France rebelled in 1358 in a revolt known as the Jacquerie, named after the everyman name of Jacques in France. This revolt stemmed from the demographic changes of the plague and their failure to result in an improved life, as well as the suffering caused by the Hundred Years War, which fell primarily on the peasant farmers who lost their crops in the fighting. Aristocrats quickly put down that rebellion, but they did not end the problems that caused it. The English peasants, led by Wat Tyler, rebelled in 1381 in response to a poll tax that unfairly charged all people the same amount, regardless of circumstances. The rebels demanded an end to serfdom, marched on London, burned buildings, and killed the archbishop of Canterbury. They did attract the attention of the young king Richard II, whom the peasants urged to protect them from the corrupt and cruel lords of their manors. While Richard was willing to speak with the rebels and eventually did expand his circle of advisors to include people from less noble backgrounds, Wat Tyler was killed and many of the rebels were executed; Richard was later pushed off the throne and assassinated (see chapter 3).

Another revolt took place during the summer of 1450, known as Jack Cade's Rebellion. Again, the rebels were incensed by the Hundred Years' War, this time by England's recent losses under Henry VI, and ideas of corruption in the advisors surrounding the king. Jack Cade led the rebels to march on London, where they looted the city and provoked a conflict with the people of London, culminating in fighting on London Bridge. Cade was arrested and died in custody, while the leaders were rounded up and tried and executed. Some historians consider this rebellion as an early skirmish in the Wars of the Roses between the houses of Lancaster and York.

Forest

The forests that covered large parts of England in the Middle Ages had their uses, as places for elites to hunt game and for peasants to let their pigs roam. Peasants collected fallen wood, cut peat for their fires, searched for food to supplement their diet such as nuts and berries, or trapped small game. Royal foresters maintained the king's forests and ensured that poachers did not illegally hunt the king's deer.

But, there is a reason that forests find a place in so many fairy tales as sites of danger. The deeper parts of the forest were associated with fairies and spirits whose stories remained from pre-Christian times. They provided cover for criminals who were notorious for robbing travelers along roads that ran through forests. Outlaws could easily hide in the heavily wooded parts of the forests, a reality that found literary life in the stories of Robin Hood, a legendary

Sherwood Forest was the subject of songs about Robin Hood. The forest could be a frightening place where outlaws might live and threaten those who passed through, but it was also a place of opportunity for several peasants. Some might gather wood, food items, hunt or trap game, or even expand farmland into the forest. (iStockPhoto.com)

figure who was the subject of cycles of poems called chansons de geste. According to the stories, a twelfth-century figure during the reign of Richard the Lionheart, who was mostly absent from England, and John I protected the common people but stole from the rich and powerful. The stories demonstrate the common feelings about the royal tax collector, corrupt reeves, and the poverty of the common people in England. These poems remained popular and gained embellishment about Robin Hood's band of followers and his romantic life.

TOWN

Towns existed slightly outside this medieval ordering system. Although they were filled with people who worked, towns grew from populations that did not need to farm for themselves but could exist off the surplus produced by rural farmers. When the surplus was sufficient, towns could grow, and the early fourteenth century was the peak for urban growth in this period, when England could boast about 690 towns. Many of these were quite small, with fewer than 2,000 residents, and only sixteen sizable English towns had more than 10,000 people. London during the first half of the four-teenth century had at least 80,000 residents, but Paris had as many as 200,000 at that time. Smaller towns, such as Exeter, had about 5,000 residents in the same period. These numbers declined mid-century during the plague and struggled to resurge until the six-teenth century (Kowaleski 2008, 1).

In the documents, towns appear to be very male, but this is due to the way information was recorded, not the reality of the towns. Skeletal evidence for York shows that 53 percent of those buried in excavated cemeteries were women, and similar findings establish the same proportion for Lincoln (Grauer 2002, 275). Women were also not insignificant members of the town, with almost 20 percent of York's households headed by women.

English town residents included merchants, those who engaged in buying and selling goods, and artisans, craftsmen and women who used their skills to make goods. For larger towns that contained a cathedral, the bishop and his cathedral canons likely shaped at least part of the town. Service industries were also important for the town, such as barbers, bankers, domestic servants, and tavern keepers. And while the majority of the population did not need to farm or tend animals, there were always a few people engaged in such work in the town.

Most significant for the towns was the organization of craftsmen into guilds, workers in the same craft who formed a community that set standards, prices, and wages. The guild members, called masters because they had mastered their craft, took on apprentices to train the next generation for the guild. Apprentices were typically children above age seven whose parents signed multiyear contracts offering their child's labor in exchange for an education in the craft, housing in the master's home for the length of the contract, meals and sometimes clothing, although parents sometimes maintained responsibility for that. At the end of the contract, the apprentice should have a working understanding of the craft and be able to work in the shop for day-wages in a position known as a "journey-man." The goal of a journeyman was to save wages to be able to open his or her own shop, at which point he or she would consider marriage and family. To join the guild, a journeyman had to dem-onstrate that his work met the standards of the guild, sometimes by producing a "masterpiece," an example of his craftsmanship that met the masters' expectations. Because of their close interaction, a journeyman considered marrying the daughter of a guild master, especially the daughter of the master who trained him. Her experience with the craft made her a suitable assistant for his own work and even made her capable to take over the shop as a widow, maintaining it for their children.

The guilds looked after their members and their families, offering charity to members who fell on hard times or to families of their members after death. They were major fundraisers for the church, sponsoring church restoration projects or funding new chapels and new church decoration. Guild funds supported the poor and provided for chantries. Guilds, alone or in concert, sponsored events for the town like the Mystery Plays in York and Coventry or church ales. The guilds were also influential politically, arranging for their members to serve on town councils and even to become mayor or other town officials. Guild members were important and weighty men in town who might stand as pledges or serve as witnesses in court cases. This was especially true for wealthier or higher-status guilds than for the opposite.

The guilds also defended their members against competition by ensuring that new members were not admitted to the guild, or permitted to open workshops, unless there was enough work to support another shop. Guild regulations were particular to a specific town, so that the carpenters' guild of London and that of York might have different expectations about prices, wages, and other standards. It also meant that some towns had reputations for certain products and that the weavers of one town could have a product superior—or inferior—to that of another. The guilds did not permit newcomers to arrive in their city, set up shop, and start selling their product without admission to the guild, as a way of protecting their members.

Guilds took very seriously their regulations about the manner in which their craftwork was conducted and did not permit the styles, methods, or techniques of another place in their town. This was in part to avoid shoddy work and inferior products and in part to avoid competition from superior methods known only to a few craftsmen and not to all, as the guild was at heart a mutual protection society. Women could run afoul of this issue as well as men, as Katherine Duchewoman—likely a foreigner working in London, given her name—found in 1374:

Henry Clerke, John Dyke, William Tanner, and Thomas Lucy, tapicers [tapestry workers, probably from the French tapissiers] and masters of the trade of the tapicers in London, caused to be brought here a coster of tapestry, wrought upon the loom after the manner of work of Arras, and made of false work by Katherine Duchewoman, in her house at Finch Lane . . . seeing that she had made it of linen thread beneath, but covered with wool above, in deceit of the people, and against the Ordinance of the trade aforesaid; and they asked that the coster might be adjudged to be false, and for that reason burnt. . . . Therefore, after due examination thereof by the Masters aforesaid, and other reputable men of the same trade, by assent of the Mayor, Recorder, and certain of the Aldermen, it was ordered that the said coster, as being false work, should be burnt. (Riley 1868, 375–376)

While most guilds were focused on artisans who made items with their skill, there were some for other trades. The mercers were cloth merchants who traded in linen, silk, and other textiles, typically those that were not created locally. By the late Middle Ages, mercers may have expanded into other goods. This was an influential trade selling anything from undergarments to accessories.

Women were influential within these guilds as the wives, daughters, and widows of guild members. Wives assisted their husbands in their work as well as in the operation of his workshop and household. They had a significant role in feeding and clothing his apprentices and servants as well as in shaping their spiritual and moral lives. After her husband's death, a widow could take over his shop in many crafts and towns, either as a full member herself or in a temporary way until her son was of age to take over. Guilds had a strong interest in marrying such widows, especially those who were young enough to have more children, within the craft, and this was a popular way for a journeyman to secure his own shop; this custom placed a lot of pressure on widows. In the late fifteenth century, some guilds pressured widows to leave the guild, especially if they remarried to a member of a different guild, making it more difficult for a man to access guild membership through marriage to a member's widow.

Daughters assisted in the shop and likely learned the craft from their fathers and could later operate on their own, depending on the craft, or become a sought-after bride for a journeyman or guild member. Several fathers left the tools of their trades to their daughters, such as Adam Hecche, armorer in York who died in 1404 and split his tools from different trades between his children: "I leave my son John all my tools relating to my craft of furbisher. . . . Also I give and leave to my daughter Agnes one of the better brass pots and all the tools of my craft pertaining to mailwork" (Goldberg 1995, 198).

Women were members of guilds in their own name and worked in a wide variety of crafts, although they tended to cluster into crafts associated with textile work. There were no guilds only for women, unlike in Paris where there was a guild for seamstresses and other such female-only crafts. Despite their significance, women rarely served in the guild offices. One exception was Marion Kent of York, who served in the mercers' guild of York as a council member in 1474–1475, after a decade of working in the guild as a widow.

Workers in a shared industry, guilds or banks or merchants, tended to live near one another, and those groupings are visible in the names of streets or sections of the town. For some industries, this was necessary because their work was messy or smelly, such as tanners, tallow makers, and butchers. This was part of the theory of miasma, the idea that foul air could spread disease. Guild members also gathered for celebrations, feasts, in honor of a dead colleague, or to celebrate holidays. There were some guildhalls that served as a gathering space for the members in some cities.

In larger cities, especially London, there were also many foreigners present. The London district of St. Martin's had a large number of aliens. Aliens might come to the city for work, but admission to the guilds could be challenging. Many of the women seen working in the lower-status industries like service or prostitution also seem to have been foreign.

Towns usually included in their charter the idea that their citizens were free, which encouraged an idea that if a serf could get away from their manor and live in a town for a year and a day, they, too, would be free. The towns thus exerted some power over the imaginations of rural villagers who sought work and found it most easily as day laborers or servants.

Work in Town

Women in medieval England worked in a wide number of fields. In towns, women worked in crafts, as merchants, as shopkeepers, as prostitutes—in some places legally, in others not. In the late Middle Ages, women have been found working in a variety of crafts, including "as tanners, skinners, curriers, glovers, saddlers, and shoemakers," all crafts involving leather or skins; "as founders, armourers, blacksmiths, ironmongers, dinners, needlers and occasionally as goldsmiths," all crafts involving metal work; "as building laborers or supplying building materials; as seamstresses, embroiderers, tailors, cappers, hosiers and dressmakers"; all textile workers; "and as candle-makers" (Ward 2006, 92). There was respectable women's work as spinsters, dressmakers, seamstresses, and so on. Women worked as hucksters, stall operators in markets. Most women's work was low status, in domestic service, brewing, spinning, helping in their fathers' or husbands' shops, or maintaining their household and raising children (See Kowaleski 1988). Medieval women worked, whether within the family business, if there was one, or outside the home, if they were lower status.

Wives were expected to work alongside their craftsmen husbands in an artisan's workshop, and their labor was so necessary that marriage was more common among artisans and merchants than among other groups. Traditionally, artisan men would wait to marry until they completed their training and fully entered their guild, using wages from their time as journeymen to open their own shop. Some men may not have wanted to wait, such as Thomas Bakester, an apprentice who agreed to marry his girlfriend if they had sex, but failed to keep his promise, which caused her to take him to court in 1384 (Goldberg 2000, 62).

Women owned businesses or ran them alongside their husbands. Johanna Hill was a bell founder with her own workshop in fifteenth-century Aldgate that she continued after her husband's death. She left her maker's stamp on bells found across southern England. When Katherine Ryche's new husband, Thomas Betson, fell ill during their first year of marriage, Katherine was the one to run the business, at fifteen years old, with the advice of Thomas's agent and her uncle. Most women who worked independently in urban crafts were single, especially widows continuing to run their husbands' workshop after their death. As widows, women might continue to train their husbands' apprentices or take on new apprentices of their own. Some women whose work was not protected by a guild, such as silk women, took on apprentices as well.

While women worked in a range of crafts, there was a larger proportion of women working with textiles. Many of these were low-status positions or crafts, but not all. Silk workers, for example, sold luxury items as trimming for wealthy women's clothing, such as ribbons. Most of these women lived in London, where they could find customers for their silken wares. In 1483, silk woman Alice Claver outfitted Richard III and Anne Neville with the trimmings for their coronation robes (Ward 2006, 91).

Textile work allowed women to support themselves while working in their own home, either as their primary employment or a by-employment for their other tasks. Women worked with flax for linen cloth, with wool, or with hemp, at all stages of the process, but typically doing the lowest-status, least well-paying work. Wool required washing, combing, and carding to remove debris. Once the raw wool was ready, it could be spun, which medieval women generally did with a distaff—a stick used for spinning—although the spinning wheel was not unknown. The distaff was so closely associated with women's work that it became a metaphor for women in general. Flax and hemp also required spinning, again using the distaff. Once spun, the thread or yarn could be used for weaving. Other steps along this path might include dyeing different colors. Much of this work could be done while minding children, waiting for food to cook, or other household chores, and women would regularly have done multiple tasks at once.

Weavers had used the vertical loom in fashion since the ancient period—the same sort of loom upon which Penelope wove a shroud for Odysseus's father Laertes—and this was still in home use in the Middle Ages. By the thirteenth century the horizontal treadle loom was in fashion in England and facilitated the weaving of long bolts. Weavers guilds operating the treadle loom tended to be male, however, and women were excluded by weaving guilds by the 1460s. In York, John Walton left to "Margaret my wife my best woolen loom with those things that pertain to it" (Goldberg 1995, 197). In Shrewsbury, even widows were only allowed to fulfill existing contracts for three months after their guild member husband's death.

Women might perform this entire process themselves, shearing wool from sheep they owned, cleaning, carding, spinning, dyeing, and weaving it entirely themselves. Or they might perform only one or a few steps along this process and sell their product on to another who would perform further steps. Those without sheep could purchase raw wool to spin; those without a loom might sell their spun yarn. This could be a process they oversaw for themselves, or a disparate group of female carders, spinners, and weavers might be overseen by a clothier who paid wages for each step in the process and then sold the finished cloth at market or in a town shop. Since men had more capital for larger-scale businesses, it was often a man who employed women for their labor in doing this piecework. For example, William Crosseby, a York dyer, in his 1466 will left "20s. To be divided by my executors for the poor women of custom working and travailing [working] in carding and spinning my wool" (Goldberg 1995, 198). Women also worked in importing or exporting cloth and other parts of the textile trade. Other textile work might be finer, such as embroidery. Mabel of Bury St. Edmunds was famous in the thirteenth century for needlework she did for the king, Henry III. Embroidery was a common pastime for elite women but might be done by towns-women as well.

It was challenging for women to enter certain professions, such as law or medicine, because these were increasingly limited to those with university educations, and universities did not admit women. For medicine, this limited women's access to high-status positions, such as physician, a medical worker who diagnosed and prescribed treatments, which was frequently regulated, requiring a medical license and a university education. There were some places where a woman might declare herself a physician, espe-cially a rural village without a university or licensing standards, but this became more difficult as time went on. There was a wide array of medical workers, however, and women could be found among all of them, as apothecaries, barbers and surgeons, mid-wives, physicians, herbalists, and wise women. Toward the end of this period, men increasingly attempted to control medical work, such as by taking a greater interest in gynecology as discussed in chapter 2, but this was not done uniformly or in an organized way. We know, for example, that the York guild of barber surgeons included female members.

Women are listed among those working in taverns or running alehouses, an occupation that makes sense, given women's associa-tion with brewing or running inns. Women who worked as huck-sters found it useful to combine these businesses, selling food and other small items alongside ale. Because of taverns' and alehouses' association with drunkenness, and the inns' association with prosti-tution, women working in these establishments are cited frequently in court records, with fines and penalties that compromised their profits.

There were also dangers for young women coming to the cities for work without much experience. Elizabeth Moring, for example, claimed to be running an embroidery shop and solicited appren-tices, but in truth she was a bawd collecting prostitutes for her brothel. Prostitution was a common form of work available to women, particularly for those who needed flexible working hours while they tended to young children and other day work or those looking to bridge a gap while searching for more regular work. We will examine prostitution more fully in chapter 5.

Women who were hired as servants tended to work in households in baking, brewing, inn keeping, or textiles, although cloth work-shops shifted to using male servants during the fifteenth century, while in the same period women servants became more attractive in merchants' shops. Servants of both sexes worked in these trades, not only doing domestic labor, although female servants were more associated with the household tasks than men were.

SINGLEWOMEN

Some women delayed marriage, especially in the late fourteenth and fifteenth centuries, or never married at all. Many of these women found work in service, with as much as 6 percent of the total English population engaged in service and as much as 11 percent of the urban population (Kowaleski 1999, 47). Women working as servants in households tended to move from rural areas to urban ones to find this work, lived in their employer's home, and remained single during the time of their contract. Singlewomen who then married typically left service, while others might renew their contracts when their term was up instead. The plague especially opened up new opportunities for singlewomen to find work, and to make marital choices without their families' interference. This availability of positions with which women might support themselves also led some women to remain single and never marry. An economic shift in the late fifteenth century, however, pushed women into poorly paid positions, which encouraged them to marry earlier and remarry when widowed.

Singlewomen working for wages were among those most likely to engage in premarital sex, especially if living apart from their families. Women might live with their employers, especially as domestic servants or older apprentices, or with other singlewomen. Several pieces of late medieval literature describe the sexual activities of singlewomen, including "The Serving-Girl's Holiday," which depicts a young woman taking a break from work to enjoy a dalliance with a lover named Jack. The girl's excitement for her time away from work was paired with her excitement to meet up with her lover, even as she is aware that her lady disapproves and is afraid of her disapproval. When she realizes she is pregnant, she fears telling her mistress, who will likely terminate her employment, meaning the loss of position, wages, housing, and food at a time she needs all. This poem is a cautionary tale for singlewomen, an education in the dangers of sexual activity. These women might have believed that their sexual relationships would lead to marriage, as a future promise followed by sex constituted a marriage, as we saw in chapter 1. Marital court cases demonstrate confusion between couples on whether marriage was actually promised before their encounter.

Some singlewomen were able to do quite well for themselves, however. Cecilia Penifader of the manor of Brigstock in the fourteenth century owned her own house as well as a significant amount of property in and around Brigstock. Cecilia never married, although her sisters did. She also was not able to access a formal education or a profession like her brother William, who likely entered the church. She eventually merged her household with that of another unmarried brother, probably relying on one another for male and female tasks, but also turning to one another for company and companionship. Cecilia's wealth permitted her to live a comfortable life, but she still gleaned illegally, perhaps shifted boundary stones to steal land, and cleared assarts. Even a wealthy *feme sole* needed to use all her tools to build a safety net.

HOUSING

Most medieval housing was modest, made of wood, stone, or wattle and daub (woven sticks and twigs held in place with mud or clay), and much less private than we expect today. Late medieval homes were modeled on a two- or three-room plan: a hall to welcome guests, dine, and conduct business; an enclosed, more personal room for sleeping and family use; and if possible, a third room for storage, animals, and/or a kitchen. In the homes of wealthier elites, additional rooms might have other functions in addition to these three spaces. In more modest houses, such as that of a peasant, the core of the home was a hearth, an open fire in the center of a room, often the hall, used for both heating and cooking. Without a chimney, a hole in the thatched roof was necessary to let out some smoke, but the inside of the house was probably quite smoky still. In the poorest of places, these three spaces were combined in one room, with animals, cooking, dining, and sleeping all together. A peasant's home had a dirt floor and either had no windows or a window without glass, only shutters.

Furnishings were simple and often of wood. Many homes used trestle tables, which could be set up for meals and put away to make space for living at other times of day. Benches, both indoors and out, provided seating and could be moved out of the way after meals. Wooden chests offered storage. A freestanding cupboard held cutlery and crockery.

The hall was an important place for building community and expressing personal or familial identity. In fifteenth-century England, the hall was a large entry space to the home, with open timber framing and heavy furniture. The idea of the hall as a meeting space open for feasting and welcoming a retinue in England goes back to "Beowulf," the eighth-century poem about a hero fighting monsters for glory and fame. In the poem, the mead hall figures prominently as a space the king can hold feasts, host his own or visiting warriors, and display the weapons and emblems that reflect his family's greatness, while his wife offered wine to the most favored guests. Late medieval English halls were places families similarly decorated to demonstrate their history and power. In a manor house, the lord might receive petitions from his tenants in his hall; in a merchant's urban house, he might transact business in his hall.

The more private family chamber was smaller than the hall and not generally a place to welcome visitors. This room had places for families to sleep, perhaps with trundle beds that could be pushed underneath traditional beds during the day. In a household with servants, this chamber was for the nuclear family, while servants could sleep in the hall or, in larger households, in another space. Beds included a headboard, canopy, and curtains, with straw or feather mattresses covered in linens and pillows. These linens could be quite elaborate, especially for special occasions such as churching, as discussed in chapter 2. The family might read, do quiet work, or pray in their shared chamber. The bed itself was a symbolic space, where people slept, consummated their marriages, conceived children, nursed their babies, cared for the ill, performed the last rites, and prepared the dead for burial.

Households included the nuclear family as well as any servants, fostering children, or apprentices. In the largest and most elite households, especially castles with significant military presence, women might have their own spaces, but in England, such spaces were for women's comfort, and they were not confined there.

CLOTHING

Medieval men and women, like their modern counterparts, used clothing to mark their gender, their class status, their profession or vocation, and even their geographical origin. Clothing provided visual clues about a medieval person's community and role within it as did their shoes, head coverings, hairstyles, and accessories. Images as well as descriptions allow us to understand the importance of clothing to medieval people.

The styles of clothing changed over time and in different regions. An interest in fashion grew in the fourteenth century, from fascination with court circles on the continent. John of Reading, a monk of Westminster Abbey, claimed that the courtiers who surrounded Edward III's queen, Philippa of Hainault, affected English fashion: "They have abandoned the old decent style of long, full garments for clothes which are short, tight, impractical, slashed, every part laced, strapped or buttoned up, with the sleeves of the gowns and the tippets of the hoods hanging down to absurd lengths, so that if the truth be told, their clothes and footwear make them look more like torturers, or even demons" (Horrox 1994, 131)· According to John and similar commentators, this obsession with clothing style, as well as form-fitting garments, committed the sin of pride.

Katherine L. French observed that "medieval fashions tended to change on two different levels: details such as edging, sleeve shape, or necklines changed frequently, while silhouette—the shape of the body created by clothing—changed more slowly" (French 2013, 198). Fashion was for those who could afford it, as embellishments and personal tailoring were expensive, as was buying new garments or altering existing ones before they wore out. As elites cast off their out-of-fashion clothing, however, a secondhand clothing market developed, making fashion more accessible to those with less wealth. The more challenging colors were those most desired, such as reds and purples, a reality that remained from Classical times. The fashion in the later fifteenth century among elite circles showed a preference for cloth-of-gold and gold embellishments set against dark cloth.

England was a land of wool, which was mostly exported to the Low Countries for weaving into cloth, and linen. These fabrics could be embroidered with silk thread or edged with different sorts of fur. Miniver, the fur of Baltic squirrels, was the most prized luxury fur and limited to certain women from the most elite circles. Even among those circles, miniver, cloth-of-gold, or cloth-of-silver were the greatest luxuries and used for the most important occasions, such as weddings, churchings, coronations, and so on.

Male and female forms of dress were distinct in the late Middle Ages, and women who cross-dressed were thought to claim male identities, as discussed in chapter 5. Women in the fourteenth and fifteenth centuries wore hose on their legs and a chemise under their clothes. Over this they wore a kirtle, a sleeveless or short-sleeved long dress. Over the kirtle they wore a tunic or tabard or, later, a gown. In the later part of this period, the kirtle developed longer sleeves, and both the kirtle and the gown became more and more form-fitting, especially with narrow waists.

Peasants wore the most basic clothing, made of wool and focused on warmth and function. Both sexes wore stockings, hooded cloaks, and leather shoes, while women wore long dresses and men wore thigh-length tunics. After the Black Death, demand increased for manufactured clothing, and especially embellishments and accessories. This is visible in the growth of specialist artisan shops, such as haberdashers and hosiers.

Hairstyles for women were strongly connected to a woman's place in the female life cycle. An unmarried woman wore her hair loose, a sign of her unmarried and thus virginal status. Once married, women covered their hair, with a linen kerchief, and if widowed, they would perhaps wear a wimple. These standards changed over time and varied in different regions. By the later Middle Ages, braided hair came into vogue, and women covered their hair less so that the plaits were visible. Women rarely cut their hair, however, and shorn hair on a woman was sometimes used as a shaming tool to punish them, or it was a way for women to mark themselves as unattractive and unavailable for marriage if they hoped to resist marital negotiations and embark instead on a holy life. In the fifteenth century women began to wear a tall conical hat with a veil draping from it, or even more elaborate versions with two points and veils.

The girdle was a woman's most significant accessory, as discussed in chapter 2. A loose belt worn low at the waist with ends that could hang quite low, almost to the floor, the girdle emphasized a woman's hips and curves, likely recalling for viewers the girdle's role in the birthing chamber. Women might attach purses to this belt, or small pouches for other purposes, rosaries, or keys.

In wills, women paid special attention to directing how their clothing should be distributed. Girdles, especially those of precious metals or elaborate decoration, often went to statues of saints like Mary, Margaret, and Dorothy in churches. Luxury clothing not already gifted to the church might similarly be donated upon the owner's death to be made into altar cloths, clothing for statues, or vestments. Other clothes might be left to daughters, relatives, or neighbors, and the lists of items in wills indicate how few garments even people of some status possessed.

Common people might have one to three changes of clothing, typically homemade by women of the household. More elite families could employ dressmakers, lacemakers, professional embroiderers, and so on to design and embellish more elaborate clothing, especially for special occasions. In addition to everyday dress, special occasions were opportunities for new clothes or ritual out-fits. White was not the standard color for a wedding dress, but brides typically wore something special for the ceremony (See chapter 1). Women would also wear a new or special dress for their churching after the birth of a child; a wealthy, high-status woman might have new and meaningful clothes for each churching along with new linens for their bed and the child's cradle (See chapter 2). Special occasion clothing was intended to be worn once and, for those who could afford it, could then be gifted to the church, where the garments were repurposed as altar cloths or priestly vestments.

The boundaries between communities were policed, in part, by legislating what people could and could not wear. In 1215, for example, the canons of the Fourth Lateran Council required Jews living in Christian Europe to wear distinguishing marks so that Christians would know they were Jewish. While the canons did not make specific requirements, Edward I and Henry III expanded and clarified the requirement to be a large yellow taffeta badge worn above the heart. See chapter 6 for further discussion.

Sumptuary laws also limited what people could wear, especially regulating luxury goods and focusing on women's clothing. These laws strictly limited what people of different status groups might wear and tried to stifle social climbing through clothing, marking certain fabrics and furs as elite and prohibiting them to those of lower stations. Such laws required prostitutes to wear clothing that would clearly demarcate them from other women so that men would not mistakenly solicit nonprostitutes. In 1351 London regu-lations required prostitutes to wear striped hoods and prohibited them from wearing fur ones. In 1363 sumptuary legislation also sought to limit social climbing, prohibiting lower social orders from dressing like higher ones. In "How the Good Wife Taught Her Daughter," the wife reminded her daughter to avoid jealousy based on her neighbor's clothing, if her neighbor happened to dress more richly than she could. She advised her to be grateful for God's gifts and to live a good life (Furnivall 1908).

Those who joined holy orders adjusted their clothing and even their hairstyle so they could immediately be recognized both as a monastic and a member of a particular order. Both male and female monastics wore a habit, a large and rather shapeless sleeved gar-ment made of wool that covered the body from head to toe. Monas-tic orders distinguished themselves in the color dye they used—or did not use—for their habits, allowing someone to instantly distin-guish a Benedictine (black wool) from a Cistercian (white wool) or a Franciscan (brown wool). Nuns wore a wimple, a veil that covered their hair and necks, to emphasize their modesty, sometimes beneath other veils. An abbess or prioress might wear the abbey's keys on a belt, an indication of her office; other abbatial officers might wear similar designations of their positions, such as the cellarer carrying keys to the storeroom.

FOOD AND DRINK

Since space in medieval homes was limited, as noted earlier, most people used wooden trestle tables and benches that could be set out for a meal and then put away when not in use. Dishes were ceramic; stone; or, for more elite diners, metal such as pewter, silver, or gold. Meals were served communally on trenchers made of bread that were also consumed or donated. Knives and spoons were in common use, but forks were rarer. Napkins and bowls of washing water were available throughout a meal. After the Black Death, a market for manufactured goods grew and featured cutlery, pewter, and tableware, with more specialized items taking particular roles on the household table, moving away from multifunctional wooden bowls.

Married women were responsible for their households' food and drink. The wife was responsible for the shopping, cooking, serving, and washing, even if only overseeing servants who performed these

Luxurious dishes and plates demonstrated to guests that a host was wealthy and able to share their good fortune with other diners. (The Metropolitan Museum of Art)

tasks. Husbands and wives were expected to eat together, and the language of marital separation indicates that the couple separated *a mensa et thoro*, or "from table and bed." Margery Kempe's refusal to dine with her husband on Fridays upset him so much that he was willing to free her from the conjugal debt if she returned to dining with him.

The food consumed was a notable marker of a household's social status and wealth. Peasants relied on a diet of grains, legumes, and whatever their kitchen gardens produced, with meat rarely consumed and boiled when it was available. This meant that bread and ale were the core of most peasant meals for both adults and children, with beans from the spring plantings; occasional fruit from the orchards such as pears and apples; and vegetables from the gardens such as turnips, onions, leeks, peas, garlic, herbs, and cabbages. Those who kept pigs, which typically ran wild in the forests until it was time to slaughter them, might add pork, bacon, and sausages; those who kept sheep and cows would have butter and cheese, although not usually milk, and rarely enjoy their meat; those who kept chickens enjoyed eggs and, more frequently, ate poultry. Villages with beehives had honey, and those with streams or ponds might have fish. Elites with hunting privileges ate a variety of game, typically roasted over a fire and served with rich sauces. Urban dwellers often relied on meals purchased outside the home, with a late medieval increase in demand on prepared food from taverns, alehouses, inns, and even shops. Servants were fed in their employer's home, but on lesser fare. English sumptuary laws regulated the food offered to servants to meat only once a day.

It is a myth that medieval people ate bland food, as they were familiar with herbs and a variety of flavors, as even a glance at a medieval garden or recipe book can show. They had common access to oil and butter, ate aliums and cheeses, and their food was flavorful. Salt was precious and valuable, but widely known. It is also a myth that they consumed rotten meat; victuallers who sold rotten meat were brought to court.

Local governments, local lords and ladies, and the royal government took roles in regulating the production and sale of food and drink, and a number of such regulations and court cases for those who violated trade regulations are extant to show the ways that cooks, butchers, fishmongers, brewers, and tapsters worked. Regulation involved taking responsibility for enforcement of standards for ale, by using ale tasters, and for punishing butchers or fishmongers who sold spoiled meat or fish. It also meant setting prices and ensuring there was no unfair price gouging. Officials were also responsible for monitoring the weights and measures to ensure that these were standard for the area and that the price charged per gallon purchased an actual gallon of the product. Violations of these regulations involved many court cases, and women might be involved in these as the victualler or as the enforcer of the regulations, as in the case of the seigneurial town of Clare in Suffolk, whose weekly market was controlled from 1314 to 1360 by Elizabeth de Burgh. Court records show that she was deeply involved in the regulation and management of this market.

Women worked in all these trades, either full time or occasionally when they produced a surplus above what their household required. The money that women could earn selling the surplus ale or beer, cheese or butter they made provided a helpful supplement to the household income, and this money also often remained under their own control.

Demographic changes following the Black Death dramatically affected the demand and consumption patterns for food in late medieval England. Previously, rye had dominated the grain supply as cheap and easily grown, but after the pandemic, grain production shifted toward barley and bread grains. Laborers began to include more meat, white bread, and ale in their diets, with animals kept for meat as well as wool, milk, butter, and cheese. Fresh fish also became more common in the English diet after the mid-fourteenth century.

The pattern of work had a great deal to do with these changes, as the status quo on agricultural estates radically changed. Peasant laborers could demand higher wages, greater mobility, fewer fees, and could move to the estates of lords who would comply with these demands and more. The need for laborers was extreme, as demonstrated by Henry Knighton, describing agricultural work in 1349: "[T]here was such a want of hands, for every kind of work, that people believed that the like shortage had never been known at any time in the past. . . . And thus the necessities of life became so dear, that what in previous times was worth 1d. now cost 4d. or 5d" (Martin 1995, 100–101). This also affected the pricing for foodstuffs, which the 1349 Ordinance of Laborers attempted to stall: "Butchers, fishmongers, hostelers, brewers, bakers, pulters, and all other sellers of all manner of victual, shall be bound to sell the same victual for a reasonable price, having respect to the price that such victual be sold at in the places adjoining, so that the same sellers have moderate gains, and not excessive, reasonably to be required according to the distance of the place from whence the said victuals be carried" (Luders 1810, 307–308).

The shift from ale to beer had a major impact on women's work as well as on the professionalization of victualizing. The church ale, mentioned at the start of this chapter as a frequent occurrence through the ritual year, was a fundraiser as well as a community gathering. Attendees purchased ale and were likely also able to purchase food they consumed while chatting with neighbors or while enjoying entertainment such as music by pipers, drummers, and singers.

Since most people drank ale, including children, it was probably not very strong, and there was a fair tolerance for it. Nonetheless, there was concern about women's drinking. Public drunkenness was shameful in either sex, but drunk women met with great disapproval. The wife in "How the Good Wife Taught Her Daughter" advised her to take care around taverns and ale, since the tavern might destroy her reputation and waste her money. The Good Wife warned that drunkenness led to shame and the loss of prosperity (Furnivall 1908). Many women were tavern owners or worked in taverns and alehouses, although this suggests that this was less respectable work.

These food patterns were also different during times of crisis, such as the Great Famine, when crops failed and animals died in large numbers. During these times, foraging became increasingly important, and families might have survived for times on diets of nuts, berries, boiled tree bark, or vermin such as rats. Poaching became more common in times of crisis. While a rabbit or two here and there might not go amiss in the lord's forests, a deer was quite noticeable, and the poacher, if caught, could face execution. People might also steal from their neighbors, gleaning when not permitted or moving boundary stones between fields or cutting more hay than their share.

MARKETS

Agricultural workers, urban artisans, merchants, and townspeople all relied on markets to buy and sell their goods. In times of surplus, agricultural workers could sustain urban dwellers by bringing wagons or boatloads of their goods to market. Craftsmen could produce commissioned goods for specific clients in their towns, but they could also produce goods intended for a general audience at the market, or gain new clients at the market itself.

Merchants often bought at one market and transported goods for sale at another, increasing the reach of artisans and making agricultural products available at some distance from their point of origin.

Hosting a market was a privilege that various institutions or town officials might control. A monastery could have the right to control a market and charge tolls and fees for including a stand, as well as a percentage of the sale, but so might a lord or a community within a town. Markets were not permanent fixtures in the market space, but operated more like the modern green market or farmer's market, hosted on specific days at specific times. A larger town might have a number of markets in different places across the urban space, with the cathedral hosting a market on Tuesdays and Saturdays, a monastery hosting one on Mondays and Wednesdays, and the town itself hosting one on Fridays, making fresh, seasonal food available throughout the week. Peasants could travel to markets based on their needs. The peasant villagers of Brigstock, for example, could travel to markets within ten miles on any day but Sunday.

The heart of the market was the agricultural produce, but producers of other goods used markets as an opportunity to connect with customers. Textiles were a fixture of the late medieval English market, including woolen cloth and secondhand clothes. Markets also provided a place for peasants to meet new people, share ideas, and perhaps form a romantic attachment with someone outside of their own village. Serfs had to pay fines to marry and leave the manor: chevage was a fee to live off the manor, and merchet was a fine for permission to marry. Manorial records show that such fines were paid, and the markets provided an opportunity to meet such a future spouse.

Women were frequent workers as hucksters, selling small items, especially food and drink. In Exeter and Coventry, women sold a variety of foods in the markets, such as butter, cheese, eggs, poultry, ale, grains, fish, and fruit as well as in smaller ways when they could not set up a stall of their own (Ward 2006, 88). Women were penalized for some of their activities in this work, especially for efforts to manipulate market prices. They might secure all of one product before it came to market so that it could fetch a higher price or purchase low-priced products in the market and then sell them later at higher costs. There were penalties on regrating, buying goods before they arrived at the market to drive up the price, and forestalling, which involved buying all of one product en route to the market and then selling them at an inflated price. This caused a lot of grief at urban markets. For example, in 1306 London, "Isabel, wife of Nicholas de Tenete, bought hens and capons coming toward the City, a jury of the venue of Bridge was summoned to say whether she was a common forestaller of victuals for the profit of her husband. The jury . . . said that she went to meet poultry at Southwark and bought it before it could come to the City. She was committed to prison. . . . Afterwards she paid 40d. fine to Richard Poterel, chamberlain" (Thomas 1924, 234). That women engaged in this sort of buying and selling shows their limited access to capital and their need to work on a small scale that skirted the edges of the law.

Also visible in the marketplaces were the punishments meted out by the courts. Medieval people were familiar with corporal punishment, which was a common penalty for all manner of crimes. For sexual crimes adjudicated by the church courts, sinners could be forced to process in a state of undress through the city, or to be whipped in public. Women proven guilty of a crime could be punished by the cucking stool, a chair on a pole that could dunk the woman under water in a lake, or the stocks, a wooden structure that locked the criminal in place by the wrists and/or ankles.

DISEASE AND DISABILITY

Women were the most common caregivers for their families or neighbors when they were ill. A physician might be called in by a wealthy family to diagnose and treat a more serious issue; a barber or surgeon might be called on to amputate a limb injured beyond repair; a midwife called on during pregnancy; and the expertise of wise women and apothecaries might be sought for tinctures, drafts, and other remedies to ingest, inhale, or fumigate the body, but for more routine injuries and illnesses, women's expertise was considered sufficient. Women were trained by their mothers in the basics of bandaging and caregiving—they would not have called this work "nursing," as that referred to wet nurses. Women were the ones tending wounds, changing sheets, and sitting bedside.

Wills sometimes reflect gratitude for this work and give us some insight into how much care was taken in a community outside of kin structures. Ellen, wife of David Holgrafe from Bothall noted in her 1403 will: "I give and leave to the three women serving me in my illness, viz. the wife of Peter Forster, the wife of John Slikborn, and Ellen de Benton, to each of them a cow" (Goldberg 1995, 179). The fact that Ellen had three cows to give to nonfamily members marks her as a relatively wealthy woman, and the fact that she made a will but listed a husband suggests that she was a widow. Also interesting is that she named two of the women not by name but by their husbands, and the change in naming Ellen de Benton suggests she was a singlewoman.

Some women performed this labor as charity in larger settings such as hospitals, which were not the medical centers open to all that we expect today, but rather charitable spaces with beds for the poor who could not afford the usual in-home care or had nobody to watch over them.

Chronic illness or disability in the Middle Ages was difficult to manage. Some people were permitted to beg alms if unable to work to support themselves, and hospitals existed to help the general poor or patients of particular illnesses, such as leprosy or disabilities such as blindness. How well a disabled or ill person thrived largely depended on the wealth and care of their family.

Saints' shrines frequently saw pilgrims who came to ask for miraculous cures for themselves or for loved ones, and the shrines recorded the saints answering these prayers. A common devotional item left at shrines was a crutch for someone whose injury or disability was miraculously cured due to their prayers. Medieval Christians believed deeply in the power of the saints to work miracles for those who were worthy of them. They also believed that charity toward the sick, the disabled, and the poor were ways to demonstrate Christian charity and worthiness.

Black Death

The outbreak of plague known as the Black Death in 1348–1350 had a devastating effect in England and killed as much as one-third of the population. Plague returned in successive waves throughout the fourteenth and fifteenth centuries and beyond. Other parts of Europe, especially Italy, eventually instituted quarantines and isolation hospitals, but England did neither. Just outside of London, special cemeteries were established in East and West Smithfield for the burial of plague bodies. Other hygiene efforts were limited. During a larger outbreak in 1467, known as the "great pestilence," some towns did try to limit the movement of visitors to their cities, especially those traveling from a place of known infection. Cities also emphasized sanitation measures such as removing waste from the streets and cleaning waterways.

Contagion theory was familiar by the late Middle Ages, and there were efforts to isolate and contain people with infectious diseases. There was no board of health, even in large cities such as London. It was the king's responsibility to determine and enforce sanitary measures within the kingdom such as by discouraging his subjects from dumping feces in the streets. The problem was not resolved, as the king kept censuring the town. Oxford was not alone, and kings ordered York, Norwich, Southwark, Cambridge, Lincoln, and others to clean up the manure, dung, and filth that clogged their streets.

DEATH, BURIAL, AFTERLIFE

Christians who were seriously ill or near the end of their lives sought the services of a priest who could perform the sacrament sometimes called the last rites or extreme unction, the anointing of the sick. This provided a final opportunity to confess unshriven sins and clear the path toward salvation. Christians believed that unrepented sins could be atoned for in purgatory and after completing that work they might go on to heaven and salvation. Souls that were beyond redemption would not go to purgatory, however, but straight to damnation in hell, a frightening place of torments. The Italian poet Dante Alighieri had composed his *Divine Comedy*, a journey through hell (*Inferno*), purgatory, and heaven (*Paradisio*), during the fourteenth century in Italian. The poem offers a glimpse into medieval thinking about the afterlife, and Dante's composition in the vernacular makes him an important contemporary and inspiration of Chaucer's.

Christian funerals in the late Middle Ages included a church service; the interment; and, the next day, a requiem mass. Medieval Christians did not practice cremation; bodies might be buried in a churchyard or, for high-status elites, within the church. Wills included details about where in the church a person wished to be laid to rest. In Alice Wyche's 1474 will she asked to be buried in the church near where she would stand for holy services, with her first husband, William Holt, rather than picking a spot where she might be buried with her second husband, a former mayor of London. Burials within the church were often within the church floor, although burial within the wall or in a freestanding tomb were also possible, if expensive. Such tombs might be a simple slab with an inscription, or more elaborate stone carving, and the records of stone masons include commissions for such work. Agnes Ramsey (d. 1399) was the daughter of the stone mason William Ramsey and continued in his craft, even creating the tomb for Queen Isabella at London Greyfriars. After the Black Death, mortuary carvings took on a particularly macabre appearance, especially those known as transi tombs, which had two levels: a statue of the body in repose on top and beneath a carving of a corpse or skeleton in some stage of decomposition. One notable example of this style is the 1475 tomb of Alice Chaucer, Duchess of Suffolk, Geoffrey Chaucer's granddaughter, at Ewelme Church in Oxfordshire.

If able, at their death, Christians donated funds to a church or monastery to say prayers or masses for their soul, either once or annually. Prayers for the dead might be said by nuns, but masses for the dead required a priest, and priests charged a fee to perform the service. Christians also often left bequests for the poor, even if poor themselves, to their servants, and for the sick in addition to their heirs, friends, and neighbors.

FOR FURTHER READING

Baildon, William Paley, ed. 1896. *Select Cases in Chancery: A. D. 1364 to 1471*. London: Bernard Quaritch.

Barron, C. M. 1996. "The Education and Training of Girls in Fifteenth-Century London." In *Courts, Counties, and the Capital in the Later Middle Ages*, edited by D. E. S. Dunn, 139–153. New York: St. Martin's Press.

Bennett, Judith M. 1994. *The Wealth of Wives: Women, Law, and Economy in Late Medieval London*. New York: Routledge.

Bennett, Judith M. 1999. *A Medieval Life: Cecilia Penifader of Brigstock, c. 1295–1344*. Boston: McGraw-Hill.

Bennett, Judith M., and Amy M. Froide, eds. 1999. *Singlewomen in the European Past, 1250–1800*. Philadelphia: University of Pennsylvania Press.

Davis, James. 2012. "Selling Food and Drink in the Aftermath of the Black Death." In *Town and Countryside in the Age of the Black Death: Essays in Honour of John Hatcher*, edited by Mark Bailey and Stephen Rigby, 351–406. Turnhout: Brepols Publishers.

Fitzherbert, Anthony. 1534. "The Book of Husbandry." Project Gutenberg. https://www.gutenberg.org/files/57457/57457-h/57457-h.htm.

French, Katherine L. 2013. "Genders and Material Culture." In *The Oxford Handbook of Women and Gender in Medieval Europe*. Oxford: Oxford University Press.

Furnivall, Frederick. 1908. "How the Good Wife Taught Her Daughter." In *The Babees' Book: Medieval Manners for the Young: Done into Modern English*, edited by Edith Rickert. London: Duffield & Co. Project Gutenberg.

Goldberg, Jeremy. 2013. "Echoes, Whispers, Ventriloquisms: On Recovering Women's Voices from the Court of York in the Later Middle Ages." In *Women, Agency and the Law, 1300–1700*, edited by Bronach Kane and Fiona Williamson, 31–41, 169–171. London: Pickering and Chatto.

Goldberg, P. J. P. 1995. *Women in England c. 1275–1525: Documentary Sources*. Manchester: Manchester University Press.

Goldberg, P. J. P. 2000. "Household and the Organization of Labour in Late Medieval Towns: Some English Evidence." In *The Household in Late Medieval Cities: Italy and Northwestern Europe Compared*, edited by Myriam Carlier and Tim Soens. Leuven: Garant.

Grauer, Anne L. 2002. "Where Were the Women?" In *Human Biologists in the Archives: Demography, Health, Nutrition and Genetics in Historical Populations*, edited by D. Ann Herring and Alan C. Swedlund, 266–288. Cambridge: Cambridge University Press.

Hanawalt, Barbara A. 1986. *The Ties That Bound: Peasant Families in Medieval England*. Oxford: Oxford University Press.

Hanawalt, Barbara A. 1993. *Growing Up in Medieval London: The Experience of Childhood in History*. Oxford: Oxford University Press.

Hanawalt, Barbara A. 2007. *The Wealth of Wives: Women, Law, and Economy in Late Medieval London*. Oxford: Oxford University Press.

Harris, Carissa M. 2018. *Obscene Pedagogies: Transgressive Talk and Sexual Education in Late Medieval Britain*. Ithaca, NY: Cornell University Press.

Horrox, Rosemary, ed. 1994. *The Black Death*. Manchester: Manchester University Press.

Hutton, Ronald. 1994. *The Rise and Fall of Merry England: The Ritual Year, 1400–1700*. Oxford: Oxford University Press.

Keene, Derek. 1994. "Tanners' Widows, 1300–1350." In *Medieval London Widows, 1300–1500*, edited by Caroline M. Barron and Anne F. Sutton, 1–28. London: Bloomsbury Academic.

Kowaleski, Maryanne. 1988. "The History of Urban Families in Medieval England." *Journal of Medieval History* 14: 47–63.

Kowaleski, Maryanne. 1999. "Singlewomen in Medieval and Early Modern Europe: The Demographic Perspective." In *Singlewomen in the European Past, 1250–1800*, edited by Judith M. Bennett and Amy M. Froide, 38–81. Philadelphia: University of Pennsylvania Press.

Kowaleski, Maryanne. 2008. *Medieval Towns: A Reader*. Toronto: University of Toronto Press.

Luders, Alexander, ed. 1810. *The Statutes of the Realm*. Vol. 1. London: Dawsons of Pall Mall.

Martin, G. H., ed. 1995. *Knighton's Chronicle, 1337–1396*. Oxford: Oxford University Press.

Oschinsky, Dorothea, ed. 1971. *Walter of Henley and Other Treatises on Estate Management and Accounting.* Oxford: Clarendon Press.

Rawclife, Carole. 2013. *Urban Bodies: Communal Health in Late Medieval English Towns and Cities.* Woodbridge: Boydell Press.

Riley, Henry Thomas. 1868. *Memorials of London and London Life, in the XIIth, XIVth, and XVth Centuries: Being a Series of Extracts, Local, Social, and Political, from the Early Archives of the City of London, A.D. 1276–1419.* London: Longmans, Green, and Co. HathiTrust.

Salisbury, Eve, ed. 2002. *The Trials and Joys of Marriage.* Kalamazoo, MI: Medieval Institute Publications. https://d.lib.rochester.edu/teams/publication/salisbury-trials-and-joys-of-marriage.

Sharpe, Reginald B., ed. 1913. *Calendar of Coroners Rolls of the City of London, A.D. 1300–1378.* London: R. Clay and Sons.

Statutes of the Realm (1101–1713). 1963. Record Commission. 11 vols. London, 1810–1828, reprinted 1963. HathiTrust.

Stone, Brian, ed. 1964. *Medieval English Verse.* New York: Penguin.

Thomas, A. H. 1924. *Calendar of Early Mayor's Court Rolls Preserved among the Archives of the Corporation of the City of London at the Guildhall A. D. 1298–1307.* Cambridge: At the University Press.

Ward, Jennifer. 2006. *Women in England in the Middle Ages.* New York: Hambledon Continuum.

5

SEX AND SEXUALITY

As Historian Ruth Mazo Karras explained, the term "sex" refers to acts, while "sexuality" is "the universe of meanings that people place on sex acts, rather than the acts themselves" (Karras 2005, 7). Sexuality might include identities or orientations as well as actions, desires, and cultural ideas about sex. Historians also distinguish between "sex," meaning the biological body, and "gender," meaning cultural and social roles and identities. While modern society distinguishes between sexual orientation, gender identity, and biological sex (making it possible to describe someone as a homosexual, cisgender woman, or a heterosexual, transgender man) these concepts were not clearly distinguished in medieval societies.[1]

Historians argue that these concepts are culturally constructed and specific to their time and place. For example, two medieval men might kiss publicly in a church, in an embrace that was quite meaningful but completely unrelated to sex or sexuality—two kings sealing a treaty or two allies making an agreement. Medieval people would not be surprised that a forty-year-old man might

---

[1] Cisgender people have a gender identity that aligns with their assigned sex at birth, while transgender people have a gender identity that differs from their assigned sex at birth. A transgender man was assigned female sex at birth, as was a cisgender woman.

have sex with a twelve-year-old girl with the consent of their families, who had arranged their marriage and share their hope and joy for a child to come of their relationship.

There are also some modern categories we use, such as heterosexuality and homosexuality, that would not make sense to medieval people. While medieval people had same-sex desire and had sex with people of the same sex, medieval people did not link desire and sexual action to identity. This can complicate the study of the history of homosexuality, as the modern meaning for this identity cannot be extended precisely into the past. Similarly, heterosexuality as an identity was not a medieval concept, and medieval people did not describe a division between heterosexual or homosexual identities. Instead, they focused on actions.

Sex was still at the root of medieval identities, but the division was based on behavior, between chastity and sexual activity. This question especially divided those whose lives were devoted to the church—priests, monks, nuns—who were prohibited from sexual activity, and those whose lives included marriage, in which sex was an obligation (if not a pleasure). Countless saints' lives depict women who desired chaste lives devoted to God whose families insisted on marriage. Typically, in these texts, God provided an opportunity for the woman to fulfill an oath of chastity and to thus pursue a holy life worthy of sainthood. Such texts inspired Margery Kempe, a married woman who begged her husband to free her from the marital debt and allow her to live a chaste life.

There were distinctions, however, between masculine and feminine roles in terms of sex. During sex acts, medieval people gendered active roles as masculine and passive roles as feminine. A man performing a passive role, whatever the sex of their partner, was participating in behavior medieval people deemed feminine. Again, the actions, not the identity of the person, were gendered in these ways.

Medieval people were not shy in discussing sex in the ways we might assume for a society so associated with religion. Marital litigation regarding consummation and impotence reveal that couples had little privacy, as friends, family, and neighbors could well testify to their sexual lives. There are graphic poems and stories, and "dirty jokes" in works of literature, including those by Geoffrey Chaucer. Sex was a matter for discussion, in sermons, literature, and in common discourse.

Anxieties about sexuality also focused on policing appropriate partners. Married women were not permitted to engage in sex work. And Jews, Muslims, and Christians all discouraged sex with members of other faiths and were especially troubled by women of their own faiths having sex with men from other groups. Jewish men were not permitted to visit Christian sex workers even where prostitution was allowed, although this was less an issue in England after 1290, since Jews were not able to be in England legally.

NORMS AND EXPECTATIONS

Modern audiences tend to portray medieval attitudes toward sex as either bawdy or repressive, and there is evidence for both notions in late medieval England. The truth is that there was a range of perspectives on sex and sexual activities and that context matters. Medieval people thought of sex as an act that an active partner did to a passive partner. The word *swiven*, "to have sex," in Middle English was most often an active verb taking an object. While medieval people recognized there was a range of sexual activities and that both men and women could be lustful—indeed, both men and women often perceived women as the more lustful sex—when medieval authors wrote about sex, they described it as a penetrative act in which one partner penetrated and the other received. Erotic acts between women were only considered sex if penetration occurred.

Medieval literature contains numerous stories of sexual enjoyment for both women and men. In one medieval song, a maiden claims, "Fayne wold I have hem bothe nyght and day," suggesting her enjoyment of sexual congress with her partner as well as her insatiability, two typical sexual attitudes attributed to medieval women (Greene 1977, song 452). Similarly, Chaucer's Wife of Bath proclaims that she will take no vow of chastity and that if her fifth husband dies, she will search for number six. She also compares her husbands' sexual prowess, remarking that her rich, older husbands were not so impressive, but that her younger fifth husband provided more joy. Regardless of her first few husbands' age, Alison claims that she did frequently demand they exhaust themselves in paying the marital debt.

The church held authority over the sexual lives of people in late medieval England and could punish those who did not adhere to rules governing sex. Penitentials listed possible sins clerics might hear from their parishioners during confession and the appropriate penance for each sin. These are useful sources for understanding the value clergy and theologians placed on particular Christian ideals and the sorts of penalties certain sins might incur. Beyond the confessional, ecclesiastical courts had jurisdiction over sexual activities including fornication, adultery, and bestiality. Fornication was closely governed and might have consequences such as fines, penance, and pressure to marry. In general, fornication referred to sex outside of marriage, but it might also prohibit some kinds of nonprocreative marital sex. Church courts punished fornication for both men and women, often with public rituals of penance such as whipping and walking naked or near-naked through the village. For example, in 1300 "John the son of Nicholas the clerk fornicated recidivously with Julia Redes. Both appear, confess, and are whipped once in the usual way through the market" (Goldberg 1995, 118). While "the usual way" does not offer many details on what befell John and Julia, it does show that their punishment was common.

Restrictions fell more heavily on women, with attitudes that women were sinful, polluting, and lustful. Because women who participated in sex were likely to become pregnant, there was a much harsher judgment of women engaged in adultery and fornication than of men who did. For the same reason, there was less concern about lesbian activity than there was for women having sex with men.

Peasants living on English manors could be charged a leyrwite fine for fornication. This is a fine that first appears in Anglo-Norman law codes but has an earlier English origin, built from the early medieval English words "leger," lying down, and "wite," fine (Bennett 2003, 132). This became a fine that by the late thirteenth century was imposed not just on fornication, but on fornication by women, often flagged by pregnancy and giving birth to an illegitimate baby. While church courts prosecuted fornication for both men and women, manorial courts largely ignored the male partner, focusing exclusively on women. The fine declined in use over the late Middle Ages and was discontinued by 1500. Penalties for fornication included public whipping and/or the payment of a fine, typically paid by the woman herself or with the assistance of a pledge.

Leyrwite may have been compensation for the lord's loss of merchet, based on the idea that a sexually active woman would be less likely to marry and pay the manorial fee of merchet for that right, but then why not also extract a fine from the man who participated in the act? The fact that manorial courts extracted this fine primarily from unmarried bondwomen demonstrates the male control of female virginity that required a financial or corporal penalty when a woman made her own sexual choices. For example, in 1320, the betrothed couple Matilda Catte and Ralph Lamb were accused of fornication before the wedding took place, and Matilda was forced to pay six pence as a leyrwite fine, a steep fine representing more than a week's wages at a time when most manorial fees were half as much (Bennett 2003, 147, 151–152). Women bore the burden of these fines and unsanctioned sexual acts, even though theologians recognized that men sometimes led women to think they were betrothed only to fornicate with them without obligation.

On the topic of seigneurial control of female sexuality, there are some pervasive myths about the Middle Ages, and one is the notion of the "Lord's First Night," or *ius primae noctis*, sometimes called the lord's privilege, or *"droit de seigneur."* According to this myth, most visibly depicted in the movie *Braveheart*, the lord had the right to have sex with his female tenants or bondwomen on their wedding night. There is no truth to this idea, however. Medieval lords held no such right to the bodies of women under their authority.

Both men and women were encouraged to be chaste, and chastity in this context meant the rejection of sex altogether, but married couples encouraged to be chaste should have sex with one another—and only one another—for the purposes of reproduction only. Further, women whose marriages included procreative sex only and who focused on a life of prayer might consider themselves on a spectrum of chastity. The only sexual act officially sanctioned by the church was intercourse and then only between married couples who could expect to procreate. Men and women who joined the church were required to be both celibate—remain unmarried— as well as chaste, avoiding sex. For unmarried women, virginity was a high expectation, both for nuns who took oaths of celibacy and for women who planned to one day marry.

Virginity was so central to the identity of premarital womanhood that young girls were often called "virgins," but it was also a marker of special status for men. In King Arthur stories, which were popular in medieval England, Arthur's knights Perceval and Galahad remained chaste and so had the purity required to go on quests in search of the Holy Grail. The Virgin Mary was the ultimate example of womanhood as a virgin mother, although an impossible model for regular women to follow. Those who had not remained virgins could still embrace chastity, and medieval stories of Mary Magdalene exemplified repentance and chastity.

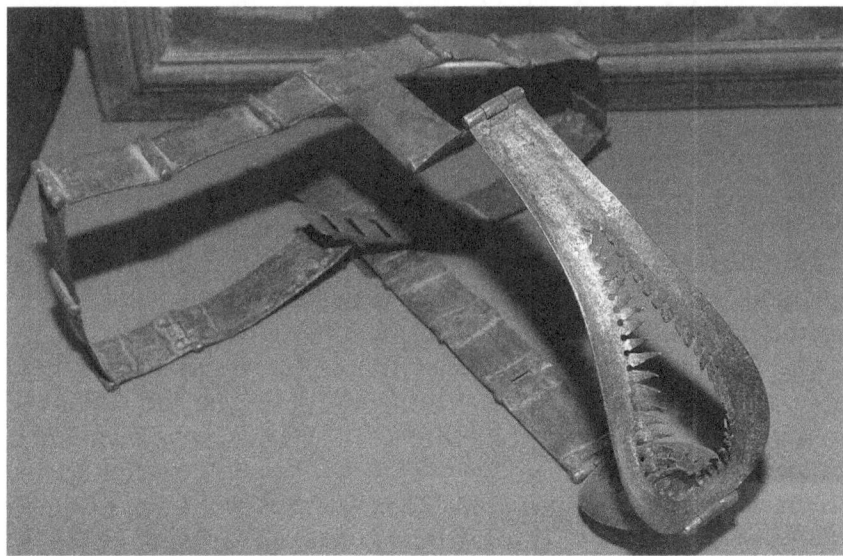

The chastity belt is a myth that is often repeated about medieval women. The idea is that men locked women in a metal chastity belt to prevent her from having sex. There is little historical evidence to support the idea, which appears to be a joke told in the fifteenth century and then repeated later as a way of depicting medieval people as repressed and backward. (Adwo/Dreamstime.com)

Widowed women also concerned the church, especially if they were young and wealthy. As we have seen earlier, there was a great deal of concern about the remarriage of wealthy widows, partially as a way of handling her property, but also to keep her from falling into sin and fornication. Widows who did remain single were expected to also remain chaste, one reason that widows found entering a monastery an attractive option.

Medieval thinkers understood that virginity and chastity were challenging expectations for both men and women. Many believed that this required even greater will for women, who had a harder time controlling lust. Theorists believed that women had a harder time resisting lust for two reasons: first, that women were weaker than men, and, second, because women had greater pleasure in sex than men did. This meant that women's chastity was more remarkable than men's, but also that women's sexual activity needed to be more tightly controlled.

Even married couples were limited in when or how they should have sex. One limitation was that menstrual blood was considered polluting, and couples were advised by doctors and theologians alike to avoid sexual contact during menstruation. The treatise *De secretes mulierum*, or "on the secrets of women," warned that engaging in sexual intercourse with a menstruating woman could cause a man to contract leprosy or cancer or become sterile. Couples who had sex too often—more than necessary for procreation—or derived too much pleasure from the experience might also be accused of fornication. There were also certain positions that were problematic, such as those that would not contribute toward reproduction.

ADULTERY AND FORNICATION

The church frowned on premarital sex, or fornication, as well as on adultery, and both were sins requiring penance. These were also the most common issues considered by the church courts in late medieval England (Butler 2007, 99). All forms of extramarital sex were punished much more heavily for women than for men, a double standard that reflected the medieval patriarchy. Heterosexual sex between single people was a sin of fornication, but less serious than adultery. As discussed later, unfree peasant women could be charged a leyrwite fine in the manorial court for premarital sex while her lover was not. The fact that many such fines exist in extant manorial court records suggests that single peasant lovers had an active sexual life even if they had to pay for it later. For example, the manor court of Halesowen included the entries for 1301:

> These were expensive fines, some of them more than others, that these unmarried women could not pay on their own and required men to pledge future payment. The focus on the women's part of a crime that involved two people is especially interesting in the case of Agnes, whose partner in crime is known and cited, but he appears to go without fine or punishment.

When men were sometimes punished for adultery, it was for violating another man's marriage by having sex with his wife, rather than for breaking his own marriage vows. Adultery was a sin against a man, the wife's husband, committed by his wife and her lover. The basis for this double standard is not hard to find: without access to DNA testing, a wife's adultery risked the paternity status of the man's heirs. This was even more significant in the later

Middle Ages, after the church had removed the option of divorce and remarriage.

Late medieval literature included numerous stories about women's adultery and fornication. Courtly love romance stories often centered on love triangles and adultery, such as the poems devoted to King Arthur/Guinevere/Lancelot and Tristan/Isolde/Mark. In both these examples, the stories revolved on the wife's adultery— Guinevere with Lancelot betraying Arthur, and Isolde with Tristan betraying Mark—as well as on the lover's betrayal of his friend or kinsman. The treachery, betrayal, and adultery make these stories dramatic and tragic. If the adultery had been Arthur's or Mark's, the story would not have been so remarkable or shocking. Geoffrey Chaucer's *The Canterbury Tales* also includes stories of adulterous women. In the "Merchant's Tale" and the "Miller's Tale," young wives married to older men take lovers, without penalty. Chaucer's stories are not meant as positive representations of these women; rather they show the licentious behavior of women in January-May romances.

The Cely letters document the love affairs the Cely merchant sons enjoyed. While George Cely's family sought a marriage partner for him, George had a series of affairs. One of his lovers, Margery, a cook, had two illegitimate children, both of whom died as infants. John Dalton, the brother of George's potential bride was aware of at least one of these babies, but he did not seem disturbed by George's behavior. His brother Richard Cely had also impregnated a woman.

Adultery and spousal abuse often accompanied one another in the ecclesiastical courts. In 1404 Thomas Tebbe was accused of adultery with Joan, servant of Peter Tebbe, and the court recorded that his affair was the cause of his abuse of his wife (Butler 2007, 100). Adultery could justify homicide for some courts. Robert of Laghscale killed John Doughty with an axe blow to the head when he came home to discover John in bed with Robert's wife. The Yorkshire jury worked in Robert's favor to see John as a trespasser in Robert's home and pardoned Robert for what they saw as justifiable murder (Butler 2007, 105). The church considered the threat of homicide as a way to rid oneself of an unwanted marriage enough of an issue to prohibit adulterers from marrying their lover. This restriction only held if the adulterer and lover both knew of the marriage and if they had promised marriage while the spouse still lived or if there was any inkling that the adulterer had had a role in their spouse's death.

MISTRESSES AND CONCUBINES

Both clerics and laymen might have concubines, women they enjoyed repeated sexual encounters with that we might refer to today as girlfriends, mistresses, or domestic partners. These might be long-term cohabitating relationships without the seal of marriage, either because one partner was already married, the man was a cleric and unable to marry, or because marriage was undesirable. These relationships might lead to marriage or not; they might last for several years. Many elite men had famous relationships with mistresses who comforted them through one or several marriages. Edward III maintained a relationship with Alice Perrers, one of his wife Philippa's ladies-in-waiting, and after Philippa's death, Alice dominated at court, even parading through the city as the "Lady of the Sun." Through Edward's gifts, Alice became fabulously wealthy and even became a patron of Geoffrey Chaucer, perhaps serving as a model for the Wife of Bath. According to reports, she even governed England in the 1370s, making her hated among the aristocracy. Alice was banished but later returned to England.

Another important example, Katharine Swynford was John of Gaunt's mistress and bore him at least four children before she became his third wife. As John was an influential person, the son of King Edward III, his children with Katharine were legitimized by royal letters, enabling them to inherit John's property. While the kings who issued and confirmed these letters did not include the right to assert a claim to the monarchy, the legitimization proved crucial for John and Katharine's great-grandson, Henry Tudor, who became King Henry VII in 1485 by defeating Richard III in battle. Other socially inferior women might not be so lucky as Katharine as to marry their elite lovers, but could instead receive gifts that would provide them with a dowry beyond what they might have anticipated previously. Several men might find that a good dowry compensated well for a sexually experienced bride.

As noted in chapter 1, priests were not permitted to marry. Any sexual domestic partnership between a cleric and a woman was illicit. For medieval priests, celibacy referred to their unmarried state, but clerics were also expected to remain chaste, avoiding sex altogether. As bridegrooms of the church itself, clerics were required to remain pure and unpolluted by sex. Throughout the Middle Ages, the church wrestled with issues of clerical concubinage, priests who engaged in sex and those who became entangled in relationships with women.

As for laymen, these might be caring, long-term relationships that closely resembled a marriage, and might produce children, but were increasingly attacked in the late medieval church. The women in the relationships were blamed as lustful and greedy temptresses who led God's clergy away from the church. Instead, these women lived as partners building domestic lives with homes and children, but without the stability or approval laymen's wives enjoyed.

The church barred clerics from marrying for several reasons. First, the church expected clerics to remain chaste, which was not possible in a marriage, since the priests would owe their wives the marital debt. Priests held a special status in the Middle Ages, and this was compromised by a mundane marital life. Emphasizing this difference between the clergy and the laity helped to establish clerical, sacred authority, which was key to seeing priests as capable of performing the miracle of the mass. Second, the church expected clerics to be devoted to their faith and their parish, not distracted by the responsibilities of a husband and father. Third, the church did not want church property to be compromised by the inheritance claims of priests' children. Despite many times issuing warnings that clerical concubinage was prohibited, the problem persisted. Indeed, in 1492, Rodrigo de Borgia became pope as Alexander VI, despite being well known as the father of four children by a long-term mistress, Vannozza Dei Cattanei. Alexander acknowledged these children openly only after his election as pope; his children then lived in the papal palace with him. Alexander was possibly the father of an additional five children by other women. While Alexander's mistresses and children did not compromise his career in the church, they were used as an example of papal corruption by sixteenth-century reformers.

As part of inspiring clerics to remain celibate, the church encouraged a new ideal of masculinity associated with celibacy: the manly priest. Since the men who became priests were often raised alongside brothers whose secular obligations included marriage and fatherhood as well as military prowess, this was an important shift in thinking. By encouraging clerics to think of themselves as waging war against their own desire and lust, theologians depicted celibacy as a masculine endeavor. This also meant that castration was an "easy way out," removing the desire and struggle that characterized priestly masculinity.

This emphasis on clerical masculinity was also accompanied by a discourse on women as polluting. Women who might have enjoyed some local status as clerical wives were now systematically depicted as concubines and termed "whores." Women lost an opportunity to be comforts and assistants to clerical spouses, as theologians also created literature emphasizing women's dangerous threat to male purity. Such rhetoric of pollution and evil connected to female sexuality played an important role in the persecution of heretics and, later, witches.

Popular depictions of priests suggest that celibacy continued to be a struggle into the late Middle Ages, and sixteenth-century Protestant reformers encouraged priests, monks, and nuns to reject their oaths of chastity and marry instead.

PROSTITUTION

The church courts declared women who were promiscuous "prostitutes," a *meretrix* in the Latin singular, whether or not they accepted money for sex. The medieval social order that divided between chastity and sexual activity did not have a category for women who engaged in sex outside of marriage, except for prostitute. For example, in 1422, a London borough court recorded that "Alice, wife of John Cheyney, and Isabel Cobham on 20 September and on many other occasions committed fornication with two priests and afterwards with various other unknown men, and that they are common whores" (Goldberg 1995, 216). The record does not claim that Alice or Isabel accepted payment for sex, but rather that they had sex with multiple people and that was sufficient to declaring them, in court, "whores."

Laymen considered prostitution a necessary evil, one that protected other women from assault by providing a place for lust. As "common women," prostitutes were available to all men. As a result, it was nearly impossible for a sex worker who was sexually assaulted to seek justice, as her consent was already implicit in her profession. While prostitution had its place and could be legal, and prostitutes were believed to be common to all men, there was an expectation that women accepted this work willingly, that they granted their consent to their employment even if they were not enthusiastic about every encounter. Despite legal and ecclesiastical opprobrium for prostitution, these women were respected authorities on male sexual performance who could appear in court as expert witnesses to verify claims of impotence, as discussed in chapter 1.

Medieval women opted for sex work for a variety of reasons, including higher wages than alternative work and lack of other opportunities. Single mothers especially had few opportunities to support themselves and might turn to prostitution. Sex work might have been a chosen profession or a temporary way to earn money. Movement between prostitution and other types of domestic or service work may have been fluid, especially in towns.

Prostitution was not legal in most of England beyond a few jurisdictions. In Smithfield, in 1382, Cock Lane was zoned for prostitution. The bishop of Winchester permitted legal brothels in Southwark, just outside London, known colloquially as "the stews," but the City of London across the Thames did not. Legal prostitution was tightly regulated, with regulation focused on the women, not their clients. The stews closed when Parliament was in session in London, and solicitation was not permitted on holidays. Beyond the brothel, some women might work on their own or in small groups working in bathhouses, taverns, alehouses, or parts of private homes. Other legal brothels were available in Sandwich and Southampton.

Neighbors remained concerned when their areas were used for illicit prostitution. Emma Hauteyn complained in 1295 that she rented a house from Richard Burdun "for the length of the present fair on condition that Richard should receive no prostitute in his row, but Richard defaulted in this agreement with her and received prostitutes" (Goldberg 1995, 217). Women from the stews were not permitted to travel across the river to practice, and in 1511, the Southampton borough court cited "a wench of the stews for coming into town without her token, 8d." (Goldberg 1995, 218). Over the course of the fifteenth century, some English towns ended legal prostitution, exiling sex workers from their cities, such as from Leicester in 1467: "Also that no brothel be holden within this town, no brothel or bawd dwelling [here], but that the townsperson dwelling nearby report them to the Court. And that they to be exiled at the first warning in pain of imprisonment and fine and ransom to the king" (Bateson 1901, 291).

York had barred accused women from the city in 1301, upon pain of imprisonment and threatened anyone who rented a house to a sex worker with the loss of its rent for a term, and then banned prostitutes from within the city walls again in 1482: "[T]he common women and other misgoverned women shall live in the suburbs outside the walls of this city and not within." A woman named Margery Gray, who went by the name of "Cherrylips" flouted this ruling in 1483, irritating "the whole parish of St Martin in Micklegate" because "she was a woman ill disposed of her body to whom ill disposed men resort to the annoyance of her neighbours" (Goldberg 1995, 213).

Coventry became so suspicious of young singlewomen working illicitly as prostitutes that they barred them from taking rooms: "[N]o singlewoman, being in good health and strong of body to work, under the age of fifty years, take or keep from henceforth houses or rooms to themselves, nor that they take any room with any other person, but that they go into service" (Goldberg 1995, 212). Coventry even imposed fines on those who rented rooms to them.

Regulations prohibited married women from working in a brothel and expelled sex workers who became pregnant, a hazard of their work that likely encouraged them to seek out the assistance of apothecaries for contraception, as discussed in chapter 2. Regulations also protected the women, guaranteeing that their rent could not be raised above fourteen pence per week and that they could not be locked out of their house or room.

There was also less official regulation of sex workers. In 1344 a London jury "found that the beadle [of Farringdon Without] took bribes from disorderly women in his ward to protect them in their practices" (Thomas 1926, 198–223, Membr. 24). Such an arrangement was not legal, and the beadle's personal protection of the women likely amounted to exploitation for his own monetary gain, but it did allow the women to work without legal repercussions, until his arrangement was discovered.

Despite regulation, sex workers did not lack for clients. While men of all status groups, professions, and origins might pay for sex, there were some groups especially noted for their interest in the availability of sex workers. Since journeymen were expected to wait to marry until gaining admission to the guild and opening their own shop, they looked to prostitutes for sexual contact during an extended bachelordom. Priests and other clergy, while expected to remain celibate, were also tempted by the presence of brothels and appear often in the records as clients. Foreign visitors to England also tended to seek out prostitutes.

Women with foreign names were common among those appearing in the courts for prostitution, especially "Doche" women. Foreign women without support, friends, or stable work in London were easy targets for bawds and procurers, as were English women moving from villages to London in the same position. A strong association between foreignness and prostitution may have encouraged more English women to adopt foreign names and dress, to attract clients.

Punishment for prostitution in London involved public shaming and exile. The shaming included a procession through the city, possibly carrying an H for harlot, wearing a striped hood, and carrying a "white rod" that symbolized prostitution. Music performed by minstrels and the banging of pots and pans ensured that crowds turned out to view the procession. Women convicted of prostitution multiple times in the fifteenth century might have their hair cut, a measure intended to make the women look more male and presumably less enticing.

Sumptuary laws defined what sex workers could wear, to ensure that they could be identified and not confused with other women, as discussed in chapter 4. The striped hood used in shaming rituals became a required garment for sex workers in some towns, as in Bristol, where a borough ordinance required that "no prostitute go about town without a striped hood" (Bickley 1900, 229).

The level of punishments imposed suggest that medieval communities found procuring more serious a crime than prostitution itself. Procuresses, or bawds, encouraged women into the profession, arranged for their clients, and took a portion—usually a large portion—of their payments. Bawds might provide housing for their employees and charge them rents. As the regulations (mentioned earlier) stipulated standards about rents and housing, we might assume that bawds were known to raise rents, to lock women out of their rooms, or to deny them access to the house altogether at times. When working for an illegal and unregulated house, these dangers were high. Procuresses did not always disclose the type of work that their employees would be doing, either, as the case of Elizabeth Moring shows.

Elizabeth Moring was brought before the London courts in 1385 for running a brothel. She was accused of enticing women into her brothel by offering them apprenticeships in an embroidery shop, which was in truth her brothel. One of her servants, Johanna, testified against Elizabeth, who claimed that "after so retaining them" as embroidery apprentices, "she incited . . . Johanna and the other women . . . to live a lewd life and to consort with friars, chaplains, and all other such men as desired to have their company, as well as in her own house in the parish of All Hallows near the Wall, in the ward of Broad Street, in London, as elsewhere." The locations are important because they were not zoned for legal prostitution. Johanna also claimed that Elizabeth had compelled her to steal when she had not been paid for her services, taking a portable breviary from a chaplain and giving it to Elizabeth who sold it. The

London borough court declared that Elizabeth was "living thus abominably and damnably, and inciting other women to live in the like manner; she herself being a common harlot and procuress" and that because of her and similar women "many scandals had befallen the said city, and great peril might through such transactions in future arise; therefore, according to the custom of the City of London in such and the like cases provided, and in order that other women might beware of doing the like, it was adjudged that the said Elizabeth should be taken from the Guildhall aforesaid to Cornhulle and put in the *thewe*, there to remain for one hour of the day, the cause thereof being publicly proclaimed. And afterwards, she was to be taken to some Gate of the City, and there to be made to forswear the City, and the liberty therof, to the effect that she would never again enter the same" (Riley 1868, 484–486). This public punishment was meant to caution, as the court said, other women from following Elizabeth's example.

While pregnancy is a logical conclusion to frequent sexual activity, there is some evidence that medieval sex workers had a low pregnancy rate. This was possibly due to sexually transmitted infections or due to the use of contraceptives, important knowledge for members of this craft to share with one another.

There was a great deal of concern among medieval European Christians about who might use the services of Christian sex workers. Jews and Muslim men were barred legally from visiting Christian sex workers in some areas, with capital punishments. This prohibition was not so strict in the other direction: Christian men might visit Jewish or Muslim sex workers. After the expulsion of the Jews from England in 1290, this was less of a concern in this kingdom than in other parts of medieval Europe, such as Spain.

SEXUAL ASSAULT AND DOMESTIC VIOLENCE

The Latin verb *rapere* meant "to seize" and originally described theft, but came to indicate ravishment and sexual assault; it is the antecedent for the word "rape." It was used in legal and historical documents to describe cases of seduction, elopement, abduction, and/or rape. As discussed in chapter 1, it is not always possible to tell from sources describing abductions as *raptus* whether these women were choosing partners for themselves, against their family's wishes, or experiencing trauma. Consensual abduction was a way to start a marriage, or a way to end one, at a time when divorce was not an option. While a modern audience views abduction without consent as a crime and terms abduction with consent "elopement," medieval courts—which included jurisdiction over adultery and fornication—saw them both as crimes.

Nonconsensual abduction and forced marriage of wealthy women or heiresses was a method for men to improve their status and wealth, and it was considered a "theft" against the woman's father or guardian. Sometimes these abductions led to marriages, especially if the abduction lasted long enough to impregnate the woman, and sometimes not. Abduction was also committed for other reasons, as in 1420, William Burton complained to the lord chancellor that a chaplain Lewis Gryville had ravished (abducted) Alice Wodeloke, a seven-year-old girl and taken her to his house at Drayton, in Oxford: "And the said Lewis still detains the same Alice, wrongfully, and against law, right and good conscience, and against the will of the said suppliant; and will not deliver the said Alice to the said suppliant unless he will make fine with the said Lewis for 40 marks and release by his writing to the said Robert [Archer] all the debt which the said Robert owes the same suppliant; wrongfully and to the damage of the said suppliant of 100 marks" (Baildon 1896, 119). Here marriage does not seem to have been the point, but rather a more typical kidnapping intended to yield cash and erase debt.

The 1382 Statute of Rapes introduced the phrase *contra voluntatem*, which indicates a "raptus" that took place "against the will" of the husband or guardian (Hawkes 1995). The inclusion of that phrase in a document can help clarify that this was a case alleging sexual assault, not seduction or elopement. In the 1390 Statute of Pardons, Parliament asked Richard II not to issue general pardons for rape, which suggests that the medieval aristocracy took sexual assault seriously.

In her research, Caroline Dunn has found a large number of "ravishment" or *raptus* cases in late medieval England. As can be seen in table 5.1, while about 40 percent of those cases were too ambiguous, more than half the cases could be clearly identified as abduction and not rape (Dunn 2013, Table 1.1, p. 22). The number of cases that could clearly be identified as rape is not unsubstantial, however, particularly given that such cases historically tend to go unreported.

Women do not seem to have been kidnapped and held for ransom, or to have been kidnapped as heiresses by those hoping to become their guardians or husbands, in significant numbers, although both these forms of kidnapping did happen frequently to men and male

Table 5.1 *Raptus* Cases in Late Medieval England

	Abduction	Rape	Ambiguous	Both
Fourteenth century	407	47	318	4
Fifteenth century	96	30	88	3
Total	503	77	406	7
Percentage of cases	**50.6**	**7.8**	**40.9**	**0.7**

wards. Women were accused of kidnapping other women, but these appear to be cases of a friend helping a woman flee her husband or of a mother taking guardianship over her daughter. Alexis Foyllet was accused of *rapuit et abduxit* her children Amalia and Christiana in 1301, and here the words indicate that she seized the girls (Dunn 2013, 21).

To prosecute an abduction in the royal courts required a writ, a document created by the royal chancery for a fee. Scribes recording the writ required the abductor's name and that of the person he had abducted, typically the complaining person's wife, daughter, or ward; writs used the formula *rapuit et abduxit*, or "seized and abducted," to describe the complaint (Dunn 2013, 5). Such documents flatten a wide variety of experiences as well as remove the emotion and the trauma women experienced, both by using the formulaic language of bureaucracy, but also by translating their language through a male plaintiff and male scribe. Notions of conception complicated the prosecution of rape when the alleged victim became pregnant. As discussed in chapter 2, the "two-seed" notion of conception common in medieval England was that a woman must experience pleasure during the sexual act to release a seed; otherwise conception would not take place. This idea suggested that a woman who became pregnant through assault had to have consented to her attacker or else she could not have released her seed. Sexual offenses in the late Middle Ages could appear in the royal courts, with jurisdiction over property and crime, or the church courts, which had jurisdiction over marriage and sin. While wives could normally not enact lawsuits independently from their husbands, they were permitted to sue for their own assault.

Status, wealth, and power factored into sexual assault. While manorial lords did not have the legal right to their bondwomen's bodies or to claim sexual rights on their wedding nights, these men's positions enabled them to coerce sexual encounters and relationships that were not sanctioned legally. Bondwomen, maidservants, and other low-status women endured sexual assault by coercion and had little legal recourse. In fact, some of these women were charged the leyrwite fine for their assaults. Some of the records of these fines open the possibility that the women were not willing participants in their fornication, as for Agnes Hulle, who was charged in 1301 when she *"violata est,"* a phrase that most easily translates to "was violated" but can more powerfully be rendered "was dishonored," "was defiled," or "was transgressed against" (Bennett 2003, 150).

Women of status as well as peasant women experienced *raptus*. Alice de Lacy, married to Thomas, Earl of Lancaster, cousin to King Edward II, was abducted twice, once during her husband's life and once after his death. And Theobald de Verdun was accused of abducting Elizabeth de Burgh, lady of Clare, from Bristol Castle, but he claimed they were betrothed and that she came with him willingly. They were married in 1316, and she honored him with requiem masses as she did her other two husbands, so it is possible this was an elopement and not an abduction (Ward 2014, 30).

Famous male authors including Geoffrey Chaucer and Thomas Malory were accused of ravishment. As noted earlier, Cecily Chaumpaigne released Geoffrey Chaucer from a charge of *raptus* in 1380, and historians have turned to Chaucer's writing to understand this incident. Chaucer's work includes a number of examples of assault or seduction. In the "Miller's Tale," part of *The Canterbury Tales*, two men whom a carpenter cheated punish him by ravishing his wife and daughter. While Chaucer depicts the women enjoying the encounter, he does not describe them desiring or consenting, as consent is besides Chaucer's point. The men's actions were intended to shame the carpenter and provide consequences for his false dealing: at the end of the "Miller's Tale," everyone was laughing: "Thus screwed was this carpenter's wife" (Benson 2008).

In another notorious case, Thomas Malory, author of the Arthurian epic the *Morte D'Arthur*, was accused of raping the wife of Hugh Smyth by breaking into their house in Monks Kirby in 1450, and then of assaulting her again later in Coventry. Malory was also accused of a string of violent robberies for which he was convicted in 1451 and sent to prison and was later pardoned by Edward IV. Malory depicted chivalrous knights who promised to protect women from rape in the *Morte D'Arthur*, which is difficult to square with his other activities, although some have argued that Malory was acting politically and targeting political opponents.

HOMOSEXUALITY

Two aspects of women's lives difficult to find in medieval English sources are homosocial relationships and same-sex desire. As we have seen in previous chapters, because records were mostly written by men or focused on their actions, female networks, female friendships, female-only spaces, and female sexual partnerships either do not appear in historical records or are sketchily reported. Male authors seem to have lacked interest in women's relationships, laws against female homosexual activity were not much enforced, and women did not write much about these aspects of their lives. There are brief examples of friendships in literature, such as Constance's conversion of Hermengild in Chaucer's "Man of Law's Tale," or Alison's friendship with her gossiping friend in the "Wife of Bath's" prologue. We also see extensive communication between women in the Paston letters, as Margaret planned for her children's weddings and alliances with similar families. But for the most part, we know little about relationships between women, even in all-female spaces such as the monastery.

This lacuna is frustrating for telling the history of female friendships, as well as of women's sexual lives without men. In contrast, we know a great deal about men's friendships, such as the contentious friendship between Thomas Becket and Henry II, or the explosive friendship between Edward III and Piers Gaveston. There is evidence of women loving other women, but distinguishing between friendly, romantic, and erotic love is a challenge—and scholars would like to know more about all three aspects of women's lives. This is not to say that there are *no* sources about women's relationships with other women; scholars must read those sources we have in new and creative ways. For example, two women's names are listed together in a fifteenth-century memorial brass in a Sussex parish church, Elizabeth Etchingham and Agnes Oxenbridge. The brass image shows the two women facing one another, names each set of parents, and shows that they died eighteen years apart, Elizabeth in 1452 and Agnes in 1480. Neither has a husband listed, but the brass is done in the style for married couples, with Elizabeth in the husband's usual position. Might this brass honor two women in a lesbian relationship? If so, it had to have the approval of both women's families, to be installed after their deaths and in Elizabeth's family's church.

Medieval women faced criticism for trouble associated with their tongues: scolding, nagging, and gossiping. The last is an important demonstration about women's active friendships, although one that led to spiritual danger so venomous that the *Ancrene Wisse* (see chapter 6) warned anchorites to "keep your ears far from all evil speech. . . . It is said of anchoresses that almost every one of them has some old woman to feed her ears, a gossip who tells her all the local tidbits, a magpie who cackles about all that she sees and hears," certainly a misogynist depiction of a friendly, happy older woman who brings local news to a woman unable to visit neighbors on her own (Savage and Watson 1991, 81). Margery Kempe recalled a visit she made to the anchoress Julian of Norwich, not to gossip, but for spiritual connection and fellowship. While these cautions were meant to condemn women's gossip, we might instead read them as demonstrations of women's friendship and conversation.

Margery Kempe described a number of her interactions with other women, some of them less friendly than her time with Julian, especially when her companions on a pilgrimage found her tears exhausting and abandoned her, but she was able to build a new friendship with Margaret Florentyne on the way to Rome. Christine de Pisan, an Italian author living in France whose *The Book of the City of Ladies* was popular throughout medieval Europe, described a community of excellent women, the "New Kingdom of Femininity," where virtue guides women in their actions and in their relationships with others.

Seeing these friendships among medieval women still leaves open the question of same-sex romantic and erotic relationships. Technically, church penitentials considered any sexual activity between women sodomy, a catch-all term for most sexual activity beyond procreative heterosexual penetrative sex. In the Penitential of Bede, there are penalties listed for women fornicating with each other and for nuns fornicating with each other using instruments, presumably a dildo. The *Ancrene Wisse* warned anchorites against both masturbation and sex with other anchoresses. Yet, there are some medical treatises that suggested a midwife could digitally stimulate an unmarried woman who was troubled by unreleased seed. While there are court cases about same-sex male sexual relationships, since sex between women did not threaten social order, property, or reproduction, the courts ignored encounters between women unless there was a phallic tool involved. Because authors were reluctant to name sodomy for fear of corrupting and enticing innocent readers, they referenced these acts as those that cannot be named.

Judith Bennett and other scholars have cautioned scholars not to require evidence of sexual activity in order to perceive homosocial relationships as evidence of same-sex desire, since that evidence is not required for perceiving heterosexual desire in male-female encounters. Bennett suggests that historians use the category of "lesbian-like" in order to see "women whose lives might have particularly offered opportunities for same-sex love; women who resisted norms of feminine behavior based on heterosexual marriage; women who lived in circumstances that allowed them to nurture and support other women" (Bennett 2000, 10–11). There are a range of "lesbian-like" activities we can perceive in sources about women, and we might instead consider what we can learn about women's lives by opening definitions in this way.

As an example, Bennett and Shannon McSheffrey discussed the case of Thomasina in the 1493 Commissary Court in London. She was accused of keeping a cross-dressing concubine in her room. The text is clear that Thomasina was a woman and that the person in her room was a woman dressed in male clothing and a concubine. Less clear is whether this was Thomasina's concubine or a concubine Thomasina sheltered, whether the two were women in a relationship using male clothing to hide their activity, whether the concubine was a trans woman, whether Thomasina was a pimp and the concubine in her employment. The court asked Thomasina to provide three witnesses to testify to her character and then dismissed the case. While it is tempting to perceive Thomasina and the concubine as possible lesbians, the available evidence leaves us more confidently in the category of lesbian-like.

Through the lenses Bennett and Lochrie suggest, the association of women's chatter with lust might be read in another way, of associating women's homosocial fellowship with homosexual activity. While there are no sexual acts involved, this is an area where women's gossip, as a promiscuous, luxurious indulgence between women exercising their tongues, is an act of resistance of feminine norms. Chaucer similarly portrays the Wife of Bath in *The Canterbury Tales* as enjoying gossip with a close friend who "knew my heart" and with whom she gossiped about her own sexual affair with a man. The Wife of Bath's friendship focuses on gossip about sexual impropriety.

One important concern is that medieval authors also did not seem to have a clear notion of a "lesbian." Instead, they imagined that sexual activity between two women must involve a sex tool such as a dildo. Nonpenetrative sex does not seem to have registered as a potential activity for women alone.

CROSS-DRESSING

There are many examples of women dressing as men, or "cross-dressing" throughout the Middle Ages. There were biblical prohibitions against cross-dressing: "A woman shall not wear anything that pertains to a man, nor shall a man put on a woman's garment; for whoever does these things is an abomination to the Lord your God" (Deuteronomy 22:5). Yet, medieval literature, hagiography, histories, and court records report examples of men and women cross-dressing for a variety of purposes. The chronicler Henry Knighton even complained that some women attended the tournaments of Edward III in male clothing, which is reminiscent of the modern Iranian women who dressed as men to attend a soccer match in Tehran, where female attendance is not permitted.

While medieval authorities did not appreciate cross-dressing that was a disguise to facilitate sin or grab for power, such as prostitution, they objected less to women who cross-dressed in order to pursue spiritual devotion, academic learning, and military careers. For medieval women, cross-dressing could be transformational, intended to make a woman more male and thereby "more perfectly human" (Bennett and McSheffrey 2014, 5). Role inversion was also a common feature of certain medieval celebrations, such as Christmas, May Day, and Shrovetide; sometimes these inversions were based on social status, but gender play was also frequent in festivals and parodies, although these tended to be male-to-female inversions. Reaching toward maleness or becoming male was a common theme for women in saints' lives and medieval literature, and this motivation for cross-dressing could be tolerated, to a point.

Early Christian saints occasionally dressed as men to avoid marriage and pursue a holy life. In the *Golden Legend*, a collection of saints' lives from the thirteenth century that circulated widely across Europe, there are several examples of female saints who dressed as men. Saints Marina and Margaret wore male clothing to join a monastery, were then accused of impregnating a woman, and suffered the consequences of that accusation rather than reveal that they were female, only to be discovered as women at their deaths. These are examples of the utility of Bennett's "lesbian-like" model: while the texts do not portray these women in a way we might say matches our normal notion of a lesbian, these women are acting outside the norms of medieval society in ways that create opportunities for homosocial and homosexual connection that were "lesbian-like."

A similar story was told about a fictional Pope Joan, who supposedly served as pope in the ninth century after passing as a man and rising through the ecclesiastical ranks to become pope. This legendary story also claims that popes were later required to sit on a chair with no seat in order to have their genitals confirmed; no such ritual existed, but its circulation demonstrates medieval anxiety about women passing as men and taking male offices.

Cross-dressing is frequently referenced in medieval literature and occasionally becomes an opportunity to express same-sex desire or even for same-sex acts to occur. In John Gower's (1408) "The Tale of Iphis," two girls, Iphis and Ianthe, shared a bed while Iphis was disguised as a boy, and they became playmates at night, exploration that Gower described as "no offense to nature" (Lochrie 2001, 82).

Women cross-dressing as men came to the attention of the late medieval courts in London, typically as a morality concern. Most of the cases found by Judith Bennett and Shannon McSheffrey suspected the accused of sexual misdeeds, of being concubines or sex workers, and using men's clothing to be in places or gain access they should not (Bennett and McSheffrey 2014, 2). Beyond wearing men's clothing, including hats to hide their hair, some of these women cut their hair. Most of the medieval women in Bennett and McSheffrey's sample did not live as men long term, except Alice Street who cross-dressed as a way to remain with her lover, a priest. Nor did these women truly pass as men, but were recognized as women in men's clothing. Indeed, some of the appeal of women dressed as men was the transgressive eroticism of the act, not intended as a successful disguise. The cross-dressing concerned the courts, but not as much as prostitution. Punishment imposed by the courts for cross-dressing included public shaming and exile, typical consequences for prostitution and procuring.

The courts also targeted male-to-female cross-dressing and similarly used prostitution charges. Eleanor Rykener, later identified as "John Rykener," was arrested in December 1394 for engaging in sex with a man in Cheapside, London, while dressed as a woman and performing a "detestable, unmentionable, and ignominious vice" (Boyd and Karras 1995, 482). Under questioning, Rykener admitted to working as a prostitute both as a man and as a woman. Rykener traveled around England, including to Oxford and Burford, pursuing encounters with both men and women, sometimes dressed as a man, sometimes as a woman. It is possible to understand Rykener as a trans woman, especially since she claimed to have spent time living and working as a woman embroideress in Oxford.

The most famous cross-dressing woman in the late medieval period was the French peasant girl Joan of Arc, who claimed she heard saints' voices. She convinced the prince of France to give her an army to fight against the English during the Hundred Years War. Joan wore her hair short like a man, wore male clothing including armor, and carried weapons. Due in part to her success, that prince was crowned King Charles VII, but he showed her little gratitude when Joan was captured and put on trial for heresy. The trial record against Joan is quite long and contains depositions from Joan herself. One area of concern for her interrogators was Joan's insistence on wearing male clothing, which troubled them immensely. Joan was forced to wear women's clothing, which upset her, and she returned to wearing men's clothing. This was seen as a relapse into heresy by her examiners. Joan was eventually convicted and burned to death for heresy in May 1431, at age nineteen. Charles later cleared her of the charge, working with Pope Calixtus III who declared Joan a martyr; in 1920 Joan became a saint and is considered a patron saint of France.

FOR FURTHER READING

Baildon, William Paley, ed. 1896. *Select Cases in Chancery: A. D. 1364 to 1471*. London: Bernard Quaritch.

Bateson, Mary, ed. 1901. *Records of the Borough of Leicester: Being a Series of Extracts from the Archives of the Corporation of Leicester*. Vol. 2. London: C. J. Clay. HathiTrust.

Bennett, Judith M. 2000. "'Lesbian-Like' and the Social History of Lesbianisms." *Journal of the History of Sexuality* 9: 1–24.

Bennett, Judith M. 2003. "Writing Fornication: Medieval Leyrwite and Its Historians: *The Prothero Lecture*." *Transactions of the Royal Historical Society* 13: 131–162.

Bennett, Judith M. 2011. "Remembering Elizabeth Etchingham and Agnes Oxenbridge." In *The Lesbian Premodern*, edited by Noreen Giffney, Michelle M. Sauer, and Diane Watt. London: Palgrave Macmillan.

Bennett, Judith M., and Shannon McSheffrey. 2014. "Early, Erotic and Alien: Women Dressed as Men in Late Medieval London." *History Workshop Journal* 77 (Spring): 1–25.

Benson, Larry D., ed. 2008. *The Riverside Chaucer*. Oxford: Oxford University Press.

Bickley, Francis B. 1900. *The Little Red Book of Bristol*. Bristol: W. C. Hemmons.

Bogage, Jacob. 2018. "Banned from Men's Soccer Matches in Iran, These Women Dressed as Men to Sneak In." *Washington Post*, May 2.

Boureau, Alain. 1998. *The Lord's First Night: The Myth of the Droit de Cuissage*. Chicago: University of Chicago Press.

Boyd, David Lorenzo, and Ruth Mazo Karras. 1995. "The Interrogation of a Male Transvestite Prostitute in Fourteenth-Century London." *GLQ* 1, no. 4: 459–465.

Brozyna, Martha A., ed. 2005. *Gender and Sexuality in the Middle Ages: A Medieval Source Documents Reader*. Jefferson, NC: McFarland.

Butler, Sara M. 2007. *The Language of Abuse: Marital Violence in Later Medieval England*. Leiden: Brill.

Cadden, Joan. 1993. *Meanings of Sex Difference in the Middle Ages: Medicine, Science, and Culture*. Cambridge: Cambridge University Press.

Dunn, Caroline. 2013. *Stolen Women in Medieval England: Rape, Abduction, and Adultery, 1100–1500*. Cambridge: Cambridge University Press.

Furnivall, Frederick James. 1908. "How the Good Wife Taught Her Daughter." In *The Babees' Book: Medieval Manners for the Young: Done into Modern English*, edited by Edith Rickert. London: Duffield & Co. Project Gutenberg.

Giffney, Noreen, Michelle M. Sauer, and Diane Watt, eds. 2011.*The Lesbian Premodern*. New York: Palgrave Macmillan.

Goldberg, P. J. P. 1995. *Women in England c. 1275–1525: Documentary Sources*. Manchester: Manchester University Press.

Green, Monica H., ed. and trans. 2001. *The Trotula: A Medieval Compendium of Women's Medicine*. Philadelphia: University of Pennsylvania Press.

Greene, Richard Leighton. 1977. *The Early English Carols*. 2nd ed. Oxford: Oxford University Press.

Hasted, Elise Bennett. 2004. "Medieval Rape: A Conceivable Defense?" *Cambridge Law Journal* 63: 743–769.

Hawkes, Emma. 1995. "'She Was Ravished against Her Will, What so Ever She Say': Female Consent in Rape and Ravishment in Late Medieval England." *Limina* I: 47–54.

Helmholz, Richard H. 1974. *Marriage Litigation in Medieval England*. Cambridge: Cambridge University Press.

Karras, Ruth Mazo. 2005. *Sexuality in Medieval Europe: Doing unto Others*. New York: Routledge.

Lochrie, Karma. 2001. "Presidential Improprieties and Medieval Categories: The Absurdity of Heterosexuality." In *Queering the Middle Ages*, edited by Glenn Burger and Steven F. Kruger, 87–96. Minneapolis: University of Minnesota Press.

Lochrie, Karma. 2003. "Between Women." In *The Cambridge Companion to Medieval Women's Writing*, edited by Carolyn Dinshaw and David Wallace, 70–88. Cambridge: Cambridge University Press.

Murray, Jacqueline. 1996. "Twice Marginal and Twice Invisible: Lesbians in the Middle Ages." In *Handbook of Medieval Sexuality*, edited by Vern L. Bullough and James A. Brundage. New York: Garland.

Riley, Henry Thomas. 1868. *Memorials of London and London Life, in the XIIth, XIVth, and XVth Centuries: Being a Series of Extracts, Local,*

Social, and Political, from the Early Archives of the City of London, A.D. 1276–1419*. London: Longmans, Green, and Co. HathiTrust.

Savage, Anne, and Nicholas Watson, trans. 1991. *Anchoritic Spirituality: "Ancrene Wisse" and Associated Works*. New York: Pauli's Press.

Thibodeaux, Jennifer D. 2015. *The Manly Priest: Clerical Celibacy, Masculinity, and Reform in England and Normandy, 1066–1300*. Philadelphia: University of Pennsylvania Press.

Thomas, A. H. 1926. *Calendar of the Plea and Memoranda Rolls of the City of London: Volume 1, 1323–1364*. London: His Majesty's Stationery Office. British History Online. https://www.british-history.ac.uk /plea-memoranda-rolls/vol1.

Ward, Jennifer. 2006. *Women in England in the Middle Ages*. New York: Hambledon Continuum.

Ward, Jennifer, ed. 2014. *Elizabeth de Burgh, Lady of Clare (1295–1360): Household and Other Records*. Woodbridge: Boydell Press.

Wogan-Brown, Jocelyn. 2001. *Saints' Lives and Women's Literary Culture c. 1150–1300: Virginity and Its Authorizations*. Oxford: Oxford University Press.

6

RELIGION

The later Middle Ages were a time of deep devotion and spirituality, with women's connections to the church and their faith taking
a central role in many of the period's religious movements. There
were increasing demands on the church in this time, demonstrations of great faith, and donations in support of grand religious
buildings and art. Beguines, anchorites, and tertiaries demanded
more and greater avenues to devote their lives to God and charity
and were often quite visible in their devotion, serving as inspirations to others. While there are examples of disagreements about
religious practice and belief, as well as examples of people who
were not enthusiastic in their devotions, there is no serious evidence
of atheism or even the capacity for atheism. Belief was woven into
the fabric of medieval life, from the way people measured time to
the way they birthed, married, and died.

Medieval Christianity was mediated through the clergy, who
were necessary to access the seven sacraments. Most Christians
were members of a parish, the smallest unit of church jurisdiction, with a church they attended regularly and clergy they knew
quite well. Priests were expected to celebrate mass at least weekly
and on the many holidays mentioned in chapter 4. The priest was
obscured from the laity during the mass by the rood screen, and
he said the words in Latin, a language not well known among the
laity by the fourteenth century. During the mass the priest expected

the attention of the congregation and to participate in the saying of the Lord's Prayer and the Nicene Creed, as well as responses for the collects. Priests delivered at least four sermons a year. Since the Fourth Lateran Council in 1215, transubstantiation was the official doctrine of the church, the belief that the bread and wine literally transformed into the body and blood of Christ. Most Christians did not take communion more than once a year, but that might have increased toward the end of the fifteenth century. The kiss of peace was given to the pax, a material object usually highly decorated, that the priest kissed and then passed around to the community so that they all might kiss it in turn.

Parish priests frequently complained that women spent their time at church services in conversation, gossiping with their fellow parishioners. The story of Tutivillus, a demon who injured himself trying to stretch out a parchment on which he was writing down women's conversations, was meant to shame the congregants into attention through humor. Similarly in "How the Good Wife Taught Her Daughter," the wife reminded her daughter that she should spend her time in church praying and not talking to friends or laughing at the people there (Furnivall 1908). She warned her to be "of good tongue," which fits with a larger pattern of associating women's failings with their tongue: gossiping, nagging, scolding, lying.

The clergy were also responsible for the religious education of the people in their parish, especially ensuring that they understood the sacraments, the Ten Commandments, the creed. Mothers taught these ideas to their children as well, but it was the clergy's responsibility if their parish became an outpost for heretical belief and practice.

In between weekly church services, Christian women prayed at home, using rosaries, images of saints, or even relics they owned privately and kept in reliquary statues or amulets. Literate women of means might have devotional books at home, especially collections of saints' lives, books of hours, or psalters. Margery Kempe could not read, but she was familiar with a range of religious texts. And while the "Wife of Bath" was written by a man, Chaucer thought his audience would find it plausible that such a woman would know Scripture and the writings of church fathers.

In order to support the church, all Christians were required to tithe, giving a tenth of their income to the church, typically in kind rather than in cash. In "How the Good Wife Taught Her Daughter," the wife advised her daughter to give her tithes "gladly"

(Furnivall 1908). Christians also paid oblations for church services, such as a "donation" for performing a baptism, marriage, or funeral. In accounts from Hornsea in 1482–1483, a parish priest received four pence for performing a wedding, six pence for his services at a funeral, and one and a half pence for a woman's churching (Heath 1964). In a rural community, the parish church also included a glebe, lands the parish set aside for the priest, and he worked this land himself in many places. Many parishes also required a mortuary payment: when a person died, their estate owed a payment to the priest, such as the second-best animal owned by that person.

The seven sacraments—baptism, Eucharist, confirmation, penance, marriage, ordination, extreme unction—provided opportunities for Christians to ritually mark their membership in the Christian community and demonstrate their devotion to God. Baptism, confirmation, and ordination were meant to take place only once, while marriage might be repeated in the case of death of one's partner. Extreme unction, or anointing of the sick, prepared the soul for death, usually at a time of sickness, and was meant to bring peace and comfort, particularly if accompanied by confession. Medieval Christians typically confessed and performed penance only once a year at Easter, but the penitential manuals written to guide priests in assigning penalties for various sins are a trove of evidence about the issues that concerned medieval people and their relative spiritual weight.

With the exception of baptism, which in extreme circumstances could be performed for a newborn by a midwife, the sacraments required the participation of ordained clergy, all of whom were male in medieval Christendom. By the fourteenth century, the Christian church in Western Europe was strictly hierarchical, with the pope, the title that recognized the bishop of Rome as the leader of the church, at the head of the organization. The pope was elected by and from a college of cardinals, who helped him oversee a network of archbishops, bishops, priests, and deacons. England held two archbishoprics, in Canterbury and York, which oversaw England's bishops, most based in major cities such as London, Lincoln, Norwich, and so on. A bishop's seat and the church that held it were known as his cathedral, and there were impressive Gothic cathedrals built during this period. Bishops supervised a large number of parish priests whose churches served the local populations in both rural and urban settings. Priests performed the sacraments, observed holy days, and delivered regular sermons. Although medieval Christians typically received communion and made confession once a year, they attended services much more frequently, engaging with their community through Christian fellowship and celebrations on an active calendar.

Women could not be ordained or become priests, and priests were not permitted to marry—although clerical concubinage was a significant problem as discussed in chapter 5. If women wanted to devote their lives to religion, their main option was to join a monastery, although some women found ways to make oaths outside of the monastery, as discussed later. Other laywomen remained active and important members of the church community even if they did not have roles in the structure of church offices. Women's prayers were understood to be particularly efficacious for the Christian community, and secular leaders deployed their wives' faith and Christian charity as companion to their strength (see chapter 3).

Noblewomen might have more direct authority over some parish churches. Since many aristocrats in England had founded churches on their manors or in other areas, there was a strong tradition of proprietary churches, in which the founder's family continued to control the advowson—the privilege to appoint the priest—of churches on their manors or those their families had built. Efforts to keep the laity out of church affairs had defined the conflicts of the eleventh and twelfth centuries' reform movement, the one that came to a head in England with the exile and then death of archbishop of Canterbury Thomas Becket, whose shrine was a major pilgrimage destination by the thirteenth century. And yet the advowson remained a privilege exercised by English families. Appointing the parish priest gave a layperson continuing authority over him. The appointed priest was known as the rector, but if the rector could not perform the job directly, as was the case when rectors had multiple appointments, a vicar could be appointed to do the more day-to-day duties of the priest in the parish, for a small portion of the rector's income. As a result, the vicars responsible for caring for the parish might be quite humble while more prestigious men in the church could collect more income and perform less work.

There were many holy women important to the Christian community, such as the Virgin Mary, Saint Margaret of Antioch, Saint Dorothy, and many others, even as there were female sinners, such as Eve, some authors drew on to condemn women's actions. Sermons might use biblical women such as Ruth and Martha to inspire women to good behavior, as Christine de Pisan's writings did.

CHARITY

Charity was a religious expectation of all Christians, one of the works of mercy listed in Matthew 25:35–37: to feed the hungry, give drink to the thirsty, give hospitality to strangers, clothe the naked, care for the sick, visit prisoners. Charity was especially bound up with ideas about proper femininity. Wills typically included some sort of charitable giving, whether to the poor, to servants, to a religious institution, or to the sick. Married women could not write wills of their own, generally, but they did also give to these same groups of people during their lives. They performed charity in order to help these people, but Christians also expected a return on their charitable investments: recipients of charity were obliged to pray for the souls of the benefactors. The prayers of some recipients were better than others, which encouraged people to give especially well to the poor (especially poor children and widows), to nuns, and to the seriously ill, such as people with leprosy. Medieval society was also clear that some people were not worthy of charity, such as fornicators, prostitutes, and single mothers.

Gifts to the poor and hungry were common, and strangers could find food at the gates of any monastery, hospital, or noble house. People of all stations gave to the poor in their wills, sometimes by giving to a hospital or almshouse or to particular recipients, sometimes setting an amount to be given randomly by the executors of the will. Some women received the poor and needy into their homes, feeding them and clothing them until they could go back into the world. In the 1350s Elizabeth de Burgh gave to the poor on Maundy Thursday, on the anniversary of her husband's death, and in her will. Gifts to a religious house could be distributed to the poor by an almoner, an officer whose responsibility focused on distributing alms.

Hospitals and almshouses were foundations intended to care for the poor, not as general health centers, since most people who could afford a physician or other medical worker would pay for their services at home or in a workshop. Hospitals were frequently religious institutions staffed by religious men and women. The hospital at St. Leonard's in York was England's largest and staffed by Augustinian canons and canonesses. It may have held as many as two hundred patients, with enough children that it had a nursery that required a supply of cow milk. A similar but smaller institution was Norwich's St. Giles' hospital. The hospital of St. Bartholomew's in London offered care to pregnant women and new

Boy received into a monastery, from Gratian's Decretum, British Library, Royal ms 10 D VIII, f. 82v. (The British Library)

mothers and took care of children whose mothers did not survive childbirth. The Augustinian canons attached to the hospitals were not paid for their work there, and other women might devote their time to caring for the patients as charitable work. Over the fourteenth century, the canons and canonesses might have taken less direct responsibility of caring for the patients, leaving this work to lay sisters or servants.

In the twelfth and thirteenth centuries, many Christians also founded leprosaria, hospitals specifically designated for the care of patients with leprosy. While people were concerned about leprosy in medieval England, they did not react to the disease with fear and horror as modern people have been led to believe by Victorian historians. Many believed that leprous people provided an opportunity for charity and devotion, as demonstrated in the many stories about Christ disguising himself as a leprous man and revealing himself only after receiving charity from the person he was testing.

St. Catherine of Siena and the Beggar is a 1460 panel from an altarpiece by Giovanni di Paolo, an Italian artist. A Dominican tertiary, Catherine gained a reputation for charity and service toward the poor and ill that served as an inspiration for Christians. (Gift of the John Huntington Art and Polytechnic Trust, The Cleveland Museum of Art)

Leprosaria appeared throughout England, but a notable house was St. Nicholas of York, a twelfth-century foundation whose residents by the fourteenth century were all women.

Hospitals were funded primarily by donations, and medieval Christians were generous toward these institutions, believing their gifts were good works and that the prayers the recipients offered would be efficacious for their salvation. Some donation charters even specified that prayers should be said for members of the donors' families.

In addition to tithing, Christians also donated to the church. Donations funded decoration programs as well as repairs, alms, and maintenance. Many Christians gave household or personal items, such as girdles for statues of the saints or churching dresses that could be repurposed as altar cloths and priestly vestments. Philippa of Hainault donated her purple velvet churching dress to Ely Cathedral after the birth of her first son in 1330. Those with land or estates or houses sometimes willed those to a church or monastery or hospital, which could then use the rents or produce as support. Sometimes the donor's children challenged those bequests, so the bequest was even better if it had the heir's approval in advance; otherwise, defending the bequest could be costly for the recipient. Another lucrative source of donation for churches and male monasteries was the chantry. A donor could attach funds or property to fund a chantry, paying a priest to say masses for the souls of the dead on a regular basis, daily, weekly, monthly, or annually. Some chantry endowments covered a period of time, such as five to twenty years, but many were "in perpetuity." Female monasteries received these donations as well, but chantries could become expensive for a female abbey, because women had to pay a priest to perform the mass, which could quickly cost more than the donation. Even poor women donated to the church, especially toward the saints. They might leave coins or fund candles burned in a saint's shrine.

LAY DEVOTION

Most Christians attended a parish church for regular church services, although wealthy families might have a private chapel in their homes. Christian jurisdictions were divided into dioceses, large units overseen by a bishop, and within the diocese into parishes, smaller units that could be served by a church and a priest with his assistants. Most churches had a main altar at which the holy offices were celebrated at set times through the day: matins, lauds, prime, terce, sext, none, vespers, and compline. The priest would perform these offices with a parish clerk who could say the responses, largely based on the psalter, or the collection of psalms from the Old Testament. The priest would also perform a daily mass at the high altar, and laymen might attend once a week or even more frequently depending on local custom and personal devotion. Larger churches might have other altars where additional masses might be performed for funerals, marriage, baptisms, or memorials, often by a chaplain rather than by the parish priest.

The faith of the parish was especially visible during a crisis. Christians turned to their faith for an explanation of the Black Death, and many believed that the plague was a punishment from God. In response, many communities rang church bells as a way of showing their devotion. Others held processions. The Flagellants were a group that traveled around Europe performing penance publicly as a way of atoning for sins and hoping to appease God. The Flagellants walked in procession wearing loincloths and carrying whips and crucifixes. They sang hymns and whipped themselves as their penance. The Flagellants were also known for vicious preaching, especially against Jewish communities they blamed for the plague. They became barred by many European communities who tried to discourage the violence their processions encouraged.

A life devoted to religion offered women almost their only opportunity to abstain from sex, marriage, and motherhood, an abstention that was desirable to some medieval women. Nuns were the most visible category of female virgins, but this was an increasingly high-status group. In the late Middle Ages, women sought other opportunities for a chaste life devoted to God by becoming beguines, tertiaries, vowesses, or anchoresses, all of which involved oaths of celibacy.

A personal description of life of a devoted, wealthy, but common, woman is fortunately available to us, a rarity in the medieval world. As detailed in her personal account, *The Book of Margery Kempe*, dictated by her to a scribe, Margery Kempe (c. 1373–c. 1438) was a married woman in Norfolk who devoted herself to religion and journeyed around England on pilgrimage, eventually going all the way to the Holy Land. Margery dictated her book to various men who wrote her words in the vernacular she used, calling herself "this creature" and describing her experience of a late medieval woman attempting to live a holy life. Her book is the earliest English autobiography we have today.

Margery lived in East Anglia, the daughter of the mayor of King's Lynn, and married about age twenty to John Kempe. Margery describes a vision of Christ that comforted her as a new mother after a difficult pregnancy and set her on a path toward a life devoted to God. Thereafter, Margery attempted to live in chastity with her husband—who long resisted giving up his claim to the marital debt but eventually agreed after they had fourteen children. He was persuaded to agree to Margery's request for a chaste marriage if she agreed to resume their meals together and if she would pay his debts. Margery then wore white, the color of virginity, which provoked criticism because of her many children. At this point her visions increased.

Margery's book describes a passionate devotion to God, filled with sobbing tears that upset her family, neighbors, and even caused some of her fellow pilgrims to abandon her en route to Rome. She took time to visit the anchoress Julian of Norwich, who agreed that Margery's experience of visions and connection to God were real. The focus on visions, on predictions of the future, and some miracles suggest that Margery and her amanuenses, the men who wrote down her words, considered her a candidate for sainthood and attempted to position her for that consideration. Much of the book focuses on Margery's challenging encounters with notable clerics, some of whom suspected her of the Lollard heresy; some dismissed her altogether, while others considered her a holy woman. Her extravagant piety, especially her wails and tears, earned her notoriety in medieval English devotional circles, to the point that one man even refused to let her attend his sermons.

As we have seen above, canon law guided a large part of a medieval woman's life, especially shaping her marital and sexual life. Medieval society in about the fourteenth century began to develop a new moral code that had important implications for the lives of women. Communities began to prosecute those who did not demonstrate personal responsibility, such as drunkards, gossips, scolds, vagrants, and gamblers. Sexual crimes, typically the jurisdiction of the church, came to increased attention of local secular leaders who took direct action, breaking into homes at night, to police fornication and adultery. The church had a variety of punishments available to inspire proper Christian behavior. Excommunication separated an individual from church services and prohibited other Christians from associating with an excommunicate. An interdict imposed a similar separation on a community. Priests had wide latitude to impose penance, although penitentials guided the clergy on the types of sin and recommended penance. Penance might include orders to pray, go on pilgrimage, fast, or involve punishments such as public shaming or flogging.

Christians continued to hold onto pagan practices and beliefs in small ways that most laypeople did not think was out of keeping with their Christian faith, even if church inquisitors disagreed. They believed that fairies existed in the deep woods, that talismans and amulets could heal and protect them, and that spells or prayers at old shrines could help them. Some Christian shrines and churches were explicitly dedicated on the sites of these older pagan holy spaces to direct this energy toward the church. Some places, such as

Stonehenge on the Salisbury Plain and standing stones elsewhere in England, were so impressive it was hard to deny their power. Celebrations of the winter solstice folded into those for Christmas, and the summer solstice folded into celebrations for John the Baptist, known as Saint John's Day or Midsummer.

Christian seasons shaped the year, as discussed in chapter 4. Christians attended church services regularly and observed festivals and holidays devotedly. Festivals raised money for the rector's fees and for repairs to the church. The most popular of these were the church ales, in which the parish gathered to enjoy ale, and the proceeds went to the church. These were community events filled with conviviality, perhaps accompanied by music and singing, and opportunities to share conversation and gossip with neighbors. They became a target of reformers in the sixteenth century, arguing that these showed corruption and exposed the sins of gluttony and lust, with public drunkenness and the fornication that followed. But for medieval people in the fourteenth and fifteenth centuries, the church ale was a time to gather with their priest and their neighbors and enjoy a festival that would benefit their church, repair its roof, and keep its priest from starving.

Several holidays became occasions for Morris dancing, such as May Day, Midsummer, Christmas, Twelfth Night, and Shrove Tuesday. Accompanied by music, the Morris dancers performed choreographed steps in groups, often wearing bells. These folk dances sometimes included characters like Robin Hood, Maid Marian, and Friar Tuck, becoming theatrical performances as well as dances. Dancers may have used tools such as long white cloths and swords or sticks. Audiences and dancers clapped rhythmically through the performance. Festivals might also have included jousts, games, and contests, popular displays that could bring nobles and common people together in celebration.

SAINTS AND PILGRIMAGE

Pilgrims especially sought mass before they left on their journey and in the churches they visited along their route. As we saw in chapter 2, many women visited saints' shrines in order to seek assistance with fertility or to pray for help in childbirth. England had several cult sites that attracted women's attention, including Walsingham and Worcester, where special attention to the cult of the Virgin Mary encouraged female devotion.

Saints

Christians had celebrated martyrs and holy people as saints since the early Middle Ages. Martyrs died for their faith during the times of persecution before Christianity became an accepted religion in the Roman Empire in the fourth century. After the era of martyrdom, holy people demonstrated their worthiness by performing charity, practicing asceticism, and working miracles, often as an imitation of Jesus and his work in the gospels. Before the twelfth century, there was no formal process for recognizing holy people as saints, so most were recognized by popular acclaim and celebrated at shrines related to their lives or deaths or those containing their relics. In Western Europe, saints' relics, parts of their actual body or items with which they had physical contact, played an important role in both religious and secular society. Church altars almost always contained a holy relic, but people also owned relics privately and even wore them in jewelry. Christians swore oaths as verbal contracts while touching a relic. Christians believed that saints were intercessors, messengers who could convey prayers directly to God as well as serve as conduits for his holy power. Saints became associated with particular places, occupations, or illnesses, specialists to whom a Christian might ask for assistance, and pilgrims traveled on pilgrimages to visit these shrines to make particular prayers or as an act of devotion.

For early Christians, martyrdom offered a way to imitate the sufferings of Christ, an idea called in Latin the *imitatio Christi*. After the era of martyrdom ended, some Christians used ascetic practices as an *imitatio Christi*. Ascetics might eat very little food for long periods, not sleep, or engage in self-mortification by whipping or harming their bodies. While one line of thought is that for medieval people, self-mortification was a way to reject the body, Caroline Walker Bynum has demonstrated instead that for some medieval women this was a way to more fully experience the body. Suffering physical torment allowed these women to feel closer to Christ and the pain he had suffered in his Passion. Asceticism continued to be a practice for exceptional religious women throughout the Middle Ages. Some theologians warned, however, about allowing pride in one's asceticism to compromise proper humility. Some of these women became saints, and the saints inspired more women to embrace lives devoted to religion.

The papacy created an office to investigate claims to sanctity and hold canonization hearings by the thirteenth century, which formalized the process of declaring someone a saint and made some saints part of the official church calendar. Part of the canonization process was recording reports of miracles worked by the saints during their lives or posthumously, often at their shrines, which were typically places where the saints' bodies were buried.

Biographies of the saints, known as *lives* or, in Latin, *vitae*, circulated widely in medieval Europe. They were read in church on the saint's feast day, usually the anniversary of the saint's death, as part of a holy day celebration. Stories of the saints also circulated in compendia, large collections of short narratives about many saints. Priests selected examples from these compendia to illustrate their sermons on a variety of topics, and literate Christians read them as acts of devotion or from interest in the stories. Hagiographers, authors who wrote the *lives* of the saints or collected tales of their miracles, emphasized the ways that the holy person was a saint, but also how he or she lived an exemplary life other Christians might emulate. These texts are rich sources historians can mine for a great deal of information about medieval ideas, especially details about illness and health, but they are also complicated to use because they are formulaic. Since the purpose of the *lives* was to convince others of the subject's sanctity or to encourage Christian belief and practice, the authors were comfortable borrowing from previous texts. Many hagiographical texts, however, were composed by people close to the saint who could have firsthand experience of their actions. For female saints, hagiographical texts commonly depicted the saint's desire to remain a virgin, often against the desire of parents to see her wed, with some sort of divine intervention to make her dream of chastity possible.

Pilgrimage

One popular act of Christian devotion was pilgrimage, a journey taken to a religious shrine of a saint. Most churches contained saints' relics, bones of the holy person or items that had had contact with the saint's body, and some pilgrims traveled to shrines to pray to these specific saints in the presence of their relics. Saints specialized in particular sorts of healing such as blindness, hurt limbs, or particular diseases. There were also established pilgrimage routes: for example, to Santiago de Compostela, to the shrines of Saint Peter and Paul in Rome, and to Jerusalem. In England, the major pilgrimage route was to the shrine of St. Thomas Becket in Canterbury and the shrine of the Virgin Mary at Walsingham in Norfolk;

the shrines of St. William of York and St. William of Norwich were also important.

Thomas Becket was a companion of Henry II who became the archbishop of Canterbury and then unexpectedly resisted Henry's efforts to assert authority over the church in England. During their dispute Thomas had fled England to France for a time and then negotiated a return to England. The harmony between Thomas and Henry did not last and—supposedly based on one of Henry's outbursts of frustration—in 1177, some of Henry's supporters murdered Thomas while he was in his cathedral at prayer. Henry performed a very public penance for his part in this murder, and Thomas was fast-tracked for sanctity, formally canonized as a saint in 1180. Thomas's shrine in Canterbury became widely known as a site for miracles. This was the main destination for Chaucer's pilgrims in *The Canterbury Tales* and a site Margery Kempe visited multiple times.

The shrine to the Virgin Mary at Walsingham in Norfolk was built by Richeldis de Faverches after a vision of Mary in the eleventh or twelfth century, on a site that became an Augustinian priory church. Many kings visited the shrine, including Edward II, Edward III, Richard II, Edward IV, and Henry VI. Traditionally pilgrims walked the final mile to the shrine barefoot to visit the "Slipper Chapel" and pray before a wooden statue of the Virgin Mary. Mary had a strong association with motherhood and fertility, and Cecily Neville, Duchess of York, mother of Edward IV and Richard III, visited Walsingham on pilgrimage for this reason. Margaret of Anjou gave an expensive gift to the shrine in 1453 while praying for a son.

The city of York was a major religious center as the seat of the archbishop of York and home of the beautiful York Minster as well as many other religious houses including Saint Leonard's hospital. Alongside the canonization program for St. Thomas Becket was a northern campaign for the canonization of St. William of York, another twelfth-century English archbishop who likely died of murder. William allegedly died of poison in 1154, and miracles were recorded at his tomb within a few months of his death. He was canonized officially in 1226, and colorful stained-glass windows devoted to him were added to York Minster. Margery Kempe cried "copiously" before his tomb during her visit, and Edward IV established a chantry of priests in his honor in the fifteenth century.

Saint William of Norwich was another important English saint. William died in 1144 as a twelve-year-old boy, and his death was described by Thomas of Monmouth as a ritual murder committed by Jews, the first English example of a series of ritual murder accusations across Europe in this period. The cult of Saint William in Norwich encouraged hostility toward the Jews even beyond their 1290 expulsion from England. This case is examined further later in this chapter.

Æthelthryth is also an important early medieval saint whose cult thrived throughout this period. Her shrine at Ely was maintained by monks who encouraged devotion to her. Rings were a popular devotional object that medieval women gifted to her shrine.

Individual saints were considered patrons for a variety of industries, areas, and activities. Medieval people more frequently celebrated the feast day of the saint in whose honor they were named—their name day—rather than their birthday and might maintain a strong connection to that saint throughout their lives. This is one reason that there were so many women named Mary or Margaret or Catherine or Anne when the cults of those saints were popular. There were patron saints for pregnancy, and women appealed to Margaret of Antioch and the Virgin Mary with special prayers while pregnant for protection during childbirth. There were also patrons for certain occupations. Local areas might develop special devotion to the saint in whose honor their church was named, celebrating his or her feast day more robustly than others, and believing that these saints protected them as their own.

Pilgrims typically traveled by foot to demonstrate the piety of their journey, and the journey could involve a great deal of time and expense. Pilgrims wore a characteristic cloak and hat, upon which they might affix pilgrimage badges they purchased at shrines along their route. Some pilgrims tossed such badges into running water when they returned home, which has made it possible to find badges when dredging the Thames or the Seine or the Ouse and have a sense of where pilgrims from that area had been.

Many who journeyed on pilgrimage sought miracles and blessings from the saints. Miracle tales collections report pilgrims who arrived and prayed to the saint for a miracle and then received one. These sources describe the repair of limbs, restoration of sight to the blind, curing of multiple diseases, and even the curing of leprosy. There were hundreds of stories of pilgrims who journeyed to a saint's shrine to ask for a miracle and then thanked the saint for his or her assistance by leaving a donation.

Pilgrimages could be major journeys that women undertook with their husbands or with their families, particularly for long trips to

Compostela, Rome, or Jerusalem. The shrine of St. James, Santiago, in Compostela, was very popular among the English in the fifteenth century. Pilgrims who journeyed to Santiago received guarantees from the crown that their property would be protected while on their pilgrimage and provided pilgrims with letters of protection. Starting in 1394, ships were given permits to carry pilgrims rather than cargo. The Holy Year of 1434 was especially popular for visits to Compostela, with fifty ships bringing more than 2,000 pilgrims from England to Spain. A guidebook compiled by William Wey in 1456 allowed those unable to travel to enjoy the wonders of the pilgrimage.

Women who were not able to visit a pilgrimage site personally could send a proxy to conduct the pilgrimage for them. Queen Elizabeth did this in the fifteenth century, as did Isabel Turnour, who died before her pilgrimage vow was completed, but her daughter fulfilled it for her.

In *The Canterbury Tales*, Geoffrey Chaucer described a group of pilgrims traveling together to Canterbury. His work, still incomplete at his death, contains a prologue describing most of the pilgrims and tales some of those pilgrims told to their group along the journey. Some of Chaucer's narrators were women: Alison, the Wife of Bath; the Prioress; and the Second Nun, but there were other female characters in the stories told by the pilgrims, including Alison from "The Miller's Tale," Griselda from "The Clerk's Tale," May from the "Merchant's Tale," Constance from the "Man of Law's Tale," and Emelye from "The Knight's Tale."

In her autobiography, Margery Kempe described multiple pilgrimages she made, including one to Jerusalem. She also traveled in a group, one that was not especially happy to have her as a member because of her frequent tears. Her companions abandoned her, only to find themselves at a disadvantage and needing to be rescued by Margery.

MONASTICISM

Women devoted themselves to lives of prayer by joining a monastery or priory or house of canonesses. Such women took vows of chastity, poverty, and obedience; wore a religious habit; and agreed to live according to a religious rule or a strict set of guidelines for monastic life. The oath of chastity was a defining feature of monastic identity for nuns, who were sometimes described as "virgins," even though some women joined monasteries later in life, as widows or as married women whose husbands also agreed to enter a monastery. The monastery was an attractive option for women who did not want to be wives or mothers or for widows with some experience with marriage and motherhood who did not wish to enjoy those institutions again.

The monastery was also an attractive part of family planning. Having a relative serving as a nun—especially one who rose to monastic office—reflected well on the family, bringing them positive attention for devotion as well as the means to secure their relative a position. Parents of large families might plan for certain children to marry and certain children to take vows as a way of finding all their children positions, and they might educate their children with these professions in mind. While child oblation had been common in the earlier part of the Middle Ages, it was no longer practiced by the fourteenth century, and most women entered a monastic house as adults or in their teens, probably not taking holy orders until at least sixteen years old. Indeed, some monastics preferred that postulants be young, about twelve years old, rather than more mature, since it was easier to train younger girls to be obedient and observe the abbey's rule. Some older women who entered monasteries as widows had expectations for their dining, privacy, and movement that did not comport well with the abbey's rule.

Orders

There were different types of monastic rules houses might follow. The Benedictine Rule was the one most widely used in the early Middle Ages, but in the twelfth century, the Cistercian Rule became quite popular, and several Cistercian houses were founded in England. With the rise of the Mendicant orders in the thirteenth century, there were some Clarissan foundations. The Gilbertine order was the only completely English one, and it was important in this period. It is worth examining the background of monasticism's development before looking more closely at some of these orders and monastic houses.

As an institution, monasticism had its roots in the first centuries of Christianity, in the Egyptian desert, when holy men and women sought to retreat from the world like Saint Anthony, by going into the desert and focusing on a life of prayer. As Christianity became an accepted religion in the Roman Empire and Christians were no longer persecuted or martyred, devout Christians sought other ways to demonstrate their faith and devote their lives to God.

Monastics formed communities where they might retreat behind monastery walls and focus on prayer and simple work, without the responsibilities of family life and secular labor. They took oaths of celibacy, poverty, and obedience. Women were important monastic founders in the early Middle Ages, establishing abbeys for women across Europe.

Initially, there were a number of rules, or sets of guidelines, guiding how these monasteries operated, but by the ninth century, the Benedictine Rule became the most popular and successful in Western Europe, guiding monastics in dividing their day into adequate time to pray, to work, and to rest and ensuring that the community would thrive with enough food. England had a number of female Benedictine houses, including Barking Abbey, a royal house founded in the seventh century and following the Benedictine Rule from the tenth century; Wilton Abbey in Wiltshire, one of England's most powerful female houses; Shaftesbury Abbey in Dorset, a ninth-century foundation that was the second wealthiest female house in England at the time of the Dissolution; St. Mary's Abbey in Winchester, founded in the ninth century; and St. Radegund's Priory in Cambridge, a twelfth-century foundation, and now a part of Jesus College, Cambridge.

Since monasteries were religious institutions, they were attractive recipients for donations, particularly in wills, but they were also typically exempt from taxes. Over centuries, successful houses could become major landholders with extensive property, and the leader of the house, abbot for monks and abbess for nuns, was increasingly required to devote time to managing estates and protecting holdings from predatory neighbors. Men and women who joined religious houses took oaths of personal poverty, but the monastery itself was not barred from acquiring these extensive lands and properties whose income would support the community. This made monasteries, especially well supported ones, important landowners, and as a result, some abbesses wielded extensive authority beyond their community.

In the late eleventh and early twelfth centuries, the success of the Benedictine order, particularly its enormous wealth, prompted some critics to conceive of new approaches to monasticism. The Cistercian order, for example, emphasized simplicity in its monastic architecture and in the simple undyed wool of monastic garments, known as habits. Initially, the Cistercians were not interested in admitting women to their order, but the excitement and demand among women who wished to become Cistercian nuns eventually won women a place in the order. There were several Cistercian abbeys in England.

Robert d'Arbrissel, a twelfth-century reformer in France, was also influential in England. He founded the abbey of Fontevraud as a double community for men and women, governed by an abbess. Fontevraud was in the county of Poitou, one of the French territories controlled by the Plantagenet family and very close to Queen Eleanor of Aquitaine's town of Poitiers. Eleanor, her husband King Henry II, and their son King Richard I were all buried at Fontevraud Abbey. Their patronage encouraged the spread of the Fontevrist order in England, with three major houses at Westwood, Amesbury, and Nuneaton.

Gilbert of Sempringham, also active in the twelfth century, founded another order significant in England. While initially interested in a Cistercian house for women in England, he found the Cistercians unhelpful and so instead established the Gilbertine order. He built a house for nuns at Sempringham that became head of a network of over twenty houses, establishing the only monastic order that came originally from England. The Gilbertines were a mix of nuns, canons, canonesses, and lay brothers and sisters.

This pattern repeated in the thirteenth century, when Saint Francis and Saint Dominic established orders known as the mendicants. Both the Franciscans and the Dominicans emphasized preaching and mobility for friars in their order, and neither was considered suitable for women. Clare of Assisi was a devoted follower of Saint Francis and founded her own order, the Clarissans, focused again on poverty but in a fixed location inside an abbey. Over the course of the thirteenth and fourteenth centuries, the Franciscans and Dominicans began to admit what they called a "third order" of nuns into their orders, calling these women "tertiaries." These women took oaths of celibacy and poverty, but they did not live communally or claim to be enclosed like the Benedictine and Cistercian nuns and often focused on charitable acts in public. Among the most famous tertiaries were Catherine of Siena and Angela of Foligno, who washed the poor and nursed the ill in marketplaces and their own homes. In the fifteenth century, however, tertiaries faced increasing pressure to live communal lives inside abbeys and to accept enclosure, which would keep them behind monastic walls.

The mendicant orders were less popular in England. There was only one Dominican house for nuns, founded by Edward III in 1346, and four houses for Franciscan nuns, known as the Second Order of

St. Francis or Minoresses, who followed a Franciscan Rule founded by Isabella of France, daughter of King Louis VIII of France and founder of the abbey of Longchamp, known as the Isabella Rule. While the Minoresses in England followed the Isabella Rule, they were very similar to the Poor Clares and often understood to be the same as the Clarissans.

All the Minoress houses in England were aristocratic foundations by women and men with close connections to French and English royalty. This may be ironic, given the Franciscan ideal of poverty, that the order thrived through those who had the greatest wealth. There was a Minoress house at Waterbeach, founded in 1294 by Denise de Montchensy, who had been sister-in-law to Stephen Langton. There was a house founded at the start of the thirteenth century just outside the walls of London at Aldgate by Blanche of Artois, dowager queen of Navarre and wife of Edmund Crouchback, Earl of Lancaster. Another house was established at Denny by Marie de St.-Pol, countess of Pembroke and grandniece of Blanche of Artois, in 1339, who transferred the community from Waterbeach to this house, although some women stayed behind, requiring an order from the pope to move to Denny; Marie chose to be buried at the Denny house. A fourth house was built in Bruisyard for Matilda of Lancaster in 1364–1366 by her daughter's husband, Lionel, Duke of Clarence, son of Edward III, and he buried his wife Elizabeth at Bruisyard. Matilda joined the house herself.

In 1415 Henry V established Syon Abbey near Sheen Palace in Isleworth as part of his "Great Work," along with Sheen Priory, a Carthusian house, and a planned Celestine house. Syon was a member of the Bridgettines Order founded by St. Bridget of Sweden and given papal approval in 1370. Henry IV had promised to build three monasteries for his role in the murders of Richard II and Archbishop Richard Scrope, but died before completing the vow, which Henry V took up for his father. Syon and Sheen were successful, but the Celestine house quickly folded after a falling out between the king and the house's French monks during the Hundred Years War. The Bridgettines were an order of double houses where nuns and monks lived in separate houses joined by their church, governed by their own superior, typically with eighty-five members, sixty nuns and twenty-five monks, which is the model Henry V designed to follow. Henry VI was generous to Syon during his reign, and it was the richest nunnery in England at the time of the Dissolution.

Life

In joining a monastery, a woman or her family made an entrance donation to the house, and while these fees were less than a typical dowry, they could be substantial and limited access to monasticism to women from wealthy and powerful families, typically of noble, gentry, or yeoman status. The entrance donation was controversial, as some saw it as simony, the buying of church offices. Religious houses also included lay sisters, who might take on more of the manual labor of the house and not take the same vows or live according to the rule. Lay sisters might come from any status group and was one way that wealthier peasant women were able to seek a monastic life.

The monastery contained a dormitory where the nuns slept; a refectory where they ate; a church where they worshipped; an infirmary where they recovered when hurt or ill; a chapter house where they met as a group; and possibly a library and scriptorium where they kept, copied, and created books. Occasionally, the abbey church was also a parish church where the nuns kept themselves separate from the local worshippers who attended services. Most monasteries had a cloister, or covered open-air walkway with a central garden, that was a place for reflection and contemplation, so central to the monastic identity that sometimes the monastery was called a "cloister." In English nunneries, these cloisters were located to the north of the abbey church, because the Virgin Mary stood to the right of Christ in church decoration and because women's bodies were associated with cold, symbolized by the north.

Nuns in the later Middle Ages were supposed to be cloistered, or enclosed, which meant that the nuns were not supposed to leave their abbey, nor were they supposed to allow others to enter. Their church might have separate doors, one for the nuns and another for all others. This rule of enclosure was often a part of monastic rules for women, but it was reinforced by Pope Boniface VIII when he decreed in 1298, in *Periculoso*, that all female monasteries must be strictly enclosed both actively—they could not leave—and passively—they could not allow others in. Scholars are divided on the question of whether monasteries truly observed these rules of enclosure, since abbesses and other nuns frequently had to leave their monasteries in order to take care of abbey business, and there is a great deal of evidence that cloisters welcomed a range of visitors with impunity. Even when the nuns were criticized for being outside their abbeys, the censure does not seem to interpret *Periculoso* strictly, as with Richard Hallam, bishop of Salisbury's 1412 "mandate to the abbess and convent of Shaftesbury forbidding the nuns to leave their house except for good cause, approved by the superior, and in the company of some senior nuns of proved character" because "several nuns have often been wandering outside the house in various places longer than is seemly and for frivolous reasons" (Horn 1982, 121). The bishop wanted the nuns' movement outside the abbey to be more thoughtful and purposeful, not curtailed altogether. Bishops also wished to eject all the visitors and lodgers who stayed on the abbey grounds—250 of them at Carrow Priory from the late fourteenth to the mid-fifteenth century!—but their continued presence, and the bishops' complaints about them, demonstrate how porous the abbey walls remained. Nonetheless, there is a clear increase in pressure on religious women to accept enclosure over the fifteenth century, including those who had never been enclosed, such as the Franciscan and Dominican tertiaries.

This does not mean that monastic women were disconnected from the world. They remained connected to their families and the events of the world. Female monasteries were often located in or near a town, for their protection, and nuns could visit families if they were nearby. Parents often selected monasteries for their children because they were local, or because other relatives were already members. These kinship networks were very important for helping new nuns feel comfortable, for encouraging devotion among the women, and for the promotion of prominent families to monastic office. These networks also helped encourage families to make donations to the monastery, knowing that their donations would support aunts, daughters, cousins, and nieces.

The largest monastic houses, abbeys, were governed by an abbess, although some smaller communities might be priories headed by a prioress. An abbey typically had at least one prioress who assisted the abbess in governing the community. Most rules required the head of the community to be elected by the women themselves, with notification to the bishop or king that an election was to take place and of the outcome, and theoretically, any woman was eligible. Nevertheless, most abbesses and prioresses, especially those of large and wealthy houses, were aristocratic women with strong connections and networks beyond the abbey.

Abbesses and prioresses met with their community once a week in chapter, a meeting often held in a special room or building designated as their chapter house, sometimes with benches for the community to sit together, read from their rule, and decide

The Prioress from *The Canterbury Tales* by Geoffrey Chaucer, woodcut from the Caxton's edition of 1485. *The Prioress's Tale* is a story of blood libel and is noted for its anti-Semitism. (Claudio Divizia/123RF)

important matters. The abbey's precentress, who directed the choir and guided the selections for the liturgical hours, was typically the third-in-command at the abbey. The abbey typically also had a cellarer who maintained the abbey's stores and supplies and a sacrist who maintained the church and a treasurer who kept track of the finances along with the abbess. The infirmarian was responsible for tending to injuries and directing care for sick nuns. An abbey with a large library could have a librarian, who might also direct the scriptorium. Another nun might have charge of the refectory, a novice-mistress took care of training the novitiates—new members of the community who had not yet taken their vows. There were also rotating positions in the community, such as who read to the nuns during mealtimes. While the top offices tended to go to noblewomen with strong connections beyond the abbey, that was not the case for other offices, where there was more of a meritocracy.

The officers responsible for the abbey's management reported to the chapter once a year: "[L]et the aforesaid treasurers, the cellaress, the sacrist, and the other nuns of the monastery holding office in the same and ministering in temporal matters, render a full account of their administrations at least once a year before the entire convent and other persons deputed for this purpose. And she who is found negligent or at fault in this respect shall be gravely punished as the office holder and absolutely expelled from that office" (Goldberg 1995, 268). Negligence, mismanagement, and corruption were serious concerns, and accusations from the nuns of any of these issues were likely to draw investigations from the bishop or other authorities.

The monastic diet was a simple one, although specifics of how much nuns ate and what sort of food differed by rule, finances, the day of the week, and the time of the year. Diets were simpler during Lent and more luxurious during Christmastide and on feast days. Most rules permitted nuns to eat meat and fish some of the days each week when it was not a fasting time and allotted some weak ale or watered wine for them to drink. Richard, bishop of Lincoln, reminded the abbess of Elstow Abbey in 1421–1422 that "every nun of the said convent have one dish of meat or of fish appropriate to the season each Monday, Wednesday, and Saturday, each dish worth a penny" (Goldberg 1995, 267), giving the cost of the meat to clarify the quality, so that the nuns had a decent piece of meat but nothing extravagant. He further noted that "each nun have five measures of superior ale every week, and that there be no distinction between the bread of the abbess and the bread of the convent, and that bread is to be 60 shillings' worth in weight" (Goldberg 1995, 267). Again, the bishop was concerned to protect the nuns by specifying the quality of the ale and bread, but also introduced a sense that abbesses might be reserving the best quality for themselves, when, as he suggests, the abbess and the nuns should have food of equal quality. Most days, their diets were simple, based on grains and vegetables produced at the abbey or on the abbey's estates, and might be seasonal.

Wealthier women who professed later in life, especially aristocratic widows, had the most challenging time accepting this simpler diet and might insist on richer fare for their own tables with an expectation of regular meat, especially game, and rich sauces. The nuns were expected to dine together in a common refectory, in silence, while a devotional chapter was read to them, but visitation records show that this was not practiced in many places, either because there was not a refectory large enough to include the entire community, because some women preferred to dine separately, or because dining spaces were more private.

Nuns were also expected to sleep in common dormitories. This was a debate across monastic houses in the later Middle Ages, in which some advocated individual cells where more private devotion was possible, and some advocated communal facilities that encouraged community between the nuns. Bishops and other authorities also preferred communal dormitories because it more easily permitted the women to monitor one another and made it more challenging for women to sin in private. As Richard, bishop of Lincoln, ordered for Elstow Abbey, "[E]ach and every one of the nuns of the said monastery, not known to be infirm or lawfully prevented, lie the whole night together in the dormitory, and that two scrutineers, without exception senior nuns, be appointed in the said monastery, who are to observe . . . that they are settled in their beds in the said dormitory at the proper hours before and after midnight, and if they find any defaulters to disclose and reveal them to the abbess without respect of persons. Let her punish and correct such defaulters according to God and the rule such that their correction and punishment serves as an example to the others" (Goldberg 1995, 270). Monasteries across Europe in the fifteenth century started to build larger refectories and dormitories in order to accommodate the entire community and build a communal spirit between the nuns and to address these sorts of concerns about illicit behavior.

The nuns' main task was to pray at prescribed times each and every day. The liturgy of the hours, as required by the Benedictine Rule and most rules after it, had seven times to pray during the day and another at night. These prayer times were:

Matins, about two hours after midnight

Lauds, at dawn or three hours after Matins, about 5 am

Prime, an hour after Lauds, about 6 am

Terce, three hours after Prime, mid-morning, about 9 am

Sext, three hours after Terce, midday, about noon

None, three hours after Sext, mid-afternoon, about 3 pm

Vespers, evening prayers, three hours after Sext, about 6 pm

Compline, nighttime prayers, said before bed, about an hour
    after Vespers

At each prayer time, the nuns gathered in their abbey church, in the choir if it was a large church, to sing hymns, psalms, and read from the Bible. On a saint's feast day, they might read from the saint's life or about his or her miracles. The intervals between prayers gave nuns about enough time for a meal, for some quiet reflection, for some light manual labor such as working in their garden or copying some texts, or meeting together in chapter. The regular pattern to the day was intended to keep the women focused on their purpose of prayer and devotion to God.

Finances

Ideally, a monastic house should have all it needed to maintain itself, with arable land, livestock, kitchen gardens to feed the nuns, and control of properties that could generate rental income. Some monasteries controlled fiefs, and the abbess even had seigneurial responsibilities for the property. The abbess might work with a steward to tend these estates and collect rents, or she might do that work directly. As time wore on, however, the initial foundation was not always sufficient to keep up with expenses, and abbeys needed to encourage new donations. This was partially offset by entrance fees from new nuns, but greater funds were necessary.

Christians frequently gave funds for charity in their wills, and often these went to the church. Donations were thought of as a good work, a good deed Christians performed that was efficacious in demonstrating merit for salvation. Monasteries were attractive institutions for charitable giving as houses of prayer whose members could remember their donors and pray for their souls in perpetuity. Founders had this in mind in creating new institutions as did many other Christians in giving to local monasteries. Abbeys might also cultivate reputations for purity or other virtues that made them attractive to new donors.

One challenge that female monasteries had in the later Middle Ages was in the shift of preference between prayers for the dead to masses for the dead. While nuns could say prayers in return for donations without any greater expense, when donors started desiring requiem masses said for their donations in perpetuity, this created an expense for the nuns. Since women could not be ordained as priests, they had to hire a priest to perform the mass. And a donation "in perpetuity" meant that this mass had to be performed annually without end, incurring expense long past the time that the donation ran out. Those donations ended up costing nuns in the long run, which is one reason why male monasteries were more financially stable than female monasteries in the late Middle Ages.

Several houses were also challenged by the Black Death, during which the numbers of professed nuns at houses declined for many, but not all houses. Syon Abbey and Shaftesbury Abbey, as major houses, maintained their numbers, and some small houses were able to maintain their numbers. Financial difficulties, partially due to the preference for requiem masses and partially due to a population peak, caused some bishops to limit the number of new nuns who could be admitted and set a cap on the total number of nuns an abbey could support. The entrance donations expected from women joining the monastery became even more important to its finances, even as the practice of expecting a donation came under attack. As Richard, bishop of Lincoln, remarked after his visit to Elstow Abbey in 1421–1422: "Also that henceforth suitable persons be received as nuns, for whose reception or entrance let no money or anything else be taken, but let them hereafter be admitted without any illicit agreement or settlement of any sum of money or of other things which used to be done by the wicked deed of simony" (Goldberg 1995, 267–268). The desperate need for "donations" came at the same time the bishops were limiting the number of nuns, causing the needed funds to grow, which meant that monasteries came to be increasingly limited to the very wealthy.

Authority

Some female abbeys did continue to thrive, however, especially those with strong connections to the monarchy and/or aristocracy. For these houses, monastic office could bring extraordinary power, especially for medieval women. Abbesses could affect both ecclesiastical and secular events with their advice and influence. Prominent abbesses of major abbeys could hold the right to run courts on their estates, correspond with leading thinkers and authorities, and influence events both local to their monastery and throughout the kingdom. This was especially true when the abbess came from a powerful or influential family, and since the professed nuns were often members of the aristocracy, this was likely. An abbess could thus draw on her personal network, as well as lean on her family's status, in protecting her abbey. Since monasteries were connected to others within their order, abbesses could likewise influence events at monastic houses throughout Europe.

Bishops had authority over most monastic houses in their jurisdiction, unless the community had an episcopal exemption. Many bishops took seriously their responsibility to ensure that all was well in these monasteries, and some kept careful records of their visitations to the abbeys. The bishops enforced discipline, ensured that the abbess was competent and managing the abbey and its estates well, that the nuns were observing their rule and their vows, and that the abbey buildings were not falling into disrepair and that the nuns were not neglected. Some of the visitation records record troubling details, such as a pregnant nun or a fornicating priest, but these were rare.

Some of the bishops' recommendations after a visitation provoke wonder at what might have been taking place in that abbey, such as when Archbishop Greenfield told the nuns of St. Mary Wilberfoss in Yorkshire not to dress as secular women by wearing red clothes with long tunics. Langley Priory was troubled in 1440 by a visitor, Lady Audley, because her twelve dogs disturbed the church, and they had to expel her despite her forty shillings in yearly rent. Richard, bishop of Lincoln, found on his 1421–1422 visit to Elstow Abbey that there were several visitors, including married people, staying in the abbey and causing problems: "[B]ecause of the stay of visitors in the said monastery, especially of married persons, the purity of religion, the sweetness of honest conversation and conduct . . . have suffered grave shipwreck" (Goldberg 1995, 267). He ordered that no visitors could stay in the monastery without the bishop's permission. Richard's successor, William Grey, found a similar problem at Godstow Abbey in 1434, ordering that "Femersham's widow with her entire household and other mature women be removed entirely from the monastery within the coming year since they are disturbing for the nuns and the occasion of bad example by reason of their dress and their visitors" (Goldberg 1995, 271).

Bishops and abbesses had the power to expel nuns who were behaving badly, which might mean simply moving them to another house, as with Alice Boyton, a nun of Kingston St. Michael, who was moved in 1414 to Bromhall "on account of her bad behavior." The bishop of Salisbury, Robert Hallam informed the prioress of Bromhall that Alice was to "be in the special custody of a mature, God-fearing nun and is to be kept from communication with secular or religious people except in the presence of this guardian" (Horn 1982, 125). Alice's infractions must have been serious, whether consorting with a man—other visitations proved that bishops were very concerned with inappropriate conversations between the women and their bailiff, with the priests who said mass for the abbey, or, for Godstow Abbey in Oxford, with the local scholars—or refusing to subject herself to her abbess's obedience. The specific prohibition on speaking to anyone without a guardian suggests that Alice was engaging in illicit conversations and behaviors. The danger is demonstrated by a papal letter of 1368 requiring the archbishop of York to investigate the case of the Gilbertine nun Alice, daughter of John de Everyngham, who had left her abbey at Haverholme to take up with James de Huthulle as if married. Alice was excommunicated but refused to appear before the master general of the Gilbertine order, William. Alice's recalcitrance in not meeting with William forced the pope to ask the archbishop to get involved.

Despite the occasional interventions of visiting bishops, the abbess had extensive authority over the women who swore formal vows to obey her as well as over the financial holdings of the monastery. This power in the hands of women was one concern of the Dissolution of the Monasteries conducted by King Henry VIII in the sixteenth century. The visitation records preparing for the Dissolution claimed that many female houses were corrupt, with abbesses charged with mismanagement, abuse, neglect, and financial crimes, as well as with permitting sexual license within the abbey to go unpunished, but most of these were probably fabrications intended to justify the Dissolution. These were an excuse to dismantle monastic houses and claim their resources for the crown, which made a fortune selling their estates, libraries, and religious objects. Even the stained-glass windows and the building stones were stripped from some houses, to be found later in the homes of elites.

Literacy and Education

Nuns were educated, especially in the liturgy, the hymnal, psalter, and in Scripture. It is likely they were able to read in English and in French and probably had some understanding of Latin. The register of Godstow Abbey from about 1460 argued that nuns should have books in English so that they would fully understand: "for default of understanding they took often times great hurt and hindrance; and, what for default of true learned men that all times be not ready to teach them and counsel . . . it were right necessary as it seems to the understanding of such religious women, that they might have, out of her Latin books, some writing in her mother tongue, whereby they might have better knowledge of her muniments, and more clearly give information to her servants, rent collectors, and receivers, in the absence of her learned counsel" (Clark 1911, 25).

Despite uncertain training in Latin, the nuns were able to read well enough to take a turn during meals and to participate in the liturgical hours, to maintain abbey records if placed in such an office. Abbeys also employed stewards who could help with record-keeping. Nuns at larger abbeys also worked in the scriptorium, copying manuscripts, illuminating them, and occasionally creating new texts of their own. Monasteries that could afford them kept psalters, books of psalms; antiphonaries, books of liturgical music; breviaries, books including the spoken and the sung elements; missals, books containing the mass and explaining changes through the liturgical year; and hagiographical books about the saints such as martyrologies and holy lives to guide the nuns in their saying of the canonical hours. The Golden Legend, by Jacobus de Voragine, was a thirteenth-century collection of saints' lives that circulated broadly. The abbey library might also include mystical works such as by or about Mechtild of Hackeborn, Catherine of Siena, and St. Bridget.

Some nuns were also authors in their own right. Katherine of Sutton, abbess of Barking Abbey from 1358 to 1376, is likely the author of the three Latin plays found in the manuscript known as University College MS 169 in Oxford. These were Easter plays, liturgical dramas suitable for monastic performance. Juliana Berners, the prioress of Saint Mary of Sopwell in Hertfordshire born circa 1388 was a little more adventurous with her writing, focusing instead on hunting and other sports in *The Book of Saint Albans*.

Given the nuns' learning and literacy, some families sent their children to be educated by them. Margaret, Duchess of Clarence, sent her daughters to learn at Dartford Abbey for three years, paying for their room, board, and servants to stay at the abbey. While this helped the nuns' financial situation, it increased the bishop's distress at the presence of visitors who distracted the nuns from their real purpose.

There has been a long-standing question among historians about the *cura monialium*, or the care for nuns. Because women cannot become priests, communities of nuns require a priest to perform the mass and offer the other sacraments. Some theologians complained that this obligation was a risk to clerical celibacy and that women ought to be avoided as much as possible. On the one hand, this fits with the depiction of women as lustful temptresses who pose a risk to male purity. On the other, the construction of a notion of clerical masculinity depended on tests, and the opportunity to face enticement and resist should prove the cleric's manliness. Historian Fiona Griffiths has demonstrated that complaints about the *cura monialium* may be only theoretical, however, since in practice men who described caring for nuns' spiritual needs found that task fulfilling.

There were also issues for male houses, since they sometimes required female assistance, such as laundresses. While male houses were less likely to be enclosed as firmly as some female houses, the oath of celibacy was a serious one, and houses took careful steps to prevent temptation. As noted in the 1422 visitation of Huntingdon Priory, the bishop of Lincoln ordered "that the women who wash clothes have no access to the claustral precinct in order to take in or return clothes to be washed, but when these washerwomen come, let them wait at the priory's outer gate and let the clothes to be washed be brought out to them and, when washed, be taken back by some secular person and under no circumstances by the canons" (Goldberg 1995, 171). The temptation to sin was too great to allow women to come into the canons' path.

Beyond the nuns themselves, several women chose to reside in monasteries without taking holy orders in their later years, as discussed in the bishops' visitations. While some widows chose to join a monastery and become a nun, others preferred to rent lodgings within the abbey enclosure. This was a suitable way for a lady to spend her final years, widowed and not wishing to rely on family resources her children desired, or interested in breaking from the social and political life to spend time instead in quiet reflection. In exchange for rent, a noblewoman might bring a modest household with her, including adult children and servants, dine on her own, and have comfortable private sleeping arrangements. She might attend the daily services and enjoy the music of the canonical hours, or miss them, praying in the church during its quiet hours. Should she become ill, she would have access to the infirmary, and she might arrange for her body to be buried in the abbey church or cemetery. This was a beneficial relationship for the nuns as well, so long as the lady and her household were not disruptive, as they had her rent as income, and she was likely to arrange her will to benefit the abbey when taking up residence there. Bequests for prayers, a requiem mass—sometimes with a chaplain prepaid and attached to the bequest—and even household goods were common. Margaret Teye gave to Barking Abbey embroidered textiles for prayers.

ANCHORESSES AND ALTERNATIVE
RELIGIOUS LIVES

Not all Christian women who wished to devote their lives to their faith could become nuns. Monasteries had a limit on how many women the house could support, and most expected entrance donations that were out of reach for any but the most elite families. In the later Middle Ages, other groups developed that enabled women to commit themselves to God outside the traditional monastery, such as anchoresses, beguines, and tertiaries.

Anchoresses, also known as anchorites, based on the Greek word for "withdraw," were monastic women who accepted enclosure within an anchor-hold to live chastely and in solitude, not moving beyond that single room, focused entirely on a life of prayer. An anchor-hold might be a cell inside a monastery or a remote hut away from society, but many were a single cell within or adjacent to churches, often centrally located urban churches, or even castles. England's anchor-holds were typically urban and attached to a church or monastery, with a window into the church so that the anchoress might observe the mass, and sometimes a window to the street where she might converse with visitors. Some anchor-holds were large enough for multiple women, but most were solitary cells.

Even as she withdrew to a life of asceticism and contemplation, an anchoress was not removed from society, and she might be visited by her confessor, fellow nuns, her family, neighbors, or even pilgrims who came quite far on purpose to see her. Anchoritism became so common in England that most people would have had contact with or knowledge of an anchorite, with an estimate of nearly 800 recorded anchorites (male and female) in England during the Middle Ages. During the fourteenth century, the phenomenon was especially popular in English cities, with twelve known anchor-holds in London, eight in York, and six in Norwich (Hughes-Edwards 2012, 7).

Such a withdrawal required the permission of a bishop and typically his participation in a ceremony of enclosure, during which the anchoress's earthly life ended, the door to her anchor-hold was sealed, and her life of asceticism began. The bishop of Lincoln in 1436 examined the Stainfield nun Beatrix Franke to determine whether to approve her request to become an anchoress in the Winterton parish church, asking her how long she had wanted to be an anchoress and if she had considered the challenges of that life.

He reported that "when the examination was over, finding her in no way either hesitant or wavering, but wanting unfailingly the life of an anchoress almost from the time of her youth, sticking the whole time to that purpose, we absolved her and caused her to be released from the yoke of obedience to her prioress of Stainfield. On St. Vincent's day, reading openly and clearly, she publicly made a new profession before the high altar of the aforesaid church during mass, and furthermore promised obedience and chastity to us, in your place, and your successors."

The ceremony included a mass, assent of the people where her anchor-hold would be, and her enclosure in a "certain house and enclosure built on the north side of the said church, and fastening the door thereof with locks, bars, and keys, we left her, as is believed by many, in joy of the Saviour, in peace and quiet of spirit" (Goldberg 1995, 278). Some licenses issued by bishops considered details such as the location and construction of the anchor-hold, the anchoress's means of support, and her new diet.

Such women gained reputations for their extraordinary devotion and holiness, and anchoresses had enormous influence on religious life in their communities. Wills show that members of the lay community admired anchoresses and donated to their support at their death, considering support of her a charitable act that would be useful for their personal salvation as well as the spirituality of other Christians. Enclosure did not mean separation from the community; instead, an anchoress's enclosure indicated a desire to focus on her spiritual life to the exclusion of all else, inside a room with a sealed door. Some anchoresses received episcopal permission to leave their cell. Emma Scherman of Pontefract even received permission to go on an annual pilgrimage (Hughes-Edwards 2012, 6).

Anchoritic handbooks written in the Middle Ages helped to guide the anchorite's experience. The guides appeared in Latin and English, which made them accessible to both men and women. The most famous of these texts is the thirteenth-century guide, the *Ancrene Wisse*, but there were several others. Even the *Ancrene Wisse* was revised several times over the course of the Middle Ages. Like a monastic rule, the text detailed how an anchoress should live her life so that she could focus on her spiritual devotion. It discouraged asceticism and specified that the anchoress should consume an adequate, although simple diet. She could have a servant but was supposed to live on donations and on funds she could raise from selling things she made. She brought with her clothes, bedding, and simple items for her household and could arrange for these to be replaced. Thus, she had what she required to focus on her spiritual life. Richard Rolle, a fourteenth-century mystic wrote guides for Margaret Kirkby, a fourteenth-century anchoress and mystic, *The Commandment* and *the Form of Living*, which also became influential on anchoresses. Rolle might have expected that Kirkby would be recognized as a saint, and several miracles were later attributed to her.

An anchoress might observe the canonical hours as a nun would, especially if attached to an abbey where she might observe and hear the nuns at prayer. The *Ancrene Wisse* encouraged her to pray throughout the day. Some anchoresses spent their days reading and writing about their experience, and several experienced visions, which their confessors helped them to write down. Emma Rawghton (d. c. 1436), an anchoress attached to All Saint's Church in York made predictions that gained attention (Hughes-Edwards 2012, 5).

The most famous anchoress in England was Julian of Norwich (c. 1342–c. 1416), a visionary living in Norwich as well as a female author writing in Middle English. Her book *Revelations of Divine Love* is the earliest-known English work by a woman (Watson 2003, 210). Julian first experienced visions at age thirty when she was ill, about 1373, and she wrote these down in an early version of *Revelations*. She then devoted herself to an anchor-hold. She named herself after the church of Saint Julian in Norwich, where she was an anchoress; her birth name is unknown. Her reputation for visions and as an excellent source of spiritual advice spread, encouraging Margery Kempe to visit her in 1413, a visit that was very important to Margery. Julian's *Revelations* examine Christ's Passion and the love of God.

This was not an easy life, and not all who committed to it were able to fulfill their vows. For example, an anchoress attached in 1329 to St. James's Church in Shere, Christine, abandoned her anchor-hold within three years (Hughes-Edwards 2012, 5).

The beguines were another group of celibate women who devoted themselves to prayer, but did so without joining a formal monastic order. Like the tertiaries, the beguines often ministered to the poor and the sick, whether in the marketplace or in hospitals. They typically lived in their own homes or in small groups with other beguines. Beguines were often drawn from elite urban families, with resources that permitted them to support these lives. The beguine life was especially popular in the cities of the Low Countries and in Northern France.

Some beguines sold their handiwork, such as weaving, to support themselves, but most focused on less remunerative work, such as caring for the sick. Marie of Oignies from what is now Belgium was the first and most famous of the beguines, a married woman who convinced her husband to take an oath of chastity alongside her. Marie became an important model for Margery Kempe. In the later Middle Ages, there was institutionalizing pressure on beguines to live in communities, but they did not accept a monastic rule or join any of the monastic orders.

Tertiaries, or "third orders," were women associated with the mendicant orders founded by St. Francis and St. Dominic that became popular in the thirteenth century. The mendicants, known as the Franciscans and Dominicans, emphasized lives of preaching and travel that were not well suited to expectations for holy women. Saint Francis's message of poverty and charity and Dominic's commitment to fighting heresy proved quite attractive to large numbers of women, posing a problem to the orders. The tertiaries were associated with the Franciscan and Dominican orders but did not fully join them, were discouraged from travel, and were not permitted to preach. Over the course of the fifteenth century, the tertiaries became increasingly pressed into monastic-like houses and enclosed, although communal living and enclosure had not been goals of the original formulation of the order.

CHURCH ARCHITECTURE

In the twelfth century, cathedrals in Europe expanded to accommodate the greater crowds of Christians attending services, especially as pilgrimage became more common, as well as to demonstrate the majesty and glory of God. While many of the earlier churches were constructed in a Romanesque style, based on the Roman basilica of a long building built with a barrel vault that limited how tall or wide the structure could be and tended to make churches dark, the Gothic style came into vogue at this time. Gothic buildings used a pointed arch with a cross vault that shifted the pressure of the stone arches from the walls to pillars. This allowed Gothic buildings to be taller and wider than Romanesque ones, particularly when the cross vaults were paired with flying buttresses, reinforcing structures added to the outside of the church that helped balance the force. With the weight and pressure shifted to pillars, architects could replace heavy stone walls with stained-glass windows, which added to the beauty of the Gothic designs. The Gothic architecture can thus be recognized by four elements: the pointed arch, cross vault, stained-glass window, and flying buttress. Some of the most famous examples of Gothic architecture are in France, including Notre-Dame of Paris, but English cathedrals were rebuilt in this style as well, including Canterbury Cathedral, Westminster Abbey, York Minster, Winchester Cathedral, and Salisbury Cathedral. Gothic architecture came into fashion in the twelfth century, but it took a long time for construction on cathedrals, and many of the notable English cathedrals remained under construction and revision through the fifteenth century. Gothic architecture in England took on a particular style of vaulting known as the fan vault, with a curve spacing fanning out the ribs, starting in the mid-fourteenth century. Gloucester Cathedral, King's College Chapel in Cambridge, parts of Canterbury Cathedral constructed under Henry VI, Christ Church in Oxford, among many others adopted this distinct style.

Parish churches were smaller buildings where the congregation could worship together, sprinkled across the English countryside and in towns. A typical parish church was based on a simple plan of a long nave with a chancel oriented, as all Christian churches were, on an east-west axis, with the chancel in the east, toward Jerusalem. The chancel contained the altar where the priest performed the mass, while the laity congregated in the nave. In most churches, a rood screen separated the chancel from the nave and obscured the view of the priest while performing the mass. Parishioners stood for the service, as fixed pews did not come into fashion until the sixteenth century and grouped themselves according to sex. It was customary for the priest to take responsibility for the maintenance of the chancel, while the parish maintained the nave.

The parish church was a space with multiple functions. In a village, the parish church's nave might become a place where the town could meet to make decisions, such as what to plant in the fields that year. It might even become a storehouse for grain or even animals as the largest and sturdiest building in the area. Christians also used parish churches as meeting places or even to conduct business, whether or not they were attending church services. When John Lely went to church for his son's christening in 1424, he also "bought a horse, accepted two homages, and terminated a dispute" (Clarke and Hicks 2016, 167).

Like the cathedrals, as the population expanded, so did the parish church. The original nave widened, adding aisles to accommodate more parishioners, and side chapels could appear where other services might take place or where quiet prayers to saints could be offered. Churches that did not already have them gained covered porches to protect those entering and exiting the church from rain and to provide further opportunities for decorating the church. Stone masons carved figures into church walls, sometimes using stock images and sometimes using models from the community. The Bible and the community of saints provided inspiration for the masons' artistry, and some design choices might be specified in contracts or negotiations. Women could usually find an image of the Virgin Mary or other female saints inside the local church and might recognize a face patterned on a neighbor or relative. Parish churches also had a bell tower and bell that could be rung during the mass, to celebrate weddings or mark deaths, and to ring the alarm. Sometimes, bells were rung to frighten away evil spirits, as was done during the plague.

Although the paint has faded, most medieval churches were painted riotous colors with murals or patterns on walls and columns, or even on ceilings. Churches might also include altarpieces, images of saints, and stained-glass windows. These images inspired devotion and reminded parishioners of the major scenes of the Bible such as the Last Supper, the Crucifixion, or the Last Judgment. The artwork of the local parish church in a village or town was probably more ornate than anything in a private home below the level of the gentry.

HERESY

In medieval Christianity in Western Europe, orthodox (right thinking) belief and practice was established by the pope, his advisors, and church councils; practices or beliefs that deviated from orthodoxy were declared "heresy." Heretics were Christians who continued to believe or practice a version of Christianity that they had been warned was heretical, not according to the orthodox faith. Those convicted of heresy could face execution, usually by burning. Medieval England was not a major outpost for heretical thinking for much of the Middle Ages, until the Lollard heresy in the fourteenth century.

The heresy originated with the ideas of John Wycliffe (d. 1384), an educated English theologian who spent much of his career in Oxford. Wycliffe attacked the special status of the clergy and emphasized the importance of Scripture, even translating the Bible so it was accessible to an audience that could only read English. He did not accept the concept of transubstantiation, which earned him a charge of heresy, and he was officially condemned by the pope in 1377. Some of his ideas, such as the supremacy of the king over clergy, were taken up two centuries later during the Protestant Reformation, although there is not a direct chain of transmission from Lollardy to Protestantism. Lollards were also dismissive of the cult of the saints and requiem masses, which allows us to use wills as some indication of orthodox or heretical beliefs in the fifteenth century. Wycliffe's ideas were initially well received in Oxford and among the gentry and petty nobility, but it was rooted out in Oxford and a rebellion by the reputed Lollard Sir John Oldcastle against the king made it politically challenging to hold to Lollard ideas, which made the heresy less popular among the nobility. Most believers after the 1420s were among the common people. Coventry and Norwich were sites of Lollard persecutions in the fifteenth and sixteenth centuries.

Lollards were a misogynist heretical group who believed that women were capable of numerous sexual perversions, particularly within monasteries where they were unsupervised by men. In a 1395 text posted to Westminster, where Parliament met, the Lollards issued a manifesto explaining their beliefs, called the *Twelve Conclusions*. In the eleventh conclusion, they questioned the "vow of continence made in our church of women," claiming nuns were not actually celibate. They accused nuns of "having sex with themselves or irrational beast or creature that bears no life surpasses those sins in worthiness to be punished by the pains of hell" and depicted these apparently terrible sins as worse than "slaying children before they are christened, abortion, and contraception by medicine." They also concluded that widows must remarry "for we cannot excuse them from secret sins," suggesting that it was all claims to female chastity and not just those of religious women that were suspect (Lochrie 2003, 79).

Some women are on record supporting Lollardy, along with their husbands, such as Sir Thomas Latimer and his wife Anne, who named a Lollard as priest at the church on their estate. Yet other wives of avowed Lollards expressed orthodox ideas in their wills. Lollards also argued that preaching and public teaching should be available to all Christians, while the Orthodox Church limited preaching to priests. Women who were attracted to Lollardy might have appreciated these ideas permitting women to preach and to have direct access to God through Scripture, not mediated by clergy, ones who valued their contributions to the church more than orthodoxy had. That association between public preaching and Lollardy put women who spoke about their faith in public, such as Margery Kempe, in danger, and indeed, Margery was accused of Lollardy.

The heresy seemed to be most popular among educated urban communities and to have spread within households, both among families and servants. Lollards met primarily in one another's homes to read and worship in English together. Given women's importance within the household and her responsibilities for managing servants and educating children, especially in terms of their faith, it is likely that women were thus heavily involved in transmitting Lollard ideas. Agnes Grebill in Tenterden in Kent was the only member of her family of four who refused to disavow her Lollard notions. Alice Rowley, wife of the mayor of Coventry, William Rowley, was a Lollard expressing her beliefs to neighbors in the 1490s, owning English books, and teaching others according to her 1511–1512 examination.

Those Lollards who were convicted of heresy were punished in a variety of ways. Some were ordered to make a procession as penitents, walking through town in a state of undress; to make a public confession admitting their error; and to make a gift to the church. The public shaming ritual was meant to draw attention to the seriousness of the offense and deter others from committing it. Some heretics received more significant sentences and were burned at the stake. Women also gave testimony against other women to accuse them of heresy. Joan Clyfland, a maid accused her employer, the wife of William Baxter, Margery, of disrespecting the saints, the crucifix, and pilgrimage. Other women convicted of Lollardy included Joan Gest and Margery Locock.

The Lollards did advocate for greater literacy and the ability of all Christians to read the Bible in the vernacular, as part of their hostility to clerical privilege and control of access to God. Because Lollardy became heretical, however, their association with vernacular Bibles made it heretical to even own English-language versions of any Scripture in the fifteenth century.

JEWS IN ENGLAND

It was unusual for England to be as homogenous as it seems in these pages, and it took some effort by the kings of England to create a kingdom of Christians. Prior to the late thirteenth century, there had been a small but significant population of Jews living in the kingdom, but they were expelled in 1290 by King Edward I and not able to return to England for centuries. The Edict of Expulsion was the end of a long period of persecution for Jews in England.

Beginning with the Norman conquest in 1066, Jews were treated as a special category, subject directly to the king rather than to a local jurisdiction. Following the requirements of the Fourth Lateran Council in 1215, which required Jews to wear distinguishing clothing, the 1218 Edict of the Badge imposed the Jewish Badge on all Jews living in England. In 1275 Edward I specified that the badge had to be yellow, six fingers long, and three fingers broad, and worn above the heart.

Because canon law prohibitions on lending money did not apply to Jews, and because Jews could not swear the Christian oaths that permitted land owning, many Jews in Christian lands were pushed into professions such as banking and moneylending, as well as working as merchants. The special status as direct subjects of the king as well as the financial status as bankers led to extensive exploitation of Jews by the king. In addition to greater and greater taxes, Henry III imposed the Statute of Jewry, which only allowed Jews to remain in England if they in some way served the king. It also prohibited the building of new synagogues and sexual relationships between Jews and Christians. It attempted to segregate and ghettoize Jews by requiring them to obtain a license to live outside already established Jewish communities.

Henry also lent belief to popular anti-Semitic myths, such as the blood libel story. According to these stories, which cropped up in many places across Europe, Jews captured Christian children and ritually murdered them in a reenactment and mockery of the Passion of Jesus. Such a story was told in Lincoln in 1255 and was remembered in the shrine of Little St. Hugh in that town, and also in Norwich, where a shrine to William of Norwich became very popular. There was no truth to these stories, but devotion to shrines of these boys encouraged the idea and encouraged hostility against Jews. Eucharistic devotion and the popularity of Corpus Christi plays also fostered another myth, that Jews convinced older Christian women to steal consecrated Eucharist wafers (in Christian belief, the literal body of Christ) and deliver them to Jews, who then attacked them with knives, stabbing Jesus. There was no evidence to this story, but it circulated and encouraged hostility toward Jews.

Such hostility turned to violence. When Richard I, an avowed Crusader, became king in 1189, false rumors spread that he had planned a pogrom against Jews in London, and mob violence began in the city's Jewish quarter. Jewish homes and business were set on fire, and the mob murdered anyone who tried to leave that part of the city. The incident embarrassed the king, but he was not able to punish many of the perpetrators. Later pogroms took place in Lynn, at Bury St. Edmunds, and at Stamford. In Lincoln, Jews were able to hide in the castle. Crusading energy brought rumors of further violence to York, where the Jews sought safety inside Clifford's Tower. When a mob indeed showed up to attack the Jews, those hiding inside the tower feared that they would be forced to convert or that their children would be forcibly baptized. The Jewish leaders killed themselves and their children before burning the tower from inside, killing the rest of the community; at least 150 people died.

These sad stories are important background for the lives of women in the fourteenth and fifteenth centuries. Christianity was a deeply held faith for many of these women, but many of them were also painfully aware that violations of orthodoxy, conformity, and obedience were dangerous. Failing to follow the dictates of their faith could also have violent, deadly consequences. Such ferocious policing of the boundaries was familiar to women as an everyday experience of patriarchy.

FOR FURTHER READING

Clark, Andrew. 1911. *The English Register of Godstow Nunnery, Near Oxford, Written about 1450*. London: EETS.

Clarke, Katie, and Michael Hicks. 2016. "What Went on in the Medieval Parish Church, 1377–1447, with Particular Reference to Churching." In *The Later Medieval Inquisitions Post Mortem: Mapping the Medieval Countryside and Rural Society*, edited by Michael Hicks. Woodbridge: Boydell Press.

Dinshaw, Carolyn. 2003. "Margery Kempe." In *The Cambridge Companion to Medieval Women's Writing*, edited by Carolyn Dinshaw and David Wallace, 222–239. Cambridge: Cambridge University Press.

Erler, Mary C. 2002. *Women, Reading and Piety in Late Medieval England*. Cambridge: Cambridge University Press.

Furnivall, Frederick James. 1908. "How the Good Wife Taught Her Daughter." In *The Babees' Book: Medieval Manners for the Young: Done into Modern English*, edited by Edith Rickert. London: Duffield & Co. Project Gutenberg.

Gilchrist, Roberta. 1994. *Gender and Material Culture: The Archaeology of Religious Women*. London: Routledge.

Goldberg, P. J. P. 1995. *Women in England c. 1275–1525: Documentary Sources*. Manchester: Manchester University Press.

Griffiths, Fiona. 2008. "The Cross and the *Cura Monialium*: Robert of Arbrissel, John the Evangelist, and the Pastoral Care of Women in the Age of Reform." *Speculum* 83, no. 2: 303–330.

Heath, Peter, ed. 1964. *Medieval Clerical Accounts*. Borthwick Papers 26. York: St. Anthony's Press.

Horn, Joyce, ed. 1982. *The Register of Robert Hallum, Bishop of Salisbury 1407–1417*. London: Boydell and Brewer.

Hughes-Edwards, Mary. 2012. *Reading Medieval Anchoritism: Ideology and Spiritual Practices*. Cardiff: University of Wales Press.

Julian of Norwich. 1978. *Revelations of Divine Love: Translated from British Library Additional MS 37790*. Translated by Frances Beer. Heidelberg: Winter.

Lochrie, Karma. 2003. "Between Women." In *The Cambridge Companion to Medieval Women's Writing*, edited by Carolyn Dinshaw and David Wallace, 70–88. Cambridge: Cambridge University Press.

Mulder-Bakker, Anneke B. 2005. *Lives of the Anchoresses: The Rise of the Urban Recluse in Medieval Europe*. Translated by Myra Heerspink Scholz. Philadelphia: University of Pennsylvania Press.

Rawcliffe, Carole. 2003. "Women, Childbirth, and Religion in Later Medieval England." In *Women and Religion in Medieval England*, edited by Diana Wood. Oxford: Oxbow Books.

Ward, Jennifer. 2006. *Women in England in the Middle Ages*. New York: Hambledon Continuum.

Watson, Nicholas. 2003. "Julian of Norwich." In *The Cambridge Companion to Medieval Women's Writing*, edited by Carolyn Dinshaw and David Wallace, 210–221. Cambridge: Cambridge University Press.

Wogan-Browne, Jocelyn. 2001. *Saints' Lives and Women's Literary Culture, c. 115–1300: Virginity and Its Authorizations*. Oxford: Oxford University Press.

FURTHER READING

INTRODUCTION

For more information about studying race in the Middle Ages, consult *Race and Medieval Studies: A Partial Bibliography*, compiled by Jonathan Hsy and Julie Orlemanski, https://docs.google.com/document /d/18JClsma1BMKYCxvgeWqwPej3ZSCrQXlAlXbL0CdqWmE/ edit, the "Recommended Readings for Early Medieval Studies" bibliography compiled by Mary Rambaran-Olm and Erik Wade, https://mrambaranolm.medium.com/race-101-for-early-medieval -studies-selected-readings-77be815f8d0f, and the Teaching Asso-ciation for Medieval Studies Featured Lesson Resource Page on Race, Racism and the Middle Ages, compiled by Carol L. Robinson, https://teams-medieval.org/?page_id=76.

Amt, Emilie, ed. 1993. *Women's Lives in Medieval Europe: A Sourcebook*. New York: Routledge.

Amt, Emilie, and Katherine Allen Smith, eds. 2018. *Medieval England 500–1500: A Reader*. 2nd ed. Toronto: University of Toronto Press.

Bennett, Judith M. 2007. *History Matters: Patriarchy and the Challenge of Feminism*. Philadelphia: University of Pennsylvania Press.

Bennett, Judith M., and Ruth Mazo Karras, eds. 2013. *The Oxford Handbook of Women & Gender in Medieval Europe*. Oxford: Oxford University Press.

Bennett, Judith M., and Ruth Mazo Karras. 2013. "Women, Gender, and Medieval Historians." In *The Oxford Handbook of Women & Gender in Medieval Europe*, edited by Judith M. Bennett and Ruth Mazo Karras, 1–20. Oxford: Oxford University Press.

Blamires, Alcuin, ed. 1992. *Woman Defamed and Woman Defended: An Anthology of Medieval Texts.* Oxford: Clarendon Press.

Bliss, W. H., and J. A. Twemlow. 1902. *Calendar of Papers Relating to Great Britain and Ireland: Volume 4, 1362–1404.* London. https://www.british -history.ac.uk/cal-papal-registers/brit-ie/vol4/pp36-47.

Clanchy, Michael T. 1993. *From Memory to Written Record: England 1066– 1307.* Oxford: Wiley-Blackwell.

Constable, Giles. 1995. *Three Studies in Medieval Religious and Social Thought.* Cambridge: Cambridge University Press.

Feminae: Medieval Women and Gender Index. University of Iowa Libraries. https://inpress.lib.uiowa.edu/feminae/.

Goldberg, P. J. P. 1995. *Women in England c. 1275–1525: Documentary Sources.* Manchester: Manchester University Press.

Goldberg, P. J. P. 2007. "Gender and Matrimonial Litigation in the Church Courts in the Later Middle Ages: The Evidence of the Court of York." *Gender & History* 19, no. 1: 43–59.

Grauer, Anne L. 2002. "Where Were the Women?" In *Human Biologists in the Archives: Demography, Health, Nutrition and Genetics in Historical Populations,* edited by D. Ann Herring and Alan C. Swedlund, 266–288. Cambridge: Cambridge University Press.

Green, Monica H. 2014. "Pandemic Disease in the Medieval World: Rethinking the Black Death." Special Issue of the *Medieval Globe* 1.

Grossman, Avraham. 2004. *Pious and Rebellious: Jewish in Medieval Europe.* Translated by Jonathan Chipman. Waltham, MA: Brandeis University Press.

Karras, Ruth Mazo. 2005. *Sexuality in Medieval Europe: Doing unto Others.* New York: Routledge.

Partner, Nancy F., ed. 1993. *Studying Medieval Women: Sex, Gender, Feminism.* Cambridge, MA: Medieval Academy of America.

Salisbury, Eve, ed. 2002. *The Trials and Joys of Marriage.* Kalamazoo, MI: Medieval Institute Publications. https://d.lib.rochester.edu/teams /publication/salisbury-trials-and-joys-of-marriage.

Schaus, Margaret, ed. 2006. *Women and Gender in Medieval Europe: An Encyclopedia.* New York: Routledge.

Ward, Jennifer. 2006. *Women in England in the Middle Ages.* New York: Hambledon Continuum.

Waymack, Anna Fore, ed. *De raptu meo,* A Website for Documents Related to Cecily Chaumpaigne. https://chaumpaigne.org/.

Wilson, Katharina M., and Nadia Margolis, eds. 2004. *Women in the Middle Ages: An Encyclopedia.* Westport, CT: Greenwood Press.

CHAPTER 1

Barron, Caroline M. 1994. "Introduction: The Widow's World in Later Medieval London." In *Medieval London Widows, 1300–1500,* edited by Caroline M. Barron and Anne F. Sutton. London: Hambledon Press.

Barron, Caroline M., and Anne F. Sutton, eds. 1994. *Medieval London Widows, 1300–1500*. London: Hambledon Press.

Beattie, Cordelia. 2007. *Medieval Single Women: The Politics of Social Classification in Late Medieval England*. Oxford: Oxford University Press.

Bennett, Judith M. 1987. *Women in the Medieval English Countryside: Gender and Household in Brigstock before the Plague*. Oxford: Oxford University Press.

Bennett, Judith M. 1999. *A Medieval Life: Cecilia Penifader of Brigstock, c. 1295–1344*. Boston: McGraw-Hill.

Bennett, Judith M. 2003. "Writing Fornication: Medieval Leyrwite and Its Historians." *Transactions of the Royal Historical Society*, 6th series, 13: 131–162.

Bennett, Judith M., and Amy M. Froide. 1999. *Singlewomen in the European Past, 1250–1800*. Philadelphia: University of Pennsylvania Press.

Benson, Larry D., ed. 2008. . Oxford: Oxford University Press.

Blamires, Alcuin, ed. 1992. *Woman Defamed and Woman Defended: An Anthology of Medieval Texts*. Oxford: Clarendon Press.

Bliss, W. H., and J. A. Twemlow. 1902. *Calendar of Papers Relating to Great Britain and Ireland: Volume 4, 1362–1404*. London. https://www.british-history.ac.uk/cal-papal-registers/brit-ie/vol4/pp36-47.

Brooke, Christopher. 1994. *The Medieval Idea of Marriage*. Oxford: Oxford University Press.

Butler, Sara M. 2007. *The Language of Abuse: Marital Violence in Later Medieval England*. Leiden: Brill.

Carlson, Cindy L., and Angela Jane Weisl, eds. 1999. *Constructions of Widowhood and Virginity in the Middle Ages*. New York: St. Martin's.

Clayton, Jane. 2019. "Elizabeth Clere and Marriage between the Clere and Paston Families in the Late Fifteenth Century." *Notes and Queries* (June): 214–216.

Coulton, G., ed. 1931. *Life in the Middle Ages*. Cambridge: Cambridge University Press.

Davis, Norman E., ed. 1976. . 2 vols. Oxford: Clarendon.

D'Avray, David. 2004. *Medieval Marriage: Symbolism and Society*. Oxford: Oxford University Press.

D'Avray, David. 2015. *Papacy, Monarchy, and Marriage, 860–1600*. Cambridge: Cambridge University Press.

Duby, Georges. 1983. *The Knight, the Lady, and the Priest: The Making of Modern Marriage in Medieval France*. Translated by Barbara Bray. New York: Pantheon.

Dunn, Caroline. 2013. *Stolen Women in Medieval England: Rape, Abduction, and Adultery, 1100–1500*. Cambridge: Cambridge University Press.

Elliott, Dyan. 1993. *Spiritual Marriage: Sexual Abstinence in Medieval Wedlock*. Princeton, NJ: Princeton University Press.

Elliott, Dyan. 1999. *Fallen Bodies: Pollution, Sexuality, and Demonology in the Middle Ages*. Philadelphia: University of Pennsylvania Press.

Erler, Mary C. 1994. "Three Fifteenth-Century Vowesses." In *Medieval London Wives, 1300–1500*, edited by Caroline M. Barron and Anne F. Sutton. London: Hambledon Press.

Fitzherbert, Anthony. 1534. "The Book of Husbandry." Project Gutenberg. https://www.gutenberg.org/files/57457/57457-h/57457-h.htm.

Furnivall, Frederick James. 1908. "How the Good Wife Taught Her Daughter." In *The Babees' Book: Medieval Manners for the Young: Done into Modern English*, edited by Edith Rickert. London: Duffield & Co. Project Gutenberg.

Goldberg, Jeremy. 2013. "Echoes, Whispers, Ventriloquisms: On Recovering Women's Voices from the Court of York in the Later Middle Ages." In *Women, Agency and the Law, 1300–1700*, edited by Bronach Kane and Fiona Williamson, 31–41, 169–171. London: Pickering and Chatto.

Goldberg, P. J. P. 1995. *Women in England c. 1275–1525: Documentary Sources*. Manchester: Manchester University Press.

Hanawalt, Barbara A. 1986. . Oxford: Oxford University Press.

Hanawalt, Barbara A. 2007. *The Wealth of Wives: Women, Law, and Economy in Late Medieval London*. Oxford: Oxford University Press.

Harris, Carissa. 2020. "The Distinguished Medieval Penis Investigators." *Narratively.com*, November 12.

Helmholz, Richard H. 1974. *Marriage Litigation in Medieval England*. Cambridge: Cambridge University Press.

Helmholz, Richard H. 1987. *Canon Law and the Law of England*. London: Hambledon Press.

Herlihy, David. 1985. *Medieval Households*. Cambridge, MA: Harvard University Press.

Kane, Bronach. 2008. *Impotence and Virginity in the Late Medieval Ecclesiastical Court of York*. Borthwick Paper 114.

Kelly, Henry Ansgar. 1975. *Love and Marriage in the Age of Chaucer*. Ithaca, NY: Cornell University Press.

Kingsford, Charles Lethbridge, ed. 1919. *The Stoner Letters and Papers, 1290–1483*, vol. 2. London: London Royal Historical Society.

Kittredge, G. L. 1960. "Chaucer's Discussion of Marriage." In *Chaucer Criticism*, edited by R. J. Schoeck and Jerome Taylor. 2 vols. Notre Dame, IN: University of Notre Dame Press.

Kowaleski, Maryanne. 1999. "Singlewomen in Medieval and Early Modern Europe: The Demographic Perspective." In *Singlewomen in the European Past, 1250–1800*, edited by Judith M. Bennett and Amy M. Froide. Philadelphia: University of Pennsylvania Press.

Massingberd, W. O., ed. 1902. *Court Rolls of the Manor of Ingoldmells in the County of Lincoln*. London: Spottiswoode.

McCarthy, Conor. 2004. *Marriage in Medieval England: Law, Literature, and Practice*. Woodbridge: Boydell and Brewer.

McCarthy, Conor, ed. 2004. *Love, Sex and Marriage in the Middle Ages: A Sourcebook*. London: Routledge.

McSheffrey, Shannon. 2006. *Marriage, Sex, and Civic Culture in Late Medieval London*. Philadelphia: University of Pennsylvania Press.

Mitchell, Linda E. 1999. *Women in Medieval Western European Culture*. New York: Garland.

Murray, Jacqueline, ed. 2001. *Love, Marriage, and Family in the Middle Ages: A Reader*. Peterborough, ON: Broadview Press.

Parish, Helen. 2010. *Clerical Celibacy in the West, c. 1100–1700*. Farnham, UK: Ashgate.

Pollock, Frederick, and F. W. Maitland. 1968. *The History of English Law before the Time of Edward I*. 2nd ed. 2 vols. Cambridge: Cambridge University Press.

Rawcliffe, Carole. 1994. "Margaret Stodeye, Lady Philipot (d. 1431)." In *Medieval London Widows, 1300–1500*, edited by Caroline M. Barron and Anne F. Sutton. London: Hambledon Press.

Reddy, William. 2012. *The Making of Romantic Love: Longing and Sexuality in Europe, South Asia, and Japan, 900–1200 CE*. Chicago: University of Chicago Press.

Salih, Sarah. 2001. *Versions of Virginity in Late Medieval England*. Woodbridge: D. S. Brewer.

Sheehan, Michael M. 1996. *Marriage, Family, and Law in Medieval Europe: Collected Studies*, edited by James K. Farge. Toronto: University of Toronto Press.

Thibodeaux, Jennifer D. 2015. *The Manly Priest: Clerical Celibacy, Masculinity, and Reform in England and Normandy, 1066–1300.* Philadelphia: University of Pennsylvania Press.

Tompkins, Laura. 2018. "Mary Percy and John de Southeray: Wardship, Marriage, and Divorce in Fourteenth-Century England." In *Fourteenth Century England*, edited by Gwilym Dodd. Cambridge: Boydell & Brewer.

Walker, Sue Sheridan. 1993. *Wife and Widow in Medieval England*. Ann Arbor: University of Michigan Press.

Walker, Susan. 1982. "Free Consent and Marriage of Feudal Wards in Medieval England." *Journal of Medieval History* 9: 123–179.

Ward, Jennifer C. 1994. "Elizabeth de Burgh, Lady of Clare (d. 1360)." In *Medieval London Widows, 1300–1500*, edited by Caroline M. Barron and Anne F. Sutton. London: Hambledon Press.

Ward, Jennifer C. 2006. *Women in England in the Middle Ages*. New York: Hambledon Continuum.

Watt, Diane, ed. 2004. *The Paston Women*. Woodbridge: D. S. Brewer.

Woolgar, C. M. 1999. *The Great Household in Medieval England*. New Haven, CT: Yale University Press.

CHAPTER 2

Bennett, Judith M. 2003. "Writing Fornication: Medieval Leyrwite and Its Historians." *Transactions of the Royal Historical Society*, 6th series, 13: 131–162.

Biller, Peter. 2003. *Measure of Multitude: Population in Medieval Thought*. Oxford: Oxford University Press.

Blumenfeld-Kosinski, Renate. 1990. *Not of Women Born: Representations of Caesarean Birth in Medieval and Renaissance Culture*. Ithaca, NY: Cornell University Press.

Cabré, Montserrat. 2008. "Women or Healers? Household Practices and the Categories of Health Care in Late Medieval Iberia." *Bulletin of the History of Medicine* 82: 18–51.

Cadden, Joan. 1993. *The Meanings of Sex Difference in the Middle Ages: Medicine, Science, and Culture*. Cambridge: Cambridge University Press.

Callan, Maeve B. 2012. "Of Vanishing Fetuses and Maidens Made-Again: Abortion, Restored Virginity, and Similar Scenarios in Medieval Irish Hagiography and Penitentials." *Journal of the History of Sexuality* 21, no. 2: 282–296.

Clarke, Katie, and Michael Hicks. 2016. "What Went on in the Medieval Parish Church, 1377–1447, with Particular Reference to Churching." In *The Later Medieval Inquisitions Post Mortem: Mapping the Medieval Countryside and Rural Society*, edited by Michael Hicks. Woodbridge: Boydell Press.

Deller, William S. 2010. "The First Rite of Passage: Baptism in Medieval Memory." *Journal of Family History* 36, no. 1: 3–14.

Donahoe, Róisín. 2021. "'A Solemn Relic Sent to Women Travailing': The Girdle in Late Medieval English Childbirth Networks." Paper Presentation at the Gender and Medieval Studies Conference, University of Surrey.

Fisher, J. D. C. 1965. "Christian Initiation: Baptism in the Medieval West." *Alcuin Club* 47: 160–163.

Furnivall, Frederick James. 1908. "How the Good Wife Taught Her Daughter." In *The Babees' Book: Medieval Manners for the Young: Done into Modern English*, edited by Edith Rickert. London: Duffield & Co. Project Gutenberg.

Gibson, Gail. 1996. "Blessing from Sun and Moon: Churching as Women's Theater." In *Bodies and Disciplines: Intersections of Literature and History in Fifteenth Century England*, edited by Barbara A. Hanawalt and David Wallace, 139–154. Minneapolis: University of Minnesota Press.

Goldberg, P. J. P. 1995. *Women in England c. 1275–1525: Documentary Sources*. Manchester: Manchester University Press.

Grauer, Anne L. 2002. "Where Were the Women?" In *Human Biologists in the Archives: Demography, Health, Nutrition and Genetics in Historical Populations*, edited by D. Ann Herring and Alan C. Swedlund, 266–288. Cambridge: Cambridge University Press.

Green, Monica H. 1988–1989. "Women's Medical Practice and Health Care in Medieval Europe." *Signs* 14: 434–473.

Green, Monica H. 1990. "Constantinus Africans and the Conflict between Religion and Science." In *The Human Embryo: Aristotle and the*

European and Arabic Traditions, edited by Gordon Dunstan, 47–69. Exeter: University of Exeter Press.

Green, Monica H., ed. and trans. 2002. *The Trotula: A Medieval Compendium of Women's Medicine*. Philadelphia: University of Pennsylvania Press.

Green, Monica H. 2008. "Gendering the History of Women's Healthcare." *Gender & History* 20: 487–518.

Green, Monica H. 2008. *Making Women's Medicine Masculine: The Rise of Male Authority in Pre-Modern Gynaecology*. Oxford: Oxford University Press.

Green, Monica H. 2013. "Caring for Gendered Bodies." In *The Oxford Handbook of Women & Gender in Medieval Europe*, edited by Judith M. Bennett and Ruth Mazo Karras, 345–361. Oxford: Oxford University Press.

Green, Monica H., and Daniel Lord Smail. 2008. "The Trial of Floreta d'Ays (1403): Jews, Christians, and Obstetrics in Later Medieval Marseille." *Journal of Medieval History* 34, no. 2 (June): 185–211.

Hanawalt, Barbara. 1986. *The Ties That Bound: Peasant Families in Medieval England*. Oxford: Oxford University Press.

Harris-Stoertz, Fiona. 2012. "Pregnancy and Childbirth in Twelfth- and Thirteenth-Century French and English Law." *Journal of the History of Sexuality* 21, no. 2 (May): 263–281.

Helmholz, Richard. 1993. "And Were There Children's Rights in Early Modern England? The Canon Law and 'Intra-family Violence' in England, 1400–1600." *International Journal of Children's Rights* 1: 23–32.

Hollingworth, T. H. 1957. "A Demographic Study of the British Ducal Families." *Population Studies* 11, no. 1: 4–26.

Jacquart Danielle, and Claude Thomasset. 1988. *Sexuality and Medicine in the Middle Ages*. Translated by Matthew Adamson. Princeton, NJ: Princeton University Press.

Julian of Norwich. 1901. *Revelations of Divine Love*. Edited by Grace Warrack. London: Methuen & Company. Project Gutenberg.

Karras, Ruth Mazo. 2005. *Sexuality in Medieval Europe: Doing unto Others*. New York: Routledge.

Koren, Sharon Faye. 2011. *Forsaken: The Menstruant in Medieval Jewish Menstruation*. Waltham, MA: Brandeis University Press.

Kowaleski, Maryanne. 2013. "Gendering Demographic Change in the Middle Ages." In *The Oxford Handbook of Women & Gender in Medieval Europe*. Edited by Judith M. Bennett and Ruth Mazo Karras. Oxford: Oxford University Press.

Legg, L. G. Wickham, ed. 1901. *English Coronation Records*. London: Archibald Constable and Co. Ltd.

L'Estrange, E. 2008. *Holy Motherhood: Gender, Dynasty, and Visual Culture in the Later Middle Ages*. Manchester: Manchester University Press, 2008.

Leyser, Henrietta. 1995. *Medieval Women: A Social History of Women in England 450–1500*. London: Orion.

Maitland, F. W., ed. 1887. *Bracton's Note Book: A Collection of Cases Decided in the King's Courts during the Reign of Henry the Third*. London: C. J. Clay & Sons.

Maurer, H. E. 2003. *Margaret of Anjou: Queenship and Power in Late Medieval England*. Woodbridge: Boydell Press.

Moreton, C. E. 1992. *The Townshend and Their World: Gentry, Law and Land in Norfolk, c. 1450–1551*. Oxford: Clarendon Press.

Mueller, Wolfgang P. 2012. *The Criminalization of Abortion in the West: Its Origins in Medieval Law*. Ithaca, NY: Cornell University Press.

Okerlund, A. N. 2009. *Elizabeth of York*. Basingstoke: Palgrave Macmillan.

Park, Katharine. 2006. *Secrets of Women: Gender, Generation, and the Origins of Human Dissection*. New York: Zone Books.

Park, Katharine. 2018. "Managing Childbirth and Fertility in Medieval Europe." In *Reproduction*, edited by Nick Hopwood, Rebecca Flemming, and Lauren Kassell, 153–166. Cambridge: Cambridge University Press.

Rawcliffe, Carole. 1995. *Medicine and Society in Later Medieval England*. Stroud: Alan Sutton.

Rawcliffe, Carole. 2003. "Women, Childbirth, and Religion in Later Medieval England." In *Women and Religion in Medieval England*, edited by Diana Wood. Oxford: Oxbow Books.

Reames, Sherry L., ed. 2003. "John Lydgate, The Lyfe of Seynt Margarete." In *Middle English Legends of Women Saints*. Kalamazoo, MI: Medieval Institute Publications.

Riddle, John M. 1992. *Contraception and Abortion from the Ancient World to the Renaissance*. Cambridge, MA: Harvard University Press.

Riddle, John M. 1997. *Eve's Herbs: A History of Contraception and Abortion in the West*. Cambridge, MA: Harvard University Press.

Rieder, Paula M. 2006. *On the Purification of Women: Churching in Northern France, 1100–1500*. New York: Palgrave Macmillan.

Shahar, Shulamith. 1990. *Childhood in the Middle Ages*. New York: Routledge.

Shenton, Caroline. 2003. "Philippa of Hainault's Churchings: the Politics of Motherhood at the Court of Edward III." In *Family and Dynasty in Late Medieval England: Proceedings of the 1997 Harlaxton Symposium*, edited by Richard Eales and Shaun Tyas. Donington: Shaun Tyas.

Ward, Jennifer. 2006. *Women in England in the Middle Ages*. New York: Hambledon Continuum.

CHAPTER 3

Adams, Tracy. 2009. "Christine de Pisan, Isabeau of Bavaria, and Female Regency." *French Historical Studies* 32, no. 1: 1–32.

Adams, Tracy. 2010. *The Life and Afterlife of Isabeau of Bavaria*. Baltimore: Johns Hopkins University Press.

Beem, C. 2006. *The Lioness Roared: The Problems of Female Rule in English History*. Basingstoke: Palgrave Macmillan.

Beem, C. 2008. *The Royal Minorities of Medieval and Early Modern England*. Basingstoke: Palgrave Macmillan.

Bennett, Judith M. 2002. "Queens, Whores, and Maidens: Women in Chaucer's England." Hayes Robinson Lecture. Royal Holloway, University of London.

Benz St. John, L. 2012. *Three Medieval Queens: Queenship and Crown in Fourteenth-Century England*. Basingstoke: Palgrave Macmillan.

Brown, E. A. R. 1974. "The Tyranny of a Concept: Feudalism and Historians of Medieval Europe." *American Historical Review* 79: 1063–1088.

Burns, E. Jane. 2013. "Performing Courtliness." In *The Oxford Handbook of Women & Gender in Medieval Europe*, edited by Judith M. Bennett and Ruth Mazo Karras, 396–413. Oxford: Oxford University Press.

Carpenter, J., and S. B. MacLean, eds. 1995. *The Power of the Weak: Studies on Medieval Women*. Urbana: University of Illinois Press.

Chaucer, Geoffrey. 1889. *The Legend of Good Women*. Edited by Walter W. Skeat. Oxford: Clarendon Press.

Chibnall, Marjorie. 1991. *The Empress Matilda: Queen Consort, Queen Mother, and Lady of the English*. Oxford: Wiley-Blackwell.

Davis, James. 2012. "Selling Food and Drink in the Aftermath of the Black Death." In *Town and Countryside in the Age of the Black Death: Essays in Honour of John Hatcher*, edited by Mark Bailey and Stephen Rigby, 351–406. Turnhout: Brepols Publishers.

Downie, F. 2006. *She Is but a Woman: Queenship in Scotland, 1424–1463*. Edinburgh: John Donald.

Dress, Joanna H. 2013. "Aristocratic Economies: Women and Family." In *The Oxford Handbook of Women & Gender in Medieval Europe*, edited by Judith M. Bennett and Ruth Mazo Karras, 327–343. Oxford: Oxford University Press.

Duggan, A. J., ed. 1997. *Queens and Queenship in Medieval Europe* Woodbridge: Boydell Press.

Duggan, A. J., ed. 2000. *Nobles and Nobility in Medieval Europe*. Woodbridge: Boydell Press.

Earenfight, Theresa. 2013. *Queenship in Medieval Europe*. London: Palgrave Macmillan.

Erler, Mary C., and Maryanne Kowaleski. 1988. *Women and Power in the Middle Ages*. Athens: University of Georgia Press.

Erler, Mary C., and Maryanne Kowaleski. 2003. *Gendering the Master Narrative: Women and Power in the Middle Ages*. Ithaca, NY: Cornell University Press.

Evergates, Theodore. 1999. *Aristocratic Women in Medieval France*. Philadelphia: University of Pennsylvania Press.

Finn, K. M. 2012. *The Last Plantagenet Consorts: Gender, Genre, and Historiography, 1440–1627*. Basingstroke: Palgrave Macmillan.

Fradenburg, L. O. Aranye, ed. 1992. *Women and Sovereignty*. Edinburgh: University of Edinburgh Press.

Furnivall, Frederick James. 1908. "How the Good Wife Taught Her Daughter." In *The Babees' Book: Medieval Manners for the Young: Done into Modern English*, edited by Edith Rickert. London: Duffield & Co. Project Gutenberg.

Gee, L. L. 2002. *Women, Art, and Patronage from Henry III to Edward III, 1216–1377*. Woodbridge: Boydell and Brewer.

Goldberg, P. J. P. 1995. *Women in England c. 1275–1525: Documentary Sources*. Manchester: Manchester University Press.

Harris, Barbara J. 2002. *English Aristocratic Women, 1450–1550*. Oxford: Oxford University Press.

Hector, L. C., and Barbara Harvey, eds. 1982. *The Westminster Chronicle, 1381–94*. Oxford: Clarendon Press.

Hilton, L. 2008. *Queens Consort: England's Medieval Queens*. London: Weidenfeld & Nicholson.

Honeycutt, Lois. 2003. *Matilda of Scotland: A Study in Medieval Queenship*. Woodbridge: Boydell Press.

Jonas, M. K., and M. G. Underwood. 1993. *The King's Mother: Lady Margaret Beaufort, Countess of Richmond and Derby*. Cambridge: Cambridge University Press.

Krueger, Roberta L. 2013. "Towards Feminism: Christine de Pizan, Female Advocacy, and Women's Textual Communities in the Late Middle Ages and Beyond." In *The Oxford Handbook of Women & Gender in Medieval Europe*, edited by Judith M. Bennett and Ruth Mazo Karras, 590–606. Oxford: Oxford University Press.

Laynesmith, J. L. 2004. *The Last Medieval Queens: English Queenship, 1445–1503*. Oxford: Oxford University Press.

Levin, C., and R. Bucholz, eds. 2009. *Queens & Power in Medieval and Early Modern England*. Lincoln: University of Nebraska Press.

Nelson, Janet L. 1999. "Medieval Queenship." In *Women in Medieval Western European Culture*, edited by Linda E. Mitchell, 179–207. New York: Garland Publishing.

Parsons, John Carmi, ed. 1993. *Medieval Queenship*. New York: St. Martin's Press.

Reynolds, Susan. 1994. *Fiefs and Vassals: The Medieval Evidence Reinterpreted*. Oxford: Clarendon Press.

Shenton, Caroline. 2003. "Philippa of Hainault's Churchings: The Politics of Motherhood at the Court of Edward III." In *Family and Dynasty in Late Medieval England: Proceedings of the 1997 Harlaxton Symposium*, edited by Richard Eales and Shaun Tyas, 105–121. Donington: Shaun Tyas.

Strohm, Paul. 1992. "Queens as Intercessors." In *Hochon's Arrow: The Social Imagination of Fourteenth-Century Texts*, 95–119. Princeton: Princeton University Press.

Taylor, Andrew. 1997 "Anne of Bohemia and the Making of Chaucer." *Studies in the Age of Chaucer* 19: 95–119.

Taylor, Craig. 2006. "The Salic Law, French Queenship and the Defence of Women in the Late Middle Ages." *French Historical Studies* 29, no. 4: 543–564.

Ward, Jennifer. 2006. *Women in England in the Middle Ages*. New York: Hambledon Continuum.

The White Princess, season 1, Starz, 2014, streaming. https://www.starz.com/us/en/series/the-white-princess/30887.

The White Princess, season 1, Starz, 2013, streaming. https://www.starz.com/us/en/series/the-white-queen/18124.

Woodacre, Elena, and Carey Fleiner, eds. 2015. *Royal Mothers and Their Ruling Children: Wielding Political Authority from Antiquity to the Early Modern Era*. New York: Palgrave Macmillan.

CHAPTER 4

Baildon, William Paley, ed. 1896. *Select Cases in Chancery: A. D. 1364 to 1471*. London: Bernard Quaritch.

Bardsley, Sandy. 1999. "Women's Work Reconsidered: Gender and Wage Differentiation in Late Medieval England." *Past & Present* 165: 3–29.

Barron, C. M. 1996. "The Education and Training of Girls in Fifteenth-Century London." In *Courts, Counties, and the Capital in the Later Middle Ages*, edited by D. E. S. Dunn, 139–153. New York: St. Martin's Press.

Barron, C. M. 2004. *London in the Later Middle Ages: Government and People, 1200–1500*. Oxford: Oxford University Press.

Beattie, Cordelia, Anna Maslakovic, and Sarah Rees Jones, eds. 2003. *The Medieval Household in Christian Europe, c. 850–1550: Managing Power, Wealth, and the Body*. Turnhout: Brepols.

Bennett, Judith M. 1987. *Women in the Medieval English Countryside: Gender and Household in Brigstock before the Plague*. Oxford: Oxford University Press.

Bennett, Judith M. 1994. *The Wealth of Wives: Women, Law, and Economy in Late Medieval London*. New York: Routledge.

Bennet, Judith M. 1996. *Ale, Beer, and Brewsters in England*. Oxford: Oxford University Press.

Bennett, Judith M. 1999. *A Medieval Life: Cecilia Penifader of Brigstock, c. 1295–1344*. Boston: McGraw-Hill.

Bennett, Judith M. 2003. "Writing Fornication: Medieval Leyrwite and Its Historians." *Transactions of the Royal Historical Society*, 6th series, 13: 131–162.

Bennett, Judith M. 2006. *History Matters: Patriarchy and the Challenge of Feminism*. Manchester: Manchester University Press.

Bennett, Judith M., and Amy M. Froide, eds. 1999. *Singlewomen in the European Past, 1250–1800*. Philadelphia: University of Pennsylvania Press.

Clanchy, Michael T. 1993. *From Memory to Written Record: England 1066–1307*. Oxford: Wiley-Blackwell.

Davidson, Clifford, ed. *The York Corpus Christi Plays*. Kalamazoo, MI: Medieval Institute Publications, available online as part of the *TEAMS* Middle English Texts Series. https://d.lib.rochester.edu/teams /publication/davidson-the-york-corpus-christi-plays.

Davis, James. 2012. "Selling Food and Drink in the Aftermath of the Black Death." In *Town and Countryside in the Age of the Black Death: Essays in Honour of John Hatcher*, edited by Mark Bailey and Stephen Rigby, 351–406. Turnhout: Brepols Publishers.

Duffy, Eamon. 1992. *The Stripping of the Altars: Traditional Religion in England, 1400–1580*. New Haven, CT: Yale University Press.

Dyer, Christopher. 1980. *Lords and Peasants in a Changing Society: The Estates of the Bishopric of Worcester, 680–1540*. Cambridge: Cambridge University Press.

Fitzherbert, Anthony. 1534. "The Book of Husbandry." Project Gutenberg. https://www.gutenberg.org/files/57457/57457-h/57457-h.htm.

Fleming, Peter. 2001. *Family and Household in Medieval England*. Basingstoke: Palgrave.

French, Katherine L. 2003. "Women in the Late Medieval English Parish." In *Gendering the Master Narrative: Women and Power in the Middle Ages*, edited by Mary C. Erler and Maryanne Kowaleski, 156–173. Ithaca, NY: Cornell University Press.

French, Katherine L. 2013. "Genders and Material Culture." In *The Oxford Handbook of Women & Gender in Medieval Europe*, edited by Judith M. Bennett and Ruth Mazo Karras, 197–212. Oxford: Oxford University Press.

Furnivall, Frederick James. 1908. "How the Good Wife Taught Her Daughter." In *The Babees' Book: Medieval Manners for the Young: Done into Modern English*, edited by Edith Rickert. London: Duffield & Co. Project Gutenberg.

Goldberg, Jeremy. 2013. "Echoes, Whispers, Ventriloquisms: On Recovering Women's Voices from the Court of York in the Later Middle Ages." In *Women, Agency and the Law, 1300–1700*, edited by Bronach Kane and Fiona Williamson, 31–41, 169–171. London: Pickering and Chatto.

Goldberg, P. J. P. 1988. "Women in Fifteenth-Century Town Life." In *Towns and Townspeople in the Fifteenth Century*, edited by John A. F. Thompson. Gloucester: Alan Sutton.

Goldberg, P. J. P. 1992. *Women, Work, and Life Cycle in a Medieval Economy: Women in York and Yorkshire, c. 1300–1520.* Oxford: Clarendon Press.

Goldberg, P. J. P. 1995. *Women in England c. 1275–1525: Documentary Sources.* Manchester: Manchester University Press.

Goldberg, P. J. P. 2000. "Household and the Organization of Labour in Late Medieval Towns: Some English Evidence." In *The Household in Late Medieval Cities: Italy and Northwestern Europe Compared,* edited by Myriam Carlier and Tim Soens. Leuven: Garant.

Gowing, Laura. 1996. *Domestic Dangers: Women, Words, and Sex in Early Modern London.* Oxford: Clarendon Press.

Grauer, Anne L. 2002. "Where Were the Women?" In *Human Biologists in the Archives: Demography, Health, Nutrition and Genetics in Historical Populations,* edited by D. Ann Herring and Alan C. Swedlund, 266–288. Cambridge: Cambridge University Press.

Hanawalt, Barbara A. 1986. *The Ties That Bound: Peasant Families in Medieval England.* Oxford: Oxford University Press.

Hanawalt, Barbara A., ed. 1986. *Women and Work in Preindustrial Europe* Bloomington: University of Indiana Press.

Hanawalt, Barbara A. 1993. *Growing Up in Medieval London: The Experience of Childhood in History.* Oxford: Oxford University Press.

Hanawalt, Barbara A., ed. 1998. *"Of Good and Ill Repute": Gender and Social Control in Medieval England.* Oxford: Oxford University Press.

Hanawalt, Barbara A. 2007. *The Wealth of Wives: Women, Law, and Economy in Late Medieval London.* Oxford: Oxford University Press.

Harris, Carissa M. 2018. *Obscene Pedagogies: Transgressive Talk and Sexual Education in Late Medieval Britain.* Ithaca, NY: Cornell University Press.

Hilton, Rodney. 1973. *Bond Men Made Free: Medieval Peasant Movements and the English Rising of 1381.* New York: Routledge.

Horrox, Rosemary, ed. 1994. *The Black Death.* Manchester: Manchester University Press.

Hutton, Ronald. 1994. *The Rise and Fall of Merry England: The Ritual Year, 1400–1700.* Oxford: Oxford University Press.

Keene, Derek. 1994. "Tanners' Widows, 1300–1350." In *Medieval London Widows, 1300–1500,* edited by Caroline M. Barron and Anne F. Sutton, 1–28. London: Bloomsbury Academic.

Kowaleski, Maryanne. 1988. "The History of Urban Families in Medieval England." *Journal of Medieval History* 14: 47–63.

Kowaleski, Maryanne. 1999. "Singlewomen in Medieval and Early Modern Europe: The Demographic Perspective." In *Singlewomen in the European Past, 1250–1800,* edited by Judith M. Bennett and Amy M. Froide, 38–81. Philadelphia: University of Pennsylvania Press.

Kowaleski, Maryanne. 2008. *Medieval Towns: A Reader.* Toronto: University of Toronto Press.

Kowaleski, Maryanne, and P. J. P. Goldberg, eds. 2008. *Medieval Domesticity: Home, Housing and Household in Medieval England*. Cambridge: Cambridge University Press.

Luders, Alexander, ed. 1810. *The Statutes of the Realm*. Vol. 1. London: Dawsons of Pall Mall.

Martin, G. H., ed. 1995. *Knighton's Chronicle, 1337–1396*. Oxford: Oxford University Press.

McIntosh, Marjorie Keniston. 1998. *Controlling Misbehavior in England 1370–1600*. Cambridge: Cambridge University Press.

McIntosh, Marjorie Keniston. 2005. *Working Women in English Society, 1300–1600*. Cambridge: Cambridge University Press.

McSheffrey, Shannon. 1999. "Men and Masculinity in Late Medieval London Civic Culture." In *Conflicted Identities and Multiple Masculinities: Men in the Medieval West*, edited by Jacqueline Murray. New York: Garland.

Oschinsky, Dorothea, ed. 1971. *Walter of Henley and Other Treatises on Estate Management and Accounting*. Oxford: Clarendon Press.

Rawclife, Carole. 2013. *Urban Bodies: Communal Health in Late Medieval English Towns and Cities*. Woodbridge: Boydell Press.

Rees Jones, Sarah. 2013. "Public and Private Space and Gender in Medieval Europe." In *The Oxford Handbook of Women & Gender in Medieval Europe*, edited by Judith M. Bennett and Ruth Mazo Karras, 246–261. Oxford: Oxford University Press.

Reyerson, Kathryn. 2013. "Urban Economies." In *The Oxford Handbook of Women & Gender in Medieval Europe*, edited by Judith M. Bennett and Ruth Mazo Karras, 295–310. Oxford: Oxford University Press.

Rigby, Susan H. 1996. *English Society in the Later Middle Ages: Class, Status and Gender*. London: Macmillan Press, Ltd.

Riley, Henry Thomas. 1868. *Memorials of London and London Life, in the XIIth, XIVth, and XVth Centuries: Being a Series of Extracts, Local, Social, and Political, from the Early Archives of the City of London, A.D. 1276–1419*. London: Longmans, Green, and Co. HathiTrust.

Salisbury, Eve, ed. 2002. *The Trials and Joys of Marriage*. Kalamazoo, MI: Medieval Institute Publications. https://d.lib.rochester.edu/teams/publication/salisbury-trials-and-joys-of-marriage.

Sharpe, Reginald B., ed. 1913. *Calendar of Coroners Rolls of the City of London, A.D. 1300–1378*. London: R. Clay and Sons.

Statutes of the Realm (1101–1713). 1963. Record Commission. 11 vols. London, 1810–1828, reprinted 1963. HathiTrust.

Stone, Brian, ed. 1964. *Medieval English Verse*. New York: Penguin.

Thomas, A. H. 1924. *Calendar of Early Mayor's Court Rolls Preserved among the Archives of the Corporation of the City of London at the Guildhall A. D. 1298–1307*. Cambridge: Cambridge University Press.

Ward, Jennifer. 2006. *Women in England in the Middle Ages*. New York: Hambledon Continuum.

Whittle, Jane. 2013. "Rural Economies." In *The Oxford Handbook of Women & Gender in Medieval Europe,* edited by Judith M. Bennett and Ruth Mazo Karras, 311–326. Oxford: Oxford University Press.

CHAPTER 5

Allen-Goss, Lucy. 2020. *Female Desire in Chaucer's* Legend of Good Women *and Middle English Romance.* Cambridge: D. S. Brewer.

Amer, Sahar. 2008. *Crossing Borders: Love between Women in Medieval French and Arabic Literatures.* Philadelphia: University of Pennsylvania Press.

Archibald, Elizabeth. 2001. *Incest and the Medieval Imagination.* Oxford: Oxford University Press.

Arnold, John H. 2013. "Heresy and Gender in the Middle Ages." In *The Oxford Handbook of Women & Gender in Medieval Europe,* edited by Judith M. Bennett and Ruth Mazo Karras, 496–510. Oxford: Oxford University Press.

Ashley, Kathleen. 2013. "Cultures of Devotion." In *The Oxford Handbook of Women & Gender in Medieval Europe,* edited by Judith M. Bennett and Ruth Mazo Karras, 511–527. Oxford: Oxford University Press.

Baildon, William Paley, ed. 1896. *Select Cases in Chancery: A.D. 1364 to 1471.* London: Bernard Quaritch.

Bateson, Mary, ed. 1901. *Records of the Borough of Leicester: Being a Series of Extracts from the Archives of the Corporation of Leicester.* Vol. 2. London: C. J. Clay. HathiTrust.

Bennett, Judith M. 2000. "'Lesbian-Like' and the Social History of Lesbianisms." *Journal of the History of Sexuality* 9: 1–24.

Bennett, Judith M. 2003. "Writing Fornication: Medieval Leyrwite and Its Historians: *The Prothero Lecture." Transactions of the Royal Historical Society* 13: 131–162.

Bennett, Judith M. 2011. "Remembering Elizabeth Etchingham and Agnes Oxenbridge." In *The Lesbian Premodern,* edited by Noreen Giffney, Michelle M. Sauer, and Diane Watt. London: Palgrave Macmillan.

Bennett, Judith M., and Shannon McSheffrey. 2014. "Early, Erotic and Alien: Women Dressed as Men in Late Medieval London." *History Workshop Journal* 77 (Spring): 1–25.

Benson, Larry D., ed. 2008. *The Riverside Chaucer.* Oxford: Oxford University Press.

Bickley, Francis B. 1900. *The Little Red Book of Bristol.* Bristol: W. C. Hemmons.

Bogage, Jacob. 2018. "Banned from Men's Soccer Matches in Iran, These Women Dressed as Men to Sneak In." *Washington Post,* May 2.

Boureau, Alain. 1998. *The Lord's First Night: The Myth of the Droit de Cuissage.* Chicago: University of Chicago Press.

Boyd, David Lorenzo, and Ruth Mazo Karras. 1995. "The Interrogation of a Male Transvestite Prostitute in Fourteenth-Century London." *GLQ* 1, no. 4: 459–465.

Brozyna, Martha A., ed. 2005. *Gender and Sexuality in the Middle Ages: A Medieval Source Documents Reader.* Jefferson, NC: McFarland.

Brundage, James A. 1987. *Law, Sex, and Christian Society in Medieval Europe.* Chicago: University of Chicago Press.

Bullough, Vern L. 1976. *Sex, Society, and History.* New York: Science History Publications.

Bullough, Vern L., and James A. Brundage, eds. 1996. *Handbook of Medieval Sexuality.* New York: Garland.

Burger, Glenn. 2003. *Chaucer's Queer Nation.* Minneapolis: University of Minnesota Press.

Burger, Glenn, and Steven F. Kruger, eds. 2001. *Queering the Middle Ages.* Minneapolis: University of Minnesota Press.

Butler, Sara M. 2006. "Women, Suicide, and the Jury in Later Medieval England." *Signs: Journal of Women in Culture and Society* 32, no. 1: 141–166.

Butler, Sara M. 2007. *The Language of Abuse: Marital Violence in Later Medieval England.* Leiden: Brill.

Cadden, Joan. 1993. *Meanings of Sex Difference in the Middle Ages: Medicine, Science, and Culture.* Cambridge: Cambridge University Press.

Camille, Michael. 1998. *The Medieval Art of Love: Objects and Subjects of Desire.* New York: Abrams.

Clark, David. 2009. *Between Medieval Men: Male Friendship and Desire in Early Medieval English Literature.* Oxford: Oxford University Press.

Dinshaw, Carolyn. 1999. *Getting Medieval: Sexualities and Communities, Pre- and Postmodern.* Durham, NC: Duke University Press.

Dunn, Caroline. 2013. *Stolen Women in Medieval England: Rape, Abduction, and Adultery, 1100–1500.* Cambridge: Cambridge University Press.

Elliott, Dyan. 1993. *Spiritual Marriage: Sexual Abstinence in Medieval Wedlock.* Princeton, NJ: Princeton University Press.

Elliott, Dyan. 2008. "The Three Ages of Joan Scott." *American Historical Review* 113: 1390–1403.

Elliott, Dyan. 2012. "Sexual Scandal and the Clergy: A Medieval Blueprint for Disaster." In *Why the Middle Ages Matter: Medieval Light on Modern Injustice,* edited by Celia Chazelle, Simon Doubleday, Felice Lifshitz, and Amy G. Remensnyder, 90–105. London: Routledge.

Furnivall, Frederick James. 1908. "How the Good Wife Taught Her Daughter." In *The Babees' Book: Medieval Manners for the Young: Done into Modern English,* edited by Edith Rickert. London: Duffield & Co. Project Gutenberg.

Giffney, Noreen, Michelle M. Sauer, and Diane Watt, eds. 2011. *The Lesbian Premodern.* New York: Palgrave Macmillan.

Goldberg, P. J. P. 1995. *Women in England c. 1275–1525: Documentary Sources.* Manchester: Manchester University Press.

Goldberg, P. J. P. 2007. *Communal Discord, Child Abduction, and Rape in the Later Middle Ages.* New York: Palgrave Macmillan.

Gravdal, Kathryn. 1991. *Ravishing Maidens: Writing Rape in Medieval French Literature and Law*. Philadelphia: University of Pennsylvania Press.

Green, Monica H., ed. and trans. 2001. *The Trotula: A Medieval Compendium of Women's Medicine*. Philadelphia: University of Pennsylvania Press.

Greene, Richard Leighton. 1977. *The Early English Carols*. 2nd ed. Oxford: Oxford University Press.

Halperin, David M. 2002. *How to Do the History of Homosexuality*. Chicago: University of Chicago Press.

Hanawalt, Barbara A. 1979. *Crime and Conflict in English Communities, 1300–1348*. Cambridge, MA: Harvard University Press.

Harper, Kyle. 2013. *From Shame to Sin: The Christian Transformation of Sexual Morality*. Cambridge, MA: Harvard University Press.

Hasted, Elise Bennett. 2004. "Medieval Rape: A Conceivable Defense?" *Cambridge Law Journal* 63: 743–769.

Hawkes, Emma. 1995. "'She Was Ravished against Her Will, What so Ever She Say': Female Consent in Rape and Ravishment in Late Medieval England." *Limina* I: 47–54.

Helmholz, Richard H. 1974. *Marriage Litigation in Medieval England*. Cambridge: Cambridge University Press.

Hopkins, Amanda, and Cory James Rushton, eds. 2007. *The Erotic in the Literature of Medieval Britain*. Woodbridge: D. S. Brewer.

Jacquart, Danielle, and Claude Thomasset. 1988. *Sexuality and Medicine in the Middle Ages*. Translated by Matthew Adamson. Princeton: Princeton University Press.

Jaeger, C. Stephen. 1999. *Ennobling Love: In Search of a Lost Sensibility*. Philadelphia: University of Pennsylvania Press.

Jordan, Mark D. 1997. *The Invention of Sodomy in Christian Theology*. Chicago: University of Chicago Press.

Karras, Ruth Mazo. 1996. *Common Women: Prostitution and Sexuality in Medieval England*. New York: Oxford University Press.

Karras, Ruth Mazo. 2005. *Sexuality in Medieval Europe: Doing unto Others*. New York: Routledge.

Linkinen, Tom. 2015. *Same-Sex Sexuality in Later Medieval English Culture*. Amsterdam: Amsterdam University Press.

Lochrie, Karma. 1997. "Mystical Acts, Queer Tendencies." In *Constructing Medieval Sexuality*, edited by Karma Lochrie, Peggy McCracken, and James A. Schultz, 180–200. Minneapolis: University of Minnesota Press.

Lochrie, Karma. 2001. "Presidential Improprieties and Medieval Categories: The Absurdity of Heterosexuality." In *Queering the Middle Ages*, edited by Glenn Burger and Steven F. Kruger, 87–96. Minneapolis: University of Minnesota Press.

Lochrie, Karma. 2003. "Between Women." In *The Cambridge Companion to Medieval Women's Writing*, edited by Carolyn Dinshaw and David Wallace, 70–88. Cambridge: Cambridge University Press.

Lochrie, Karma. 2005. *Heterosyncrasies: Female Sexuality When Normal Wastn't.* Minneapolis: University of Minnesota Press.

McDougall, Sara. 2013. "Women and Gender in Canon Law." In *The Oxford Handbook of Women & Gender in Medieval Europe,* edited by Judith M. Bennett and Ruth Mazo Karras. Oxford: Oxford University Press.

McLaughlin, Megan. 2010. *Sex, Gender, and Episcopal Authority in an Age of Reform, 1000–1122.* Cambridge: Cambridge University Press.

Mulder-Bakker, Anneke B. 2013. "Devoted Holiness in the Lay World." In *The Oxford Handbook of Women & Gender in Medieval Europe,* edited by Judith M. Bennett and Ruth Mazo Karras, 464–479. Oxford: Oxford University Press.

Murray, Jacqueline. 1996. "Twice Marginal and Twice Invisible: Lesbians in the Middle Ages." In *Handbook of Medieval Sexuality,* edited by Vern L. Bullough and James A. Brundage. New York: Garland.

Murray, Jacqueline, and Konrad Eisenbichler, eds. 1996. *Desire and Discipline: Sex and Sexuality in the Pre-Modern West.* Toronto: University of Toronto Press.

Phillips, Kim M. 2003. "Four Virgin's Tales: Sex and Power in Medieval Law." In *Medieval Virginities,* edited by Anke Bernau, Ruth Evans, and Sarah Salih, 80–101. Toronto: University of Toronto Press.

Puff, Helmut. 2013. "Same-Sex Possibilities." In *The Oxford Handbook of Women & Gender in Medieval Europe,* edited by Judith M. Bennett and Ruth Mazo Karras, 379–395. Oxford: Oxford University Press.

Pugh, Tison. 2008. *Sexuality and Its Queer Discontents in Middle English Literature.* New York: Palgrave Macmillan.

Riley, Henry Thomas. 1868. *Memorials of London and London Life, in the XIIth, XIVth, and XVth Centuries: Being a Series of Extracts, Local, Social, and Political, from the Early Archives of the City of London, A.D. 1276–1419.* London: Longmans, Green, and Co. HathiTrust.

Robertson, Elizabeth, and Christine M. Rose, eds. 2001. *Representing Rape in Medieval and Early Modern Literature.* New York: Palgrave.

Rubin, Miri. 2013. "Cults of Saints." In *The Oxford Handbook of Women & Gender in Medieval Europe,* edited by Judith M. Bennett and Ruth Mazo Karras, 480–495. Oxford: Oxford University Press.

Savage, Anne, and Nicholas Watson, trans. 1991. *Anchoritic Spirituality: 'Ancrene Wisse' and Associated Works.* New York: Pauli's Press.

Schultz, James. 2008. *Courtly Love, the Love of Courtliness, and the History of Sexuality.* New York: Routledge.

Thibodeaux, Jennifer D. 2015. *The Manly Priest: Clerical Celibacy, Masculinity, and Reform in England and Normandy, 1066–1300.* Philadelphia: University of Pennsylvania Press.

Thomas, A. H. 1926. *Calendar of the Plea and Memoranda Rolls of the City of London: Volume 1, 1323–1364.* London: His Majesty's Stationery Office. British History Online. https://www.british-history.ac.uk/plea-memoranda-rolls/vol1.

Ward, Jennifer. 2006. *Women in England in the Middle Ages*. New York: Hambledon Continuum.

Ward, Jennifer, ed. 2014. *Elizabeth de Burgh, Lady of Clare (1295–1360): Household and Other Records*. Boydell Press.

Wogan-Brown, Jocelyn. 2001. *Saints' Lives and Women's Literary Culture c. 1150–1300: Virginity and Its Authorizations*. Oxford: Oxford University Press.

Wolfthal, Diane. 2010. *In and Out of the Marital Bed: Seeing Sex in Renaissance Europe*. New Haven, CT: Yale University Press.

CHAPTER 6

Bale, Anthony. 2006. *The Jew in the Medieval Book: English Antisemitisms, 1350–1500*. Cambridge: Cambridge University Press.

Burton, J. E. 1979. *The Yorkshire Nunneries in the Twelfth and Thirteenth Centuries*. York: Borthwick Institute of Historical Research.

Bynum, Caroline Walker. 2011. *Christian Materiality: An Essay on Religion in Late-Medieval Europe*. New York: Zone Books.

Campbell, Anna. 2017. "Franciscan Nuns in England, the Minoress Foundations and Their Patrons, 1281–1367." In *The English Province of the Franciscans (1224–c. 1350)*, edited by Michael Robson, 426–447. Leiden: Brill.

Clark, Andrew. 1911. *The English Register of Godstow Nunnery, Near Oxford, Written about 1450*. London: EETS.

Clarke, Katie, and Michael Hicks. 2016. "What Went on in the Medieval Parish Church, 1377–1447, with Particular Reference to Churching." In *The Later Medieval Inquisitions Post Mortem: Mapping the Medieval Countryside and Rural Society*, edited by Michael Hicks. Woodbridge: Boydell Press.

Craig, Leigh Ann. 2009. *Wandering Women and Holy Matrons: Women as Pilgrims in the Later Middle Ages*. Leiden: Brill.

Crouch, David J. F. 2000. *Piety, Fraternity, and Power: Religious Gilds in Late Medieval Yorkshire, 1389–1547*. York: York Medieval Press.

Cullum, P. H. 1991. *Cremetts and Corrodies: Care of the Poor and Sick at St Leonard's Hospital, York, in the Middle Ages*. York: Borthwick Institute of Historical Research.

Cullum, P. H. 1996. "Vowesses and Female Lay Piety in the Province of York, 1300–1530." *Northern History* 32: 21–41.

Cullum, P. H., and P. J. P. Goldberg. 1993. "Charitable Provision in Late Medieval York: 'To the Praise of God and the Use of the Poor.'" *Northern History* 29: 24–39.

Dinshaw, Carolyn. 2003. "Margery Kempe." In *The Cambridge Companion to Medieval Women's Writing*, edited by Carolyn Dinshaw and David Wallace, 222–239. Cambridge: Cambridge University Press.

Duffy, Eamon. 1992. *The Stripping of the Altars: Traditional Religion in England, 1400–1580.* New Haven, CT: Yale University Press.

Edwards, Jennifer C. 2019. *Superior Women: Medieval Female Authority in Poitiers' Abbey of Sainte-Croix.* Oxford: Oxford University Press.

Elliott, Dyan. 2011. *The Bride of Christ Goes to Hell: Metaphor and Embodiment in the Lives of Religious Women, ca. 200–1461.* Philadelphia: University of Pennsylvania Press.

Erler, Mary C. 2002. *Women, Reading and Piety in Late Medieval England.* Cambridge: Cambridge University Press.

Finucane, Ronald C. 1978. *Miracles and Pilgrims: Popular Beliefs in Medieval England.* Totowa, NJ: Rowman and Littlefield.

Foot, Sarah. 2000. *Veiled Women.* 2 vols. Aldershot: Ashgate.

Foster-Campbell, Megan H. 2011. "Pilgrimage through the Pages: Pilgrims' Badges in Late Medieval Devotional Manuscripts." In *Push Me, Pull You: Imaginative and Emotional Interaction in Late Medieval and Renaissance Art*, edited by Sarah Blick and Laura D. Gelfand, 227–274. Leiden: Brill.

French, Katherine L. 2008. *The Good Women of the Parish: Gender and Religion after the Black Death.* Philadelphia: University of Pennsylvania Press.

Furnivall, Frederick James. 1908. "How the Good Wife Taught Her Daughter." In *The Babees' Book: Medieval Manners for the Young: Done into Modern English*, edited by Edith Rickert. London: Duffield & Co. Project Gutenberg.

Gilchrist, Roberta. 1994. *Gender and Material Culture: The Archaeology of Religious Women.* London: Routledge.

Goldberg, P. J. P. 1995. *Women in England c. 1275–1525: Documentary Sources.* Manchester: Manchester University Press.

Golding, B. 1995. *Gilbert of Sempringham and the Gilbertine Order, c. 1130–1300.* Oxford: Clarendon Press.

Griffiths, Fiona. 2008. "The Cross and the *Cura Monialium*: Robert of Arbrissel, John the Evangelist, and the Pastoral Care of Women in the Age of Reform." *Speculum* 83, no. 2: 303–330.

Harrison, M. J. 2001. *The Nunnery of Nun Appleton.* York: Borthwick Institute of Historical Research.

Heath, Peter, ed. 1964. *Medieval Clerical Accounts.* Borthwick Paper 26. York: St. Anthony's Press.

Horn, Joyce, ed. 1982. *The Register of Robert Hallum, Bishop of Salisbury 1407–1417.* London: Boydell and Brewer.

Hughes-Edwards, Mary. 2012. *Reading Medieval Anchoritism: Ideology and Spiritual Practices.* Cardiff: University of Wales Press.

Jansen, Katherine Ludwig. 2000. *The Making of the Magdalen: Preaching and Popular Devotion in the Later Middle Ages.* Princeton, NJ: Princeton University Press.

Julian of Norwich. 1978. *Revelations of Divine Love: Translated from British Library Additional MS 37790.* Translated by Frances Beer. Heidelberg: Winter.

Lee, Paul. 2001. *Nunneries, Learning and Spirituality in Late Medieval English Society: The Dominican Priory of Dartford.* Woodbridge: York Medieval Press.

Licence, Tom. 2013. *Hermits and Recluses in English Society, 950–1200.* Oxford: Oxford University Press.

Lochrie, Karma. 2003. "Between Women." In *The Cambridge Companion to Medieval Women's Writing,* edited by Carolyn Dinshaw and David Wallace, 70–88. Cambridge: Cambridge University Press.

McAvoy, Liz Herbert. 2011. *Medieval Anchoritisms: Gender, Space and the Solitary Life.* Woodbridge: Boydell and Brewer.

McNamara, Jo Ann. 1996. *Sisters in Arms: Catholic Nuns through Two Millennia.* Cambridge, MA: Harvard University Press.

McSheffrey, Shannon. 1995. *Gender and Heresy: Women and Men in Lollard Communities, 1420–1530.* Philadelphia: University of Pennsylvania Press.

McSheffrey, Shannon, and Norman Tanner, ed. and trans. 2003. *Lollards of Coventry, 1486–1522.* Cambridge: Cambridge University Press.

Mulder-Bakker, Anneke B. 2005. *Lives of the Anchoresses: The Rise of the Urban Recluse in Medieval Europe.* Translated by Myra Heerspink Scholz. Philadelphia: University of Pennsylvania Press.

Mullins, Edwin. 2000. *The Pilgrimage to Santiago.* Oxford: Signal Books, Ltd.

Oliva, Marilyn. 1998. *The Convent and the Community in Late Medieval England: Female Monasteries in the Diocese of Norwich, 1350–1540.* Woodbridge: Boydell Press.

Rawcliffe, Carole. 2003. "Women, Childbirth, and Religion in Later Medieval England." In *Women and Religion in Medieval England,* edited by Diana Wood. Oxford: Oxbow Books.

Rose, E. M. 2015. *The Murder of William of Norwich: The Origins of Blood Libel in Medieval Europe.* Oxford: Oxford University Press.

Schulenberg, Jane Tibbetts. 1998. *Forgetful of Their Sex: Female Sanctity and Society, ca. 500–1100.* Chicago: University of Chicago Press.

Skinner, Patricia, ed. 2003. *The Jews in Medieval Britain: Historical, Literary, and Archaeological Perspectives.* Woodbridge: Boydell and Brewer.

Swanson, R. N. 1989. *Church and Society in Late Medieval England.* Oxford: Basil Blackwell.

Swanson, R. N. 1995. *Religion and Devotion in Europe, c. 1215–c. 1515.* New York: Cambridge University Press.

Ward, Jennifer. 2006. *Women in England in the Middle Ages.* New York: Hambledon Continuum.

Watson, Nicholas. 2003. "Julian of Norwich." In *The Cambridge Companion to Medieval Women's Writing*, edited by Carolyn Dinshaw and David Wallace, 210–221. Cambridge: Cambridge University Press.

Winstead, Karen A. 1997. *Virgin Martyrs: Legends of Sainthood in Late Medieval England*. Ithaca, NY: Cornell University Press.

Wogan-Browne, Jocelyn. 2001. *Saints' Lives and Women's Literary Culture, c. 115–1300: Virginity and Its Authorizations*. Oxford: Oxford University Press.

INDEX

Page numbers in *italics* indicate photos.

About the Author

Jennifer C. Edwards is professor and chair of history at Manhattan College in Riverdale, New York, where she teaches medieval and ancient history. She is the author of *Superior Women: Medieval Female Authority in Poitiers' Abbey of Sainte-Croix* (2019). She earned her PhD and MA from the University of Illinois at Urbana-Champaign and BA from the University of Massachusetts at Amherst. She is an associate editor for the *Medieval Feminist Forum* and serves on the Advisory Board of the Society for Medieval Feminist Scholarship. She is working currently on a book project, *Holy Healing: Saints and Leprosy in the Middle Ages*, examining the treatment of leprosy in the medieval cult of the saints.

www.ingramcontent.com/pod-product-compliance
Lightning Source LLC
Chambersburg PA
CBHW051144030726
47504CB00004B/1031